ORPHAN BLACK

IDW

Facebook: **facebook.com/idwpublishing**
Twitter: **@idwpublishing**
YouTube: **youtube.com/idwpublishing**
Tumblr: **tumblr.idwpublishing.com**
Instagram: **instagram.com/idwpublishing**

COVER ART BY
CORBYN KERN

ISBN: 978-1-63140-583-9   19 18 17 16   2 3 4 5

COLLECTION EDITS BY
JUSTIN EISINGER
AND ALONZO SIMON

COLLECTION DESIGN BY
JEFF POWELL

PUBLISHER
TED ADAMS

TEMPLE STREET PRODUCTIONS

Originally published as ORPHAN BLACK: HELSINKI issues #1–5.

Ted Adams, CEO & Publisher
Greg Goldstein, President & COO
Robbie Robbins, EVP/Sr. Graphic Artist
Chris Ryall, Chief Creative Officer/Editor-in-Chief
Matthew Ruzicka, CPA, Chief Financial Officer
Dirk Wood, VP of Marketing
Lorelei Bunjes, VP of Digital Services
Jeff Webber, VP of Digital and Subsidiary Rights
Jerry Bennington, VP of New Product Development

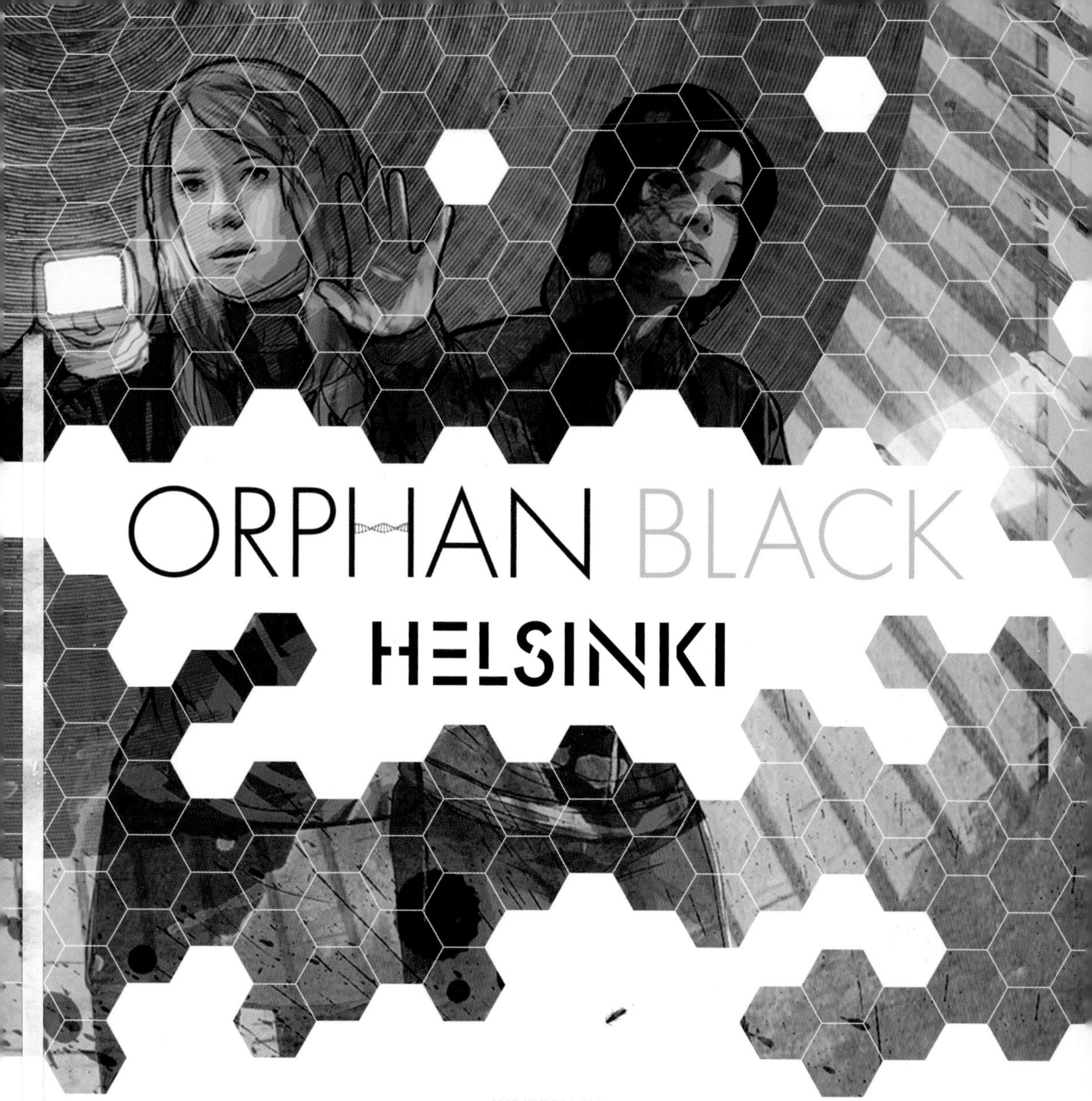

ORPHAN BLACK

HELSINKI

WRITTEN BY

JOHN FAWCETT, GRAEME MANSON AND HELI KENNEDY

PART 1	PARTS 2-5
ART BY ALAN QUAH INKING ASSIST BY JEFFREY HUET	ART BY WAYNE NICHOLS AND FICO OSSIO

COLORS BY

CHRIS FENOGLIO, ANDREW ELDER, AND SEBASTIAN CHENG

STORY EDITS BY

MACKENZIE DONALDSON AND KERRY APPLEYARD

LETTERS BY

NEIL UYETAKE

SERIES EDITS BY

DENTON J. TIPTON

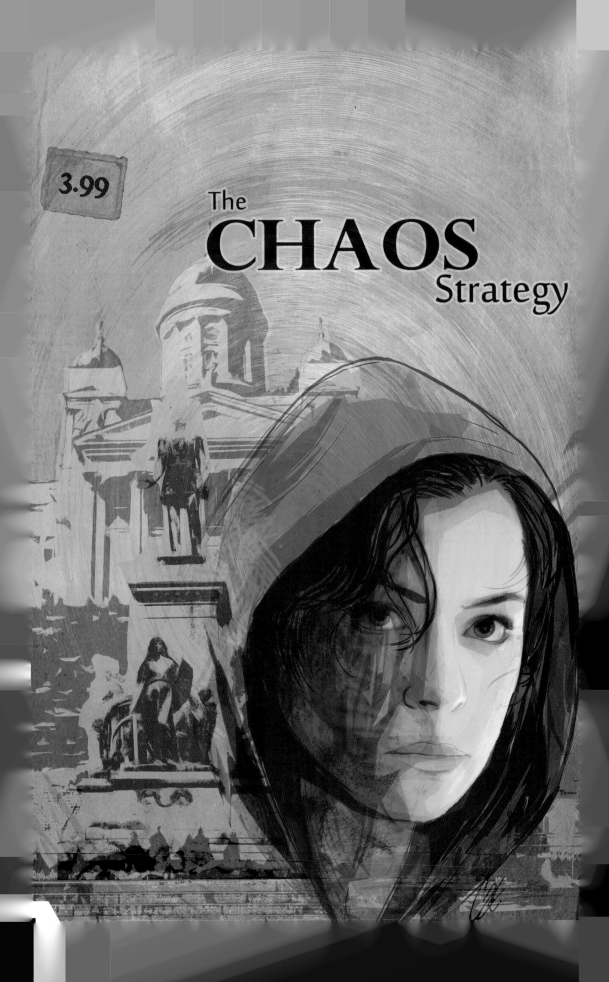

3.99

The
CHAOS
Strategy

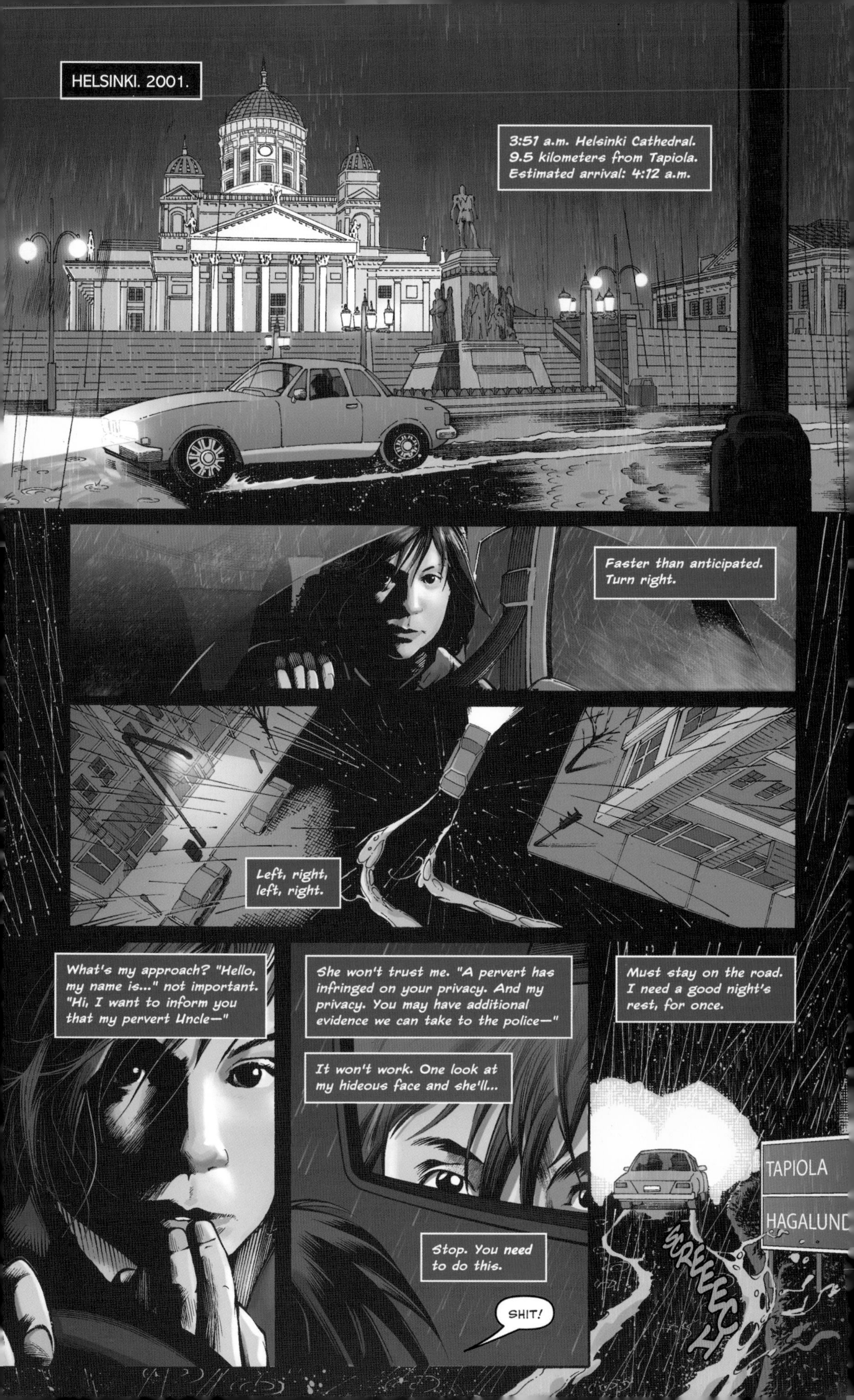
HELSINKI. 2001.
3:51 a.m. Helsinki Cathedral. 9.5 kilometers from Tapiola. Estimated arrival: 4:12 a.m.
Faster than anticipated. Turn right.
Left, right, left, right.
What's my approach? "Hello, my name is..." not important. "Hi, I want to inform you that my pervert Uncle—"
She won't trust me. "A pervert has infringed on your privacy. And my privacy. You may have additional evidence we can take to the police—"
It won't work. One look at my hideous face and she'll...
Stop. You need to do this.
SHIT!
Must stay on the road. I need a good night's rest, for once.
TAPIOLA
HAGALUND
SCREEEECH

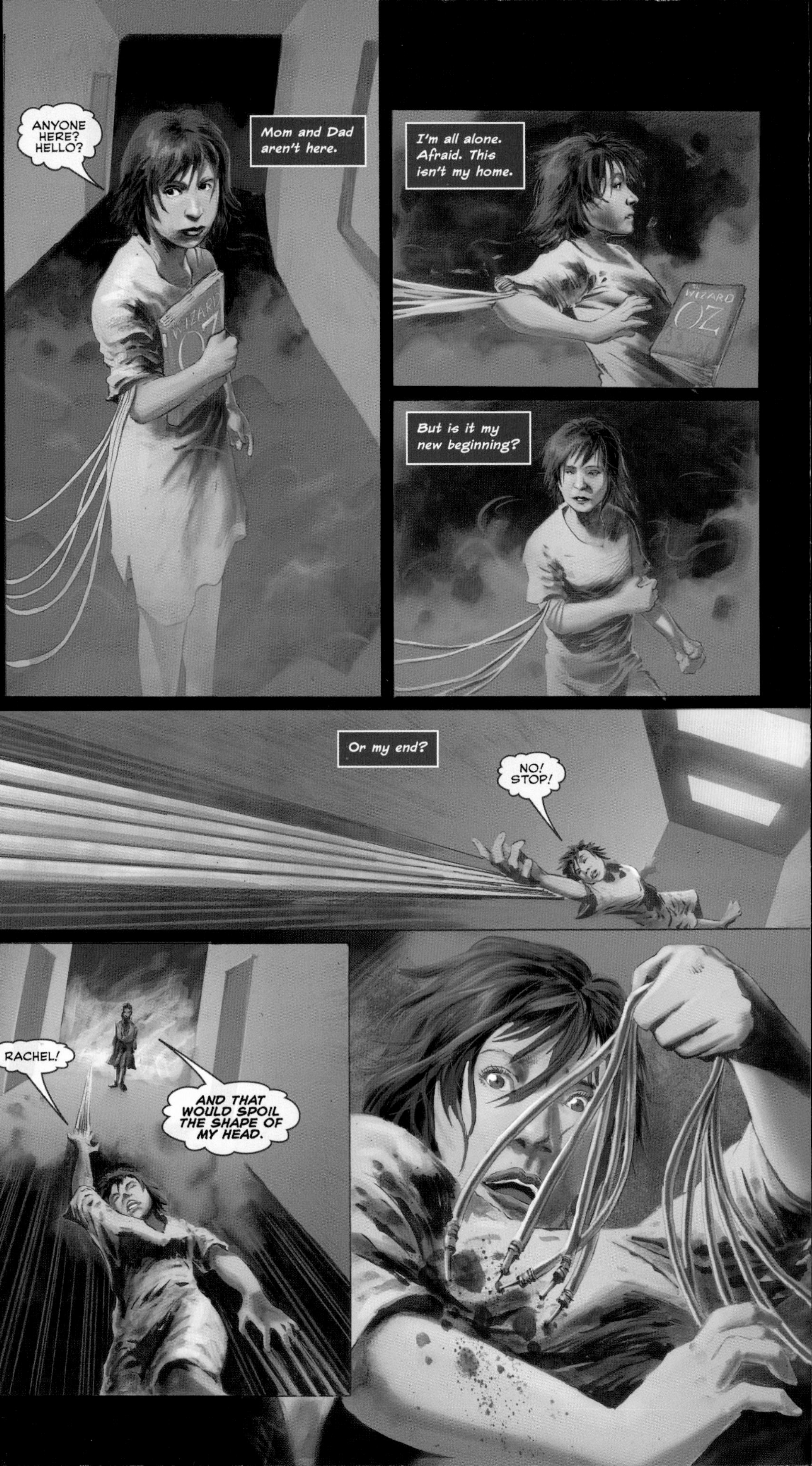
ANYONE HERE? HELLO?
Mom and Dad aren't here.
WIZARD OZ
I'm all alone. Afraid. This isn't my home.
WIZARD OZ
But is it my new beginning?
Or my end?
NO! STOP!
RACHEL!
AND THAT WOULD SPOIL THE SHAPE OF MY HEAD.

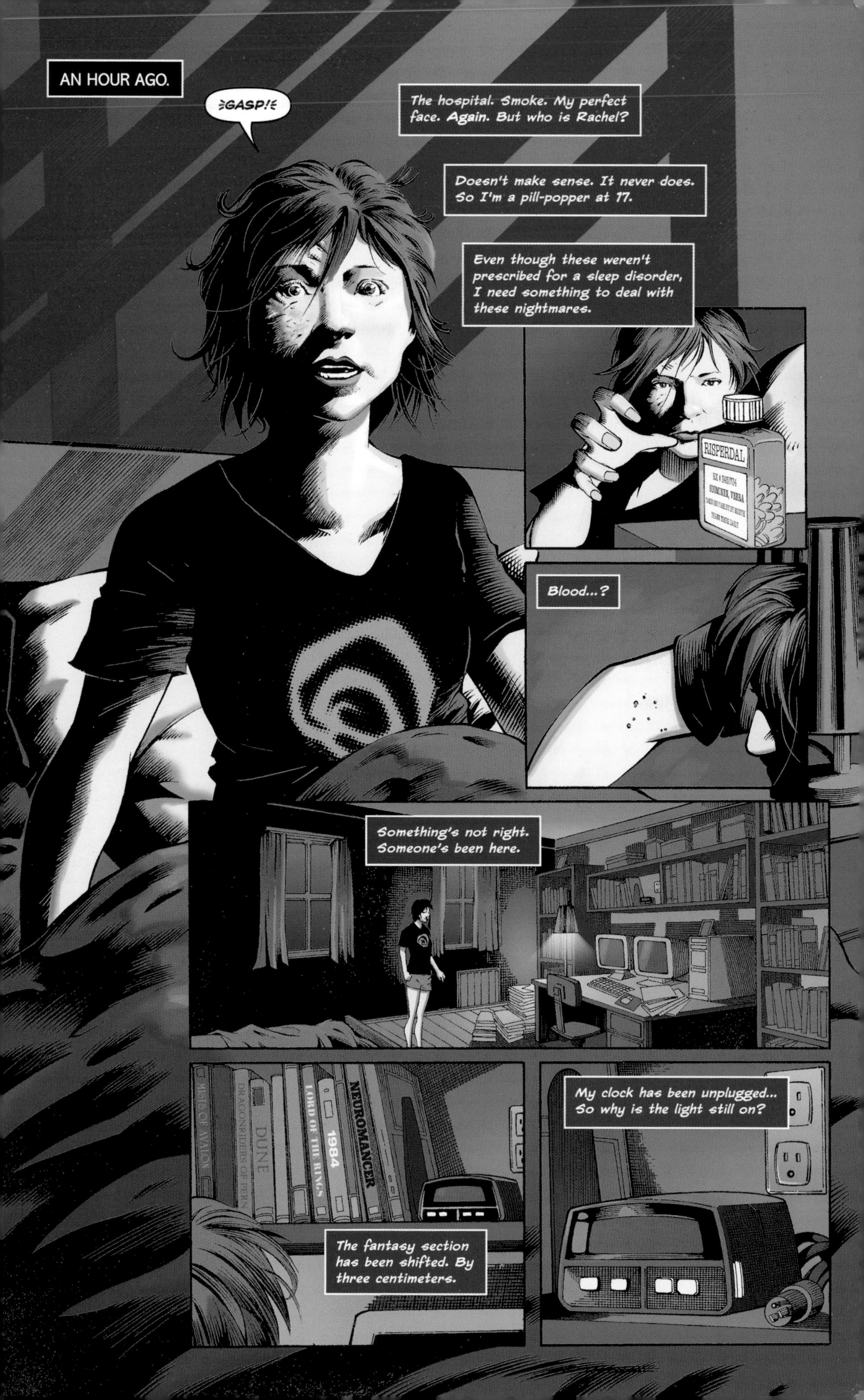
AN HOUR AGO.
GASP!
The hospital. Smoke. My perfect face. Again. But who is Rachel?
Doesn't make sense. It never does. So I'm a pill-popper at 17.
Even though these weren't prescribed for a sleep disorder, I need something to deal with these nightmares.
RISPERDAL
Blood...?
Something's not right. Someone's been here.
MISTS OF AVALON
DRAGONRIDERS OF PERN
DUNE
LORD OF THE RINGS
1984
NEUROMANCER
The fantasy section has been shifted. By three centimeters.
My clock has been unplugged... So why is the light still on?

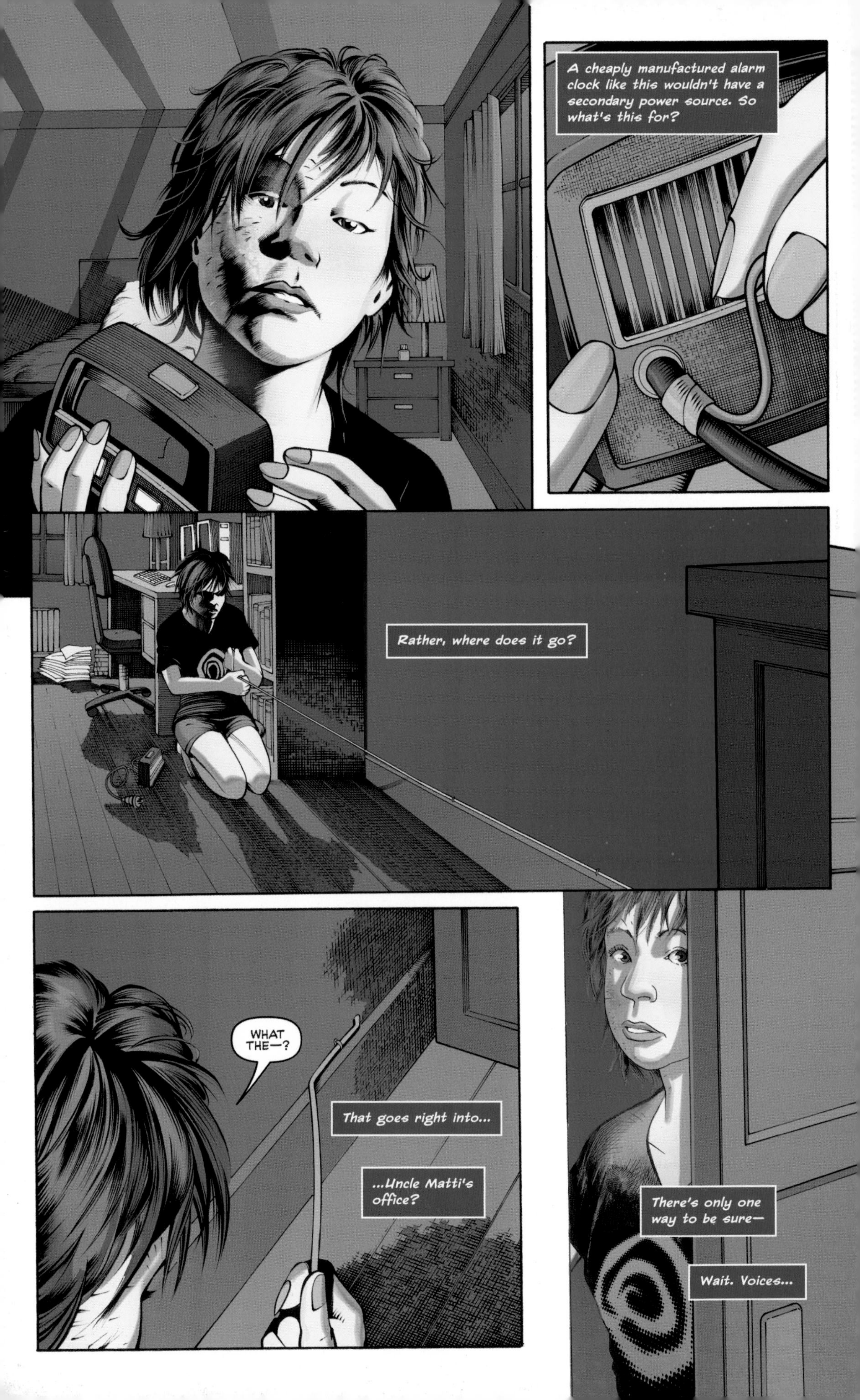
A cheaply manufactured alarm clock like this wouldn't have a secondary power source. So what's this for?
Rather, where does it go?
WHAT THE—?
That goes right into...
...Uncle Matti's office?
There's only one way to be sure—
Wait. Voices...

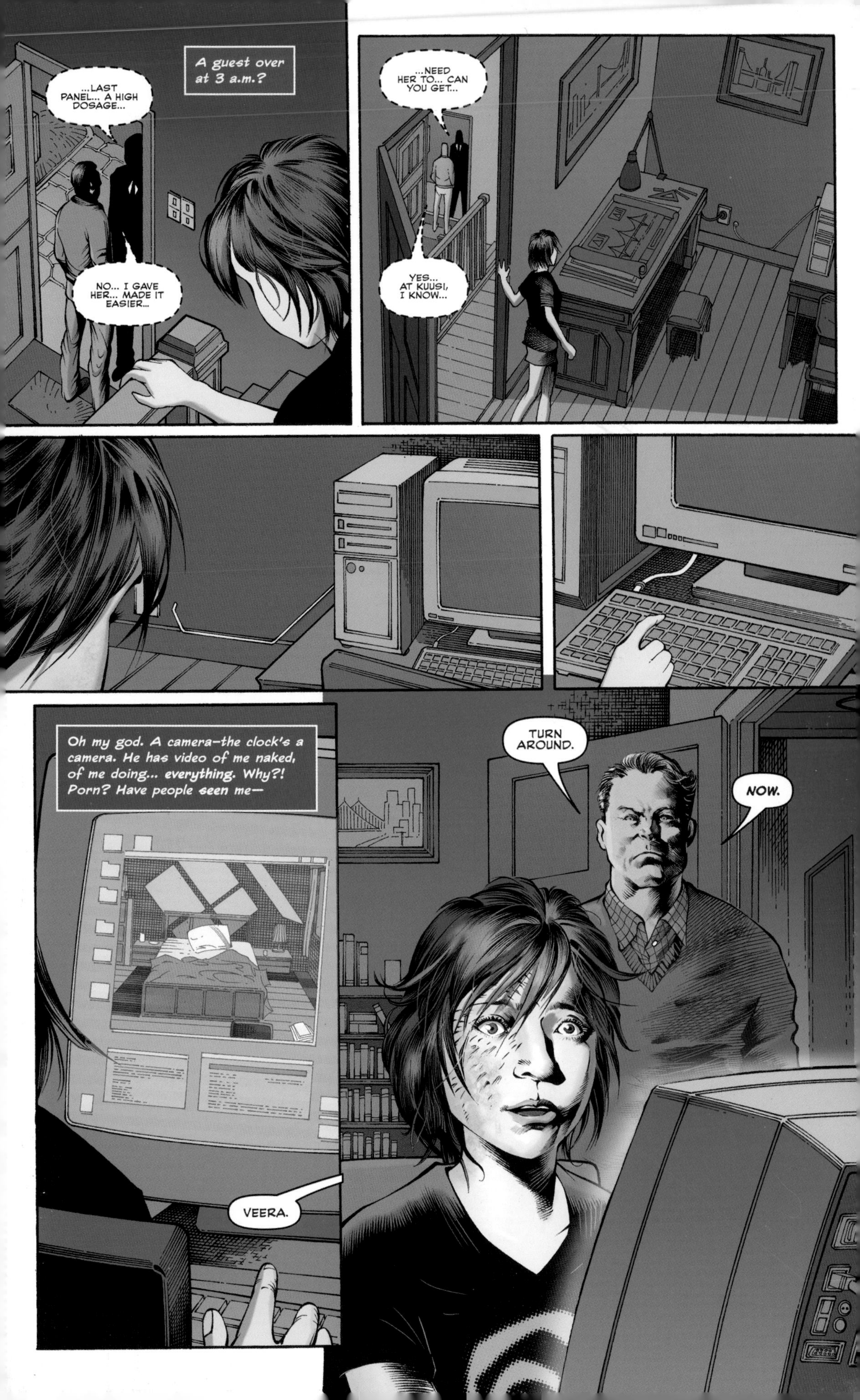
A guest over at 3 a.m.?
...LAST PANEL... A HIGH DOSAGE...
NO... I GAVE HER... MADE IT EASIER...
...NEED HER TO... CAN YOU GET...
YES... AT KUUSI, I KNOW...
Oh my god. A camera—the clock's a camera. He has video of me naked, of me doing... everything. Why?! Porn? Have people seen me—
VEERA.
TURN AROUND.
NOW.

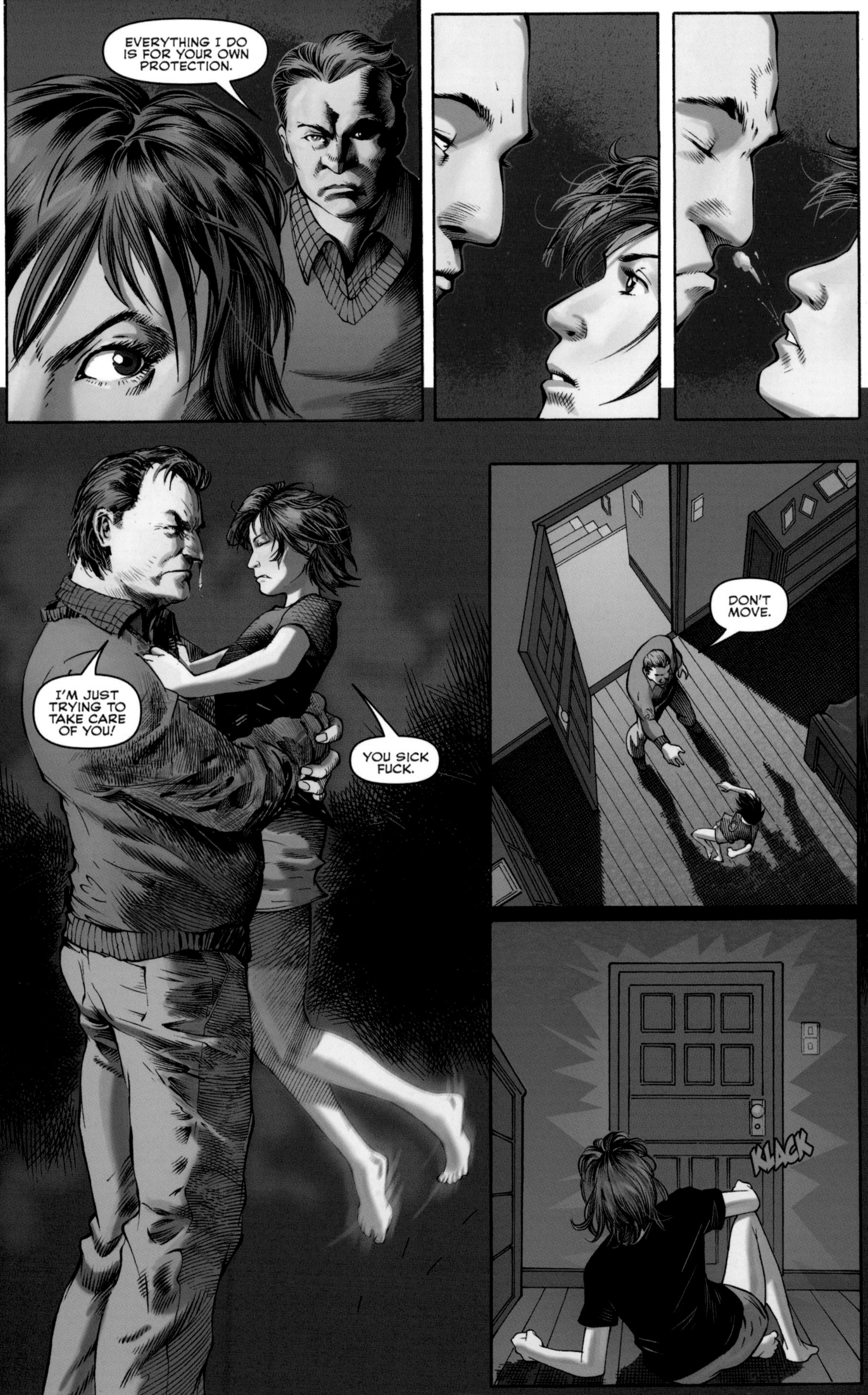
EVERYTHING I DO IS FOR YOUR OWN PROTECTION.
I'M JUST TRYING TO TAKE CARE OF YOU!
YOU SICK FUCK.
DON'T MOVE.
KLACK

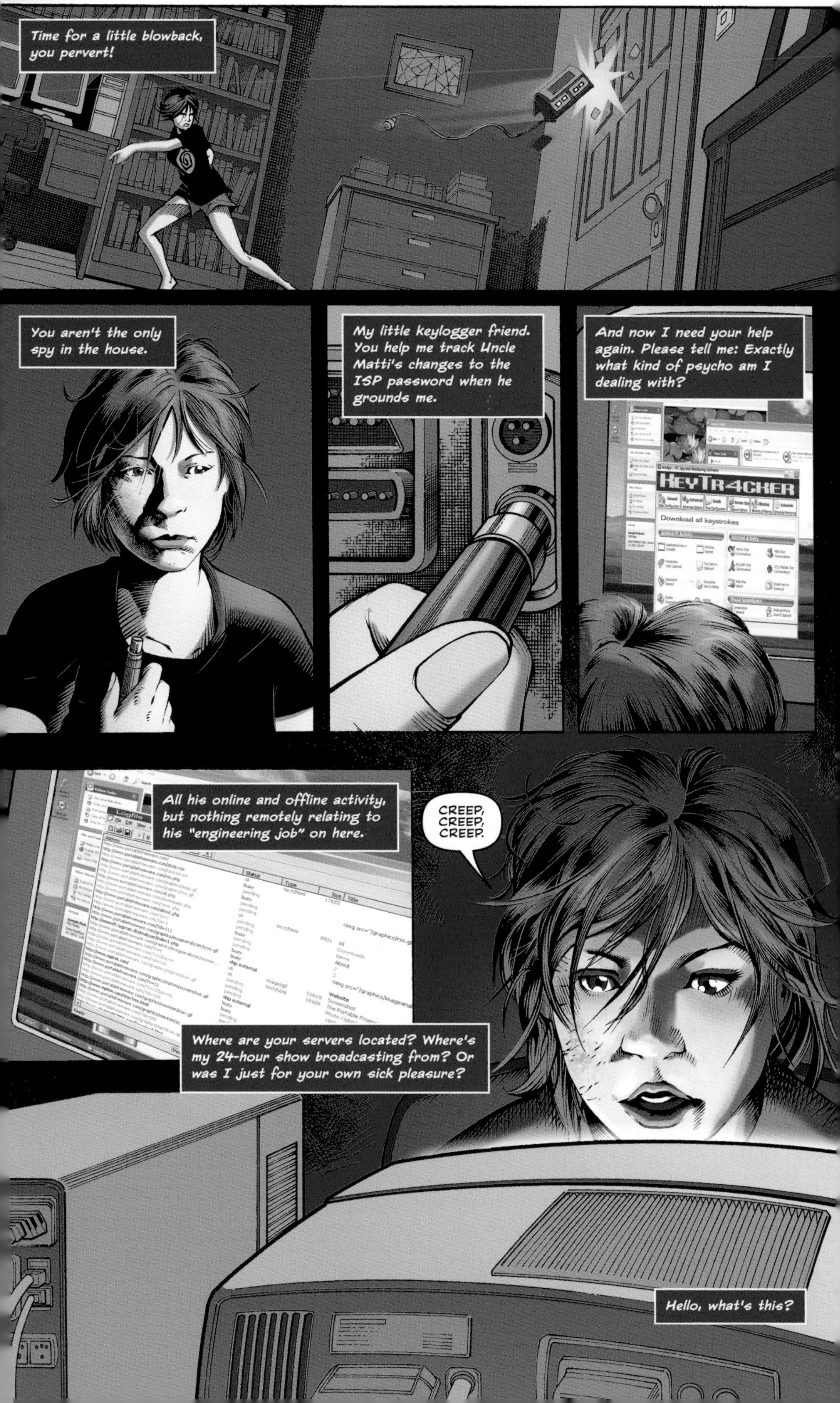
Time for a little blowback, you pervert!
You aren't the only spy in the house.
My little keylogger friend. You help me track Uncle Matti's changes to the ISP password when he grounds me.
And now I need your help again. Please tell me: Exactly what kind of psycho am I dealing with?
KEYTR4CKER
Download all keystrokes
All his online and offline activity, but nothing remotely relating to his "engineering job" on here.
CREEP, CREEP, CREEP.
Where are your servers located? Where's my 24-hour show broadcasting from? Or was I just for your own sick pleasure?
Hello, what's this?

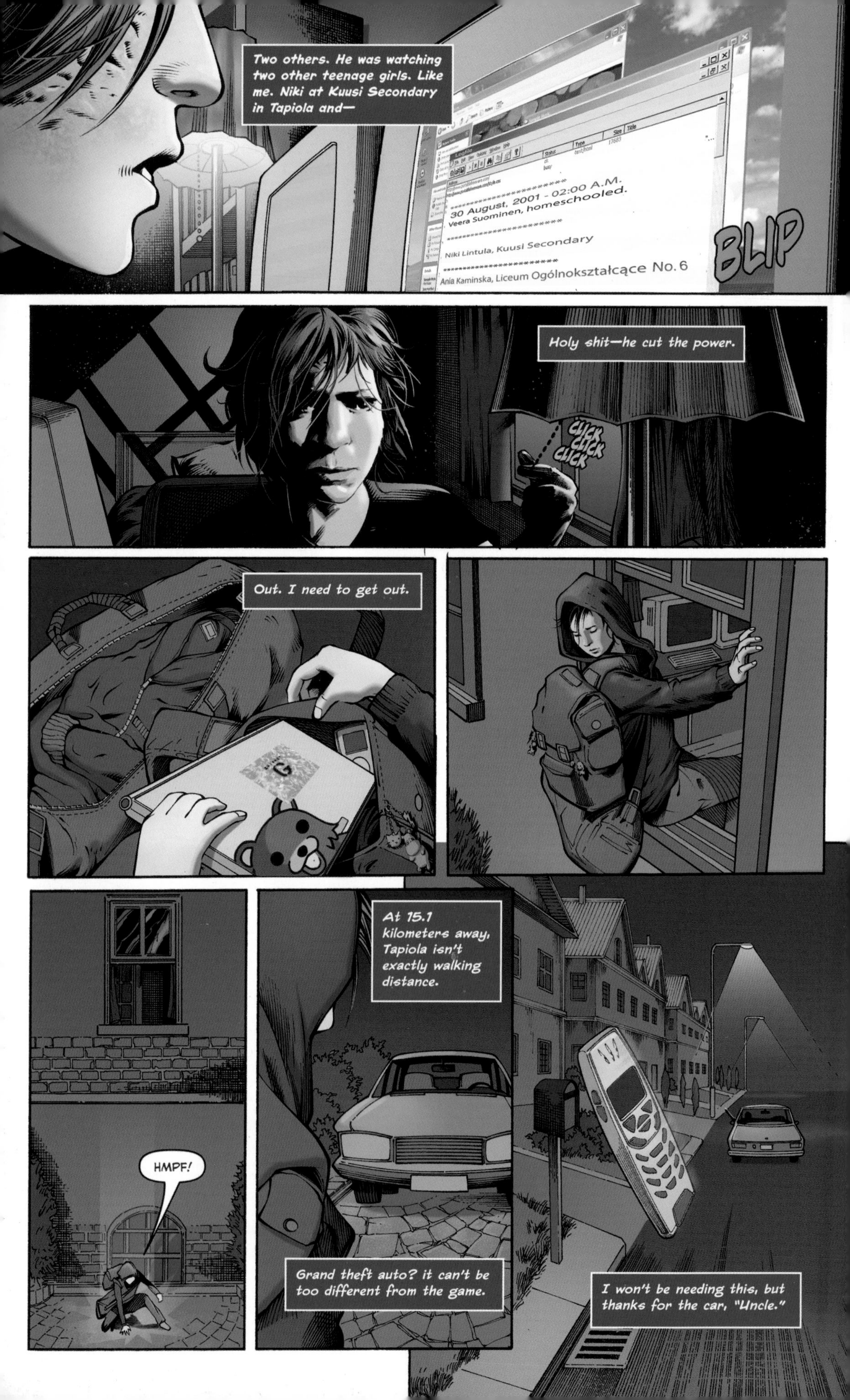

Two others. He was watching two other teenage girls. Like me. Niki at Kuusi Secondary in Tapiola and—
30 August, 2001 - 02:00 A.M.
Veera Suominen, homeschooled.
Niki Lintula, Kuusi Secondary
Ania Kaminska, Liceum Ogólnokształcące No. 6
BLIP
Holy shit—he cut the power.
CLICK CLICK CLICK
Out. I need to get out.
HMPF!
At 15.1 kilometers away, Tapiola isn't exactly walking distance.
Grand theft auto? it can't be too different from the game.
I won't be needing this, but thanks for the car, "Uncle."

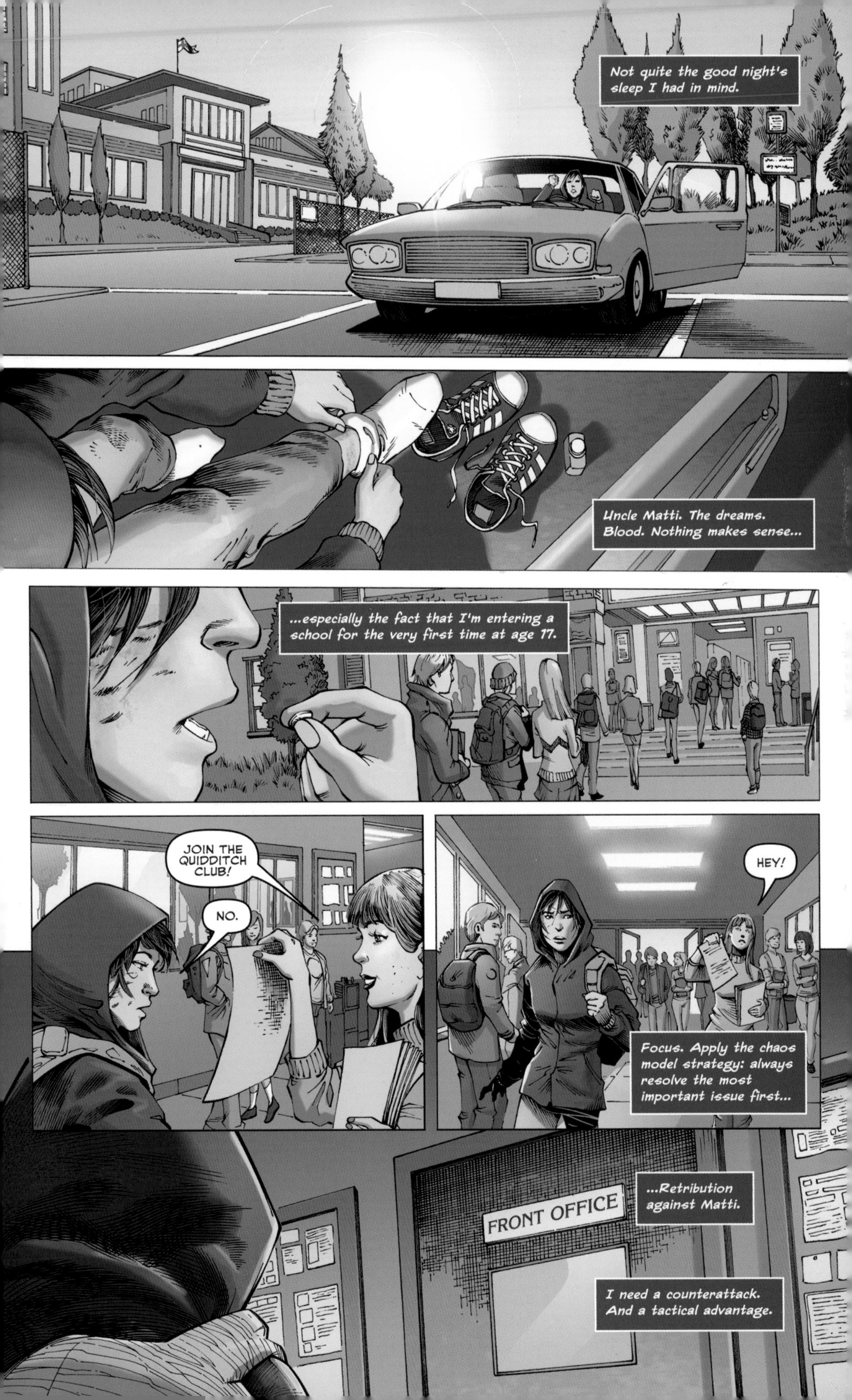
Not quite the good night's sleep I had in mind.
Uncle Matti. The dreams. Blood. Nothing makes sense...
...especially the fact that I'm entering a school for the very first time at age 17.
JOIN THE QUIDDITCH CLUB!
NO.
HEY!
Focus. Apply the chaos model strategy: always resolve the most important issue first...
FRONT OFFICE
...Retribution against Matti.
I need a counterattack. And a tactical advantage.

Strategy: find these girls + gather evidence of what's being done to us + bring Matti to justice = stability.

Niki Lintula, you're my first step. Where are you?

Got it: Biology.

LINTULA, NIKI

DOB:
1 APRIL, 1984
ADDRESS:
KAARINAPOLKU 36
02100, ESPOO
CLASS SCHEDULE:
PERIOD 1: BIOLOGY
PERIOD 2: HISTORY
PERIOD 3: ENGL
PERIOD 4: F
PERIOD 5
PERIO
PER

EXCUSE ME, WHAT ARE YOU DOING?

"I am newly enrolled in school here, and was having trouble finding my way to my class. Someone failed to give me a timetable, so I came to the office for help." Come on, get the words out. Say something...

I'M... I'M... I'M...

...NEW.

NEW STUDENTS ARE MY SPECIALTY. I'M OONA HOLMSTROM, GUIDANCE COUNSELOR. I'LL *GUIDE* YOU TO CLASS.

SORRY, BAD JOKE.

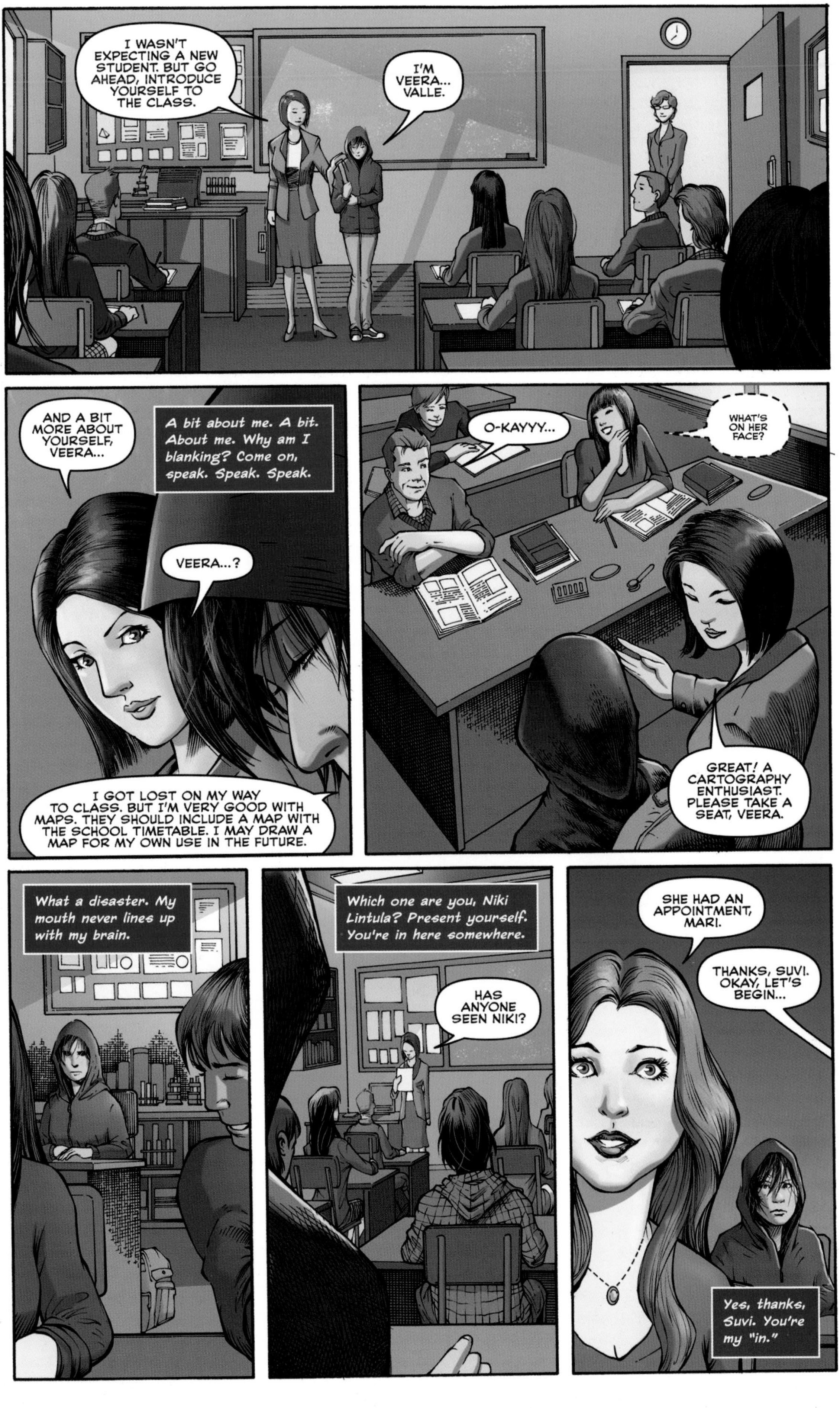
I WASN'T EXPECTING A NEW STUDENT. BUT GO AHEAD, INTRODUCE YOURSELF TO THE CLASS.
I'M VEERA... VALLE.
AND A BIT MORE ABOUT YOURSELF, VEERA...
A bit about me. A bit. About me. Why am I blanking? Come on, speak. Speak. Speak.
VEERA...?
I GOT LOST ON MY WAY TO CLASS. BUT I'M VERY GOOD WITH MAPS. THEY SHOULD INCLUDE A MAP WITH THE SCHOOL TIMETABLE. I MAY DRAW A MAP FOR MY OWN USE IN THE FUTURE.
O-KAYYY...
WHAT'S ON HER FACE?
GREAT! A CARTOGRAPHY ENTHUSIAST. PLEASE TAKE A SEAT, VEERA.
What a disaster. My mouth never lines up with my brain.
Which one are you, Niki Lintula? Present yourself. You're in here somewhere.
HAS ANYONE SEEN NIKI?
SHE HAD AN APPOINTMENT, MARI.
THANKS, SUVI. OKAY, LET'S BEGIN...
Yes, thanks, Suvi. You're my "in."

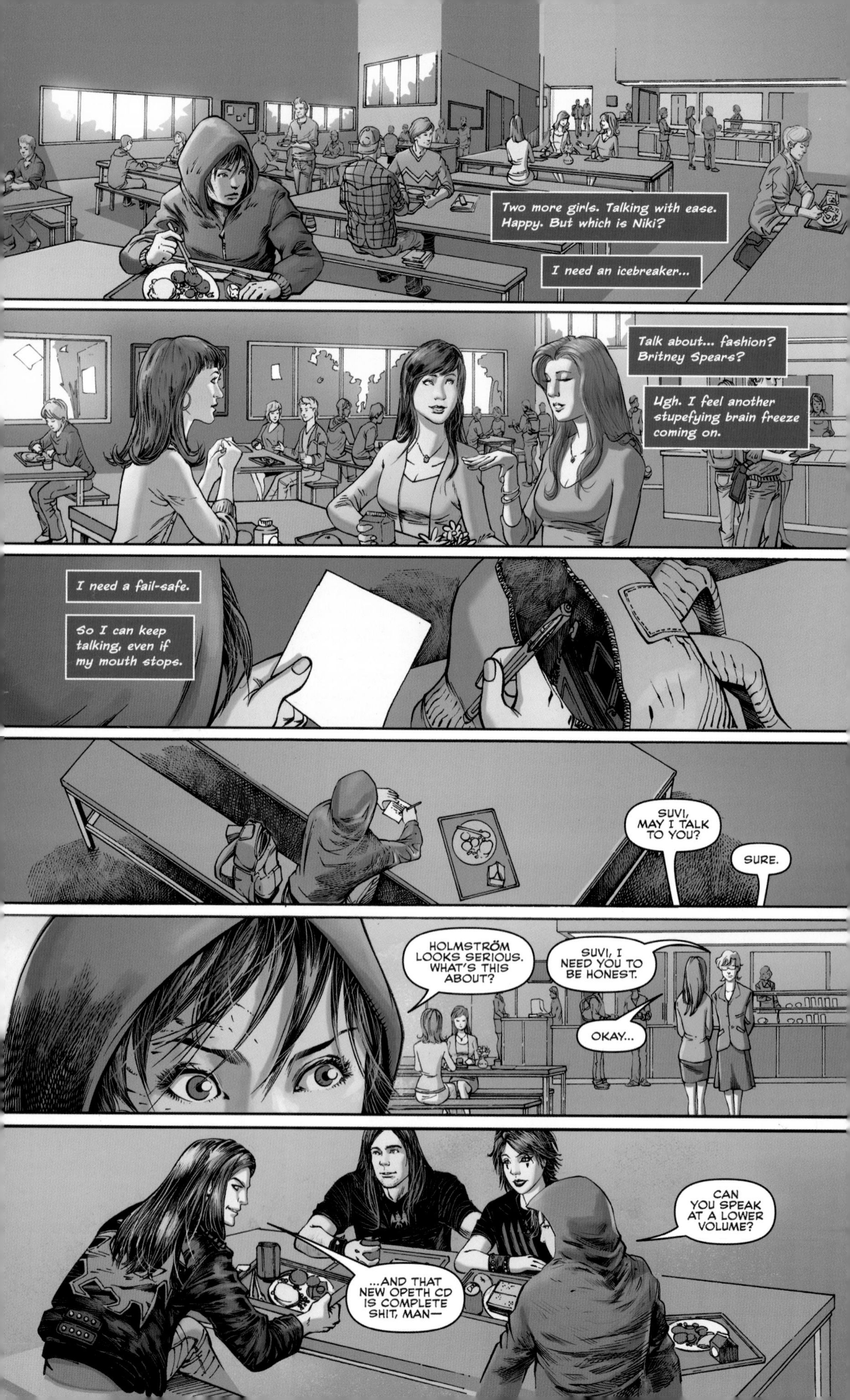
Two more girls. Talking with ease. Happy. But which is Niki?
I need an icebreaker...
Talk about... fashion? Britney Spears?
Ugh. I feel another stupefying brain freeze coming on.
I need a fail-safe.
So I can keep talking, even if my mouth stops.
SUVI, MAY I TALK TO YOU?
SURE.
HOLMSTRÖM LOOKS SERIOUS. WHAT'S THIS ABOUT?
SUVI, I NEED YOU TO BE HONEST.
OKAY...
CAN YOU SPEAK AT A LOWER VOLUME?
...AND THAT NEW OPETH CD IS COMPLETE SHIT, MAN—

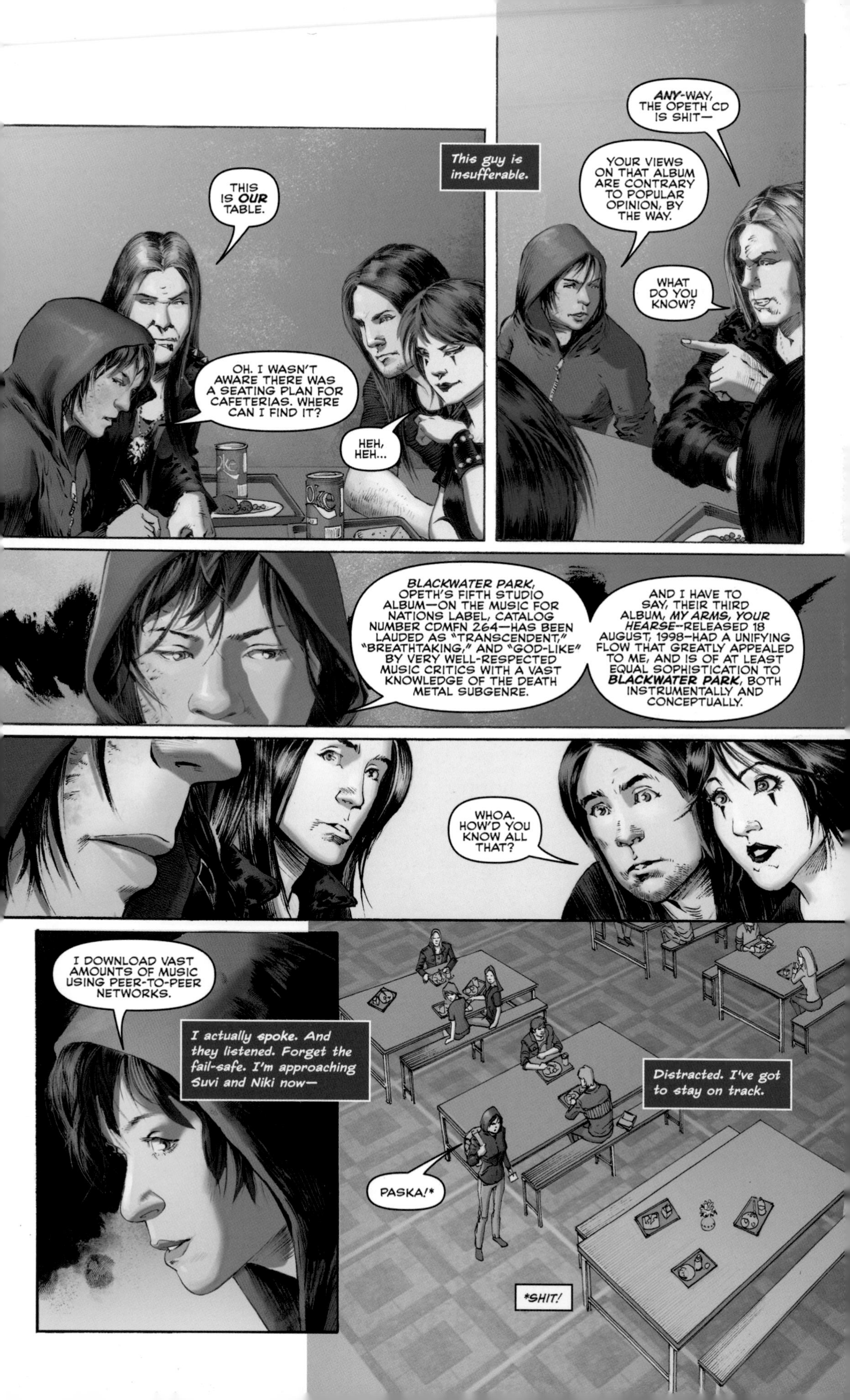
THIS IS *OUR* TABLE.
OH. I WASN'T AWARE THERE WAS A SEATING PLAN FOR CAFETERIAS. WHERE CAN I FIND IT?
HEH, HEH...
This guy is insufferable.
ANY-WAY, THE OPETH CD IS SHIT—
YOUR VIEWS ON THAT ALBUM ARE CONTRARY TO POPULAR OPINION, BY THE WAY.
WHAT DO YOU KNOW?
BLACKWATER PARK, OPETH'S FIFTH STUDIO ALBUM—ON THE MUSIC FOR NATIONS LABEL, CATALOG NUMBER CDMFN 264—HAS BEEN LAUDED AS "TRANSCENDENT," "BREATHTAKING," AND "GOD-LIKE" BY VERY WELL-RESPECTED MUSIC CRITICS WITH A VAST KNOWLEDGE OF THE DEATH METAL SUBGENRE.
AND I HAVE TO SAY, THEIR THIRD ALBUM, *MY ARMS, YOUR HEARSE*--RELEASED 18 AUGUST, 1998--HAD A UNIFYING FLOW THAT GREATLY APPEALED TO ME, AND IS OF AT LEAST EQUAL SOPHISTICATION TO ***BLACKWATER PARK,*** BOTH INSTRUMENTALLY AND CONCEPTUALLY.
WHOA. HOW'D YOU KNOW ALL THAT?
I DOWNLOAD VAST AMOUNTS OF MUSIC USING PEER-TO-PEER NETWORKS.
I actually spoke. And they listened. Forget the fail-safe. I'm approaching Suvi and Niki now—
Distracted. I've got to stay on track.
PASKA!*
*SHIT!

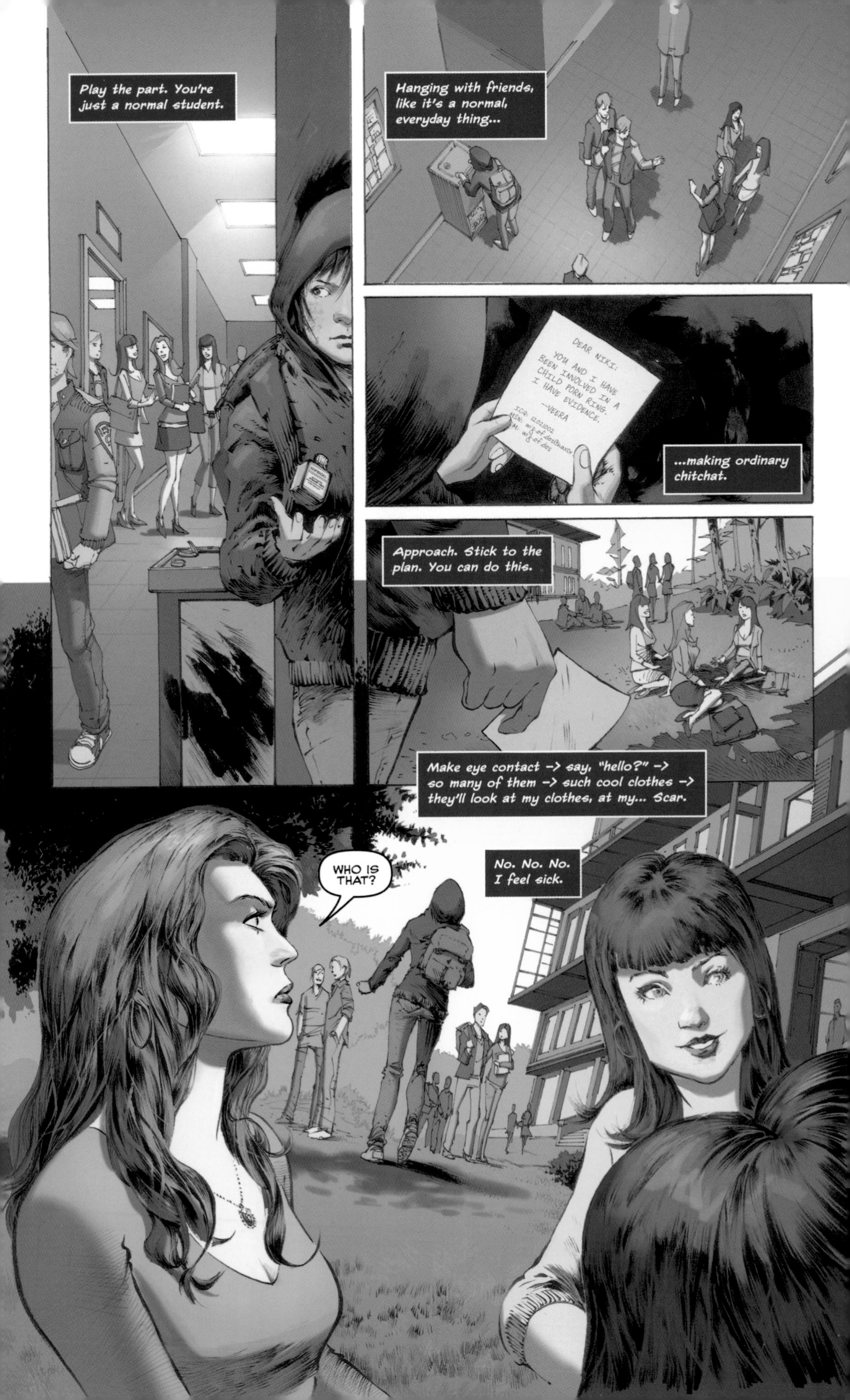
Play the part. You're just a normal student.
Hanging with friends, like it's a normal, everyday thing...
DEAR NIKI:
YOU AND I HAVE BEEN INVOLVED IN A CHILD PORN RING. I HAVE EVIDENCE.
—VEERA
ICQ: 12021002
...making ordinary chitchat.
Approach. Stick to the plan. You can do this.
Make eye contact -> say, "hello?" -> so many of them -> such cool clothes -> they'll look at my clothes, at my... Scar.
WHO IS THAT?
No. No. No. I feel sick.

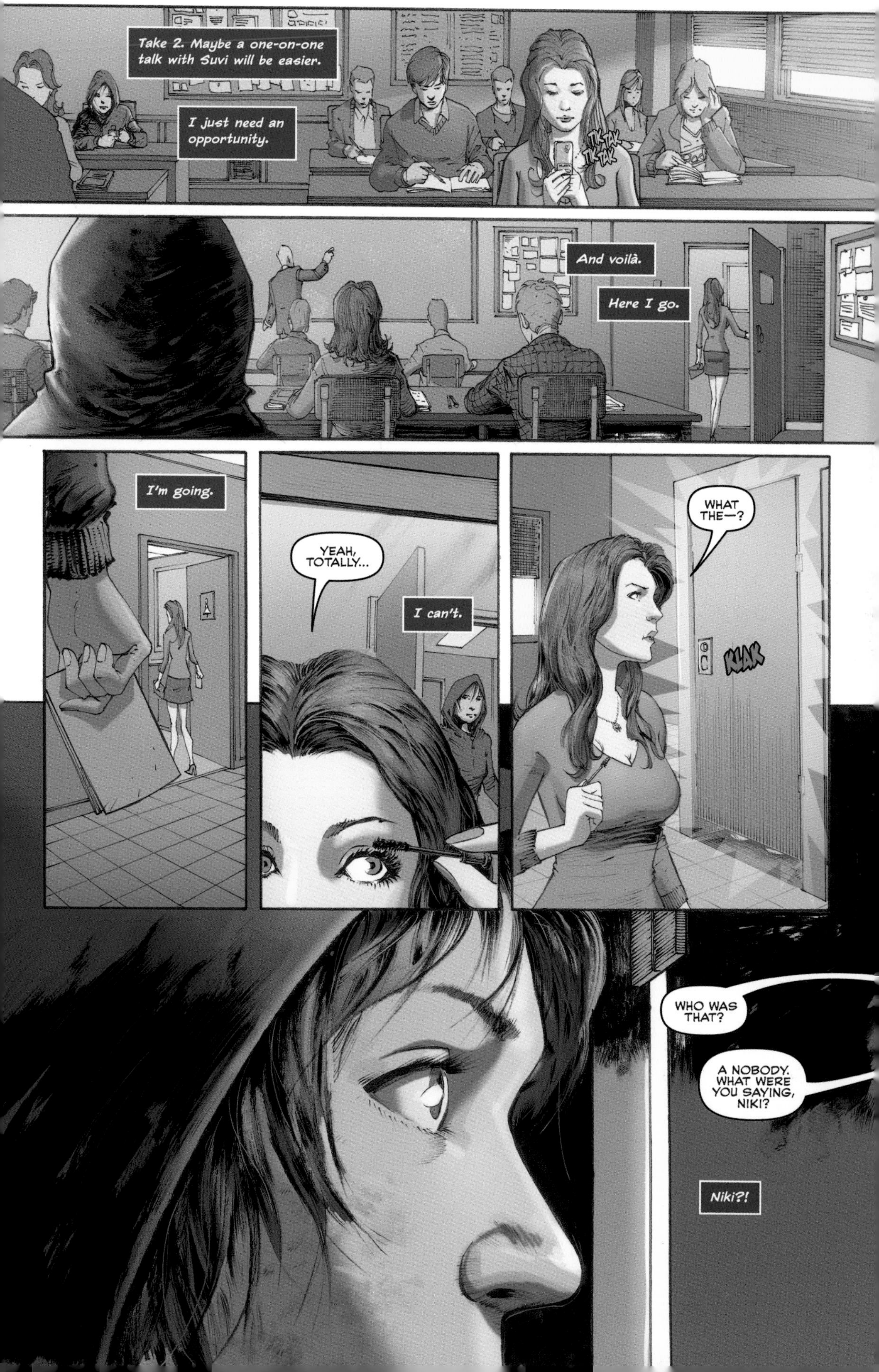
Take 2. Maybe a one-on-one talk with Suvi will be easier.
I just need an opportunity.
TIK TAK TIK TAK
And voilà.
Here I go.
I'm going.
YEAH, TOTALLY...
I can't.
WHAT THE—?
KLAK
WHO WAS THAT?
A NOBODY. WHAT WERE YOU SAYING, NIKI?
Niki?!

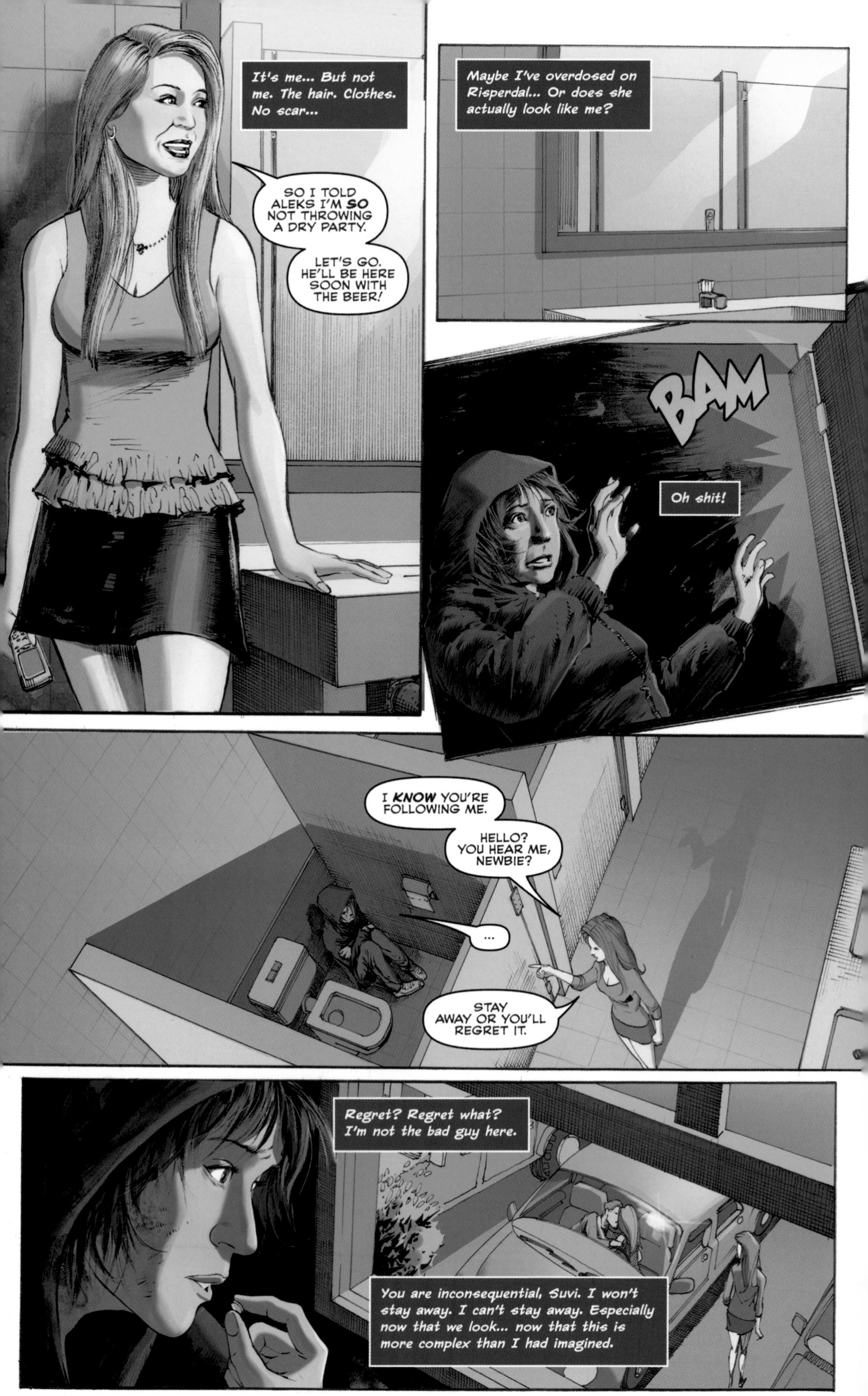

It's me... But not me. The hair. Clothes. No scar...
SO I TOLD ALEKS I'M **SO** NOT THROWING A DRY PARTY.
LET'S GO. HE'LL BE HERE SOON WITH THE BEER!
Maybe I've overdosed on Risperdal... Or does she actually look like me?
BAM
Oh shit!
I **KNOW** YOU'RE FOLLOWING ME.
HELLO? YOU HEAR ME, NEWBIE?
...
STAY AWAY OR YOU'LL REGRET IT.
Regret? Regret what? I'm not the bad guy here.
You are inconsequential, Suvi. I won't stay away. I can't stay away. Especially now that we look... now that this is more complex than I had imagined.

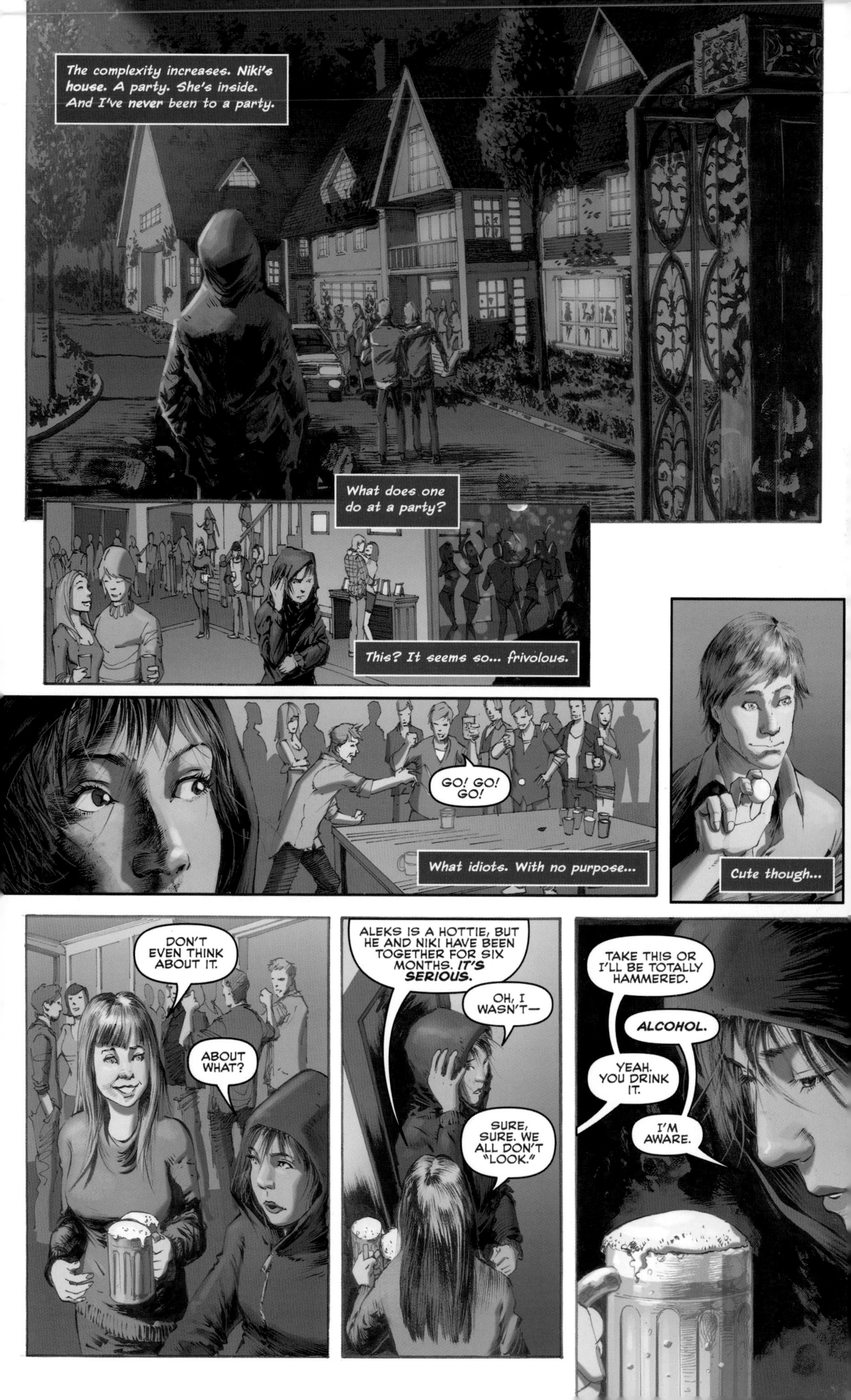
The complexity increases. Niki's house. A party. She's inside. And I've never been to a party.
What does one do at a party?
This? It seems so... frivolous.
GO! GO! GO!
What idiots. With no purpose...
Cute though...
DON'T EVEN THINK ABOUT IT.
ABOUT WHAT?
ALEKS IS A HOTTIE, BUT HE AND NIKI HAVE BEEN TOGETHER FOR SIX MONTHS. *IT'S SERIOUS.*
OH, I WASN'T—
SURE, SURE. WE ALL DON'T "LOOK."
TAKE THIS OR I'LL BE TOTALLY HAMMERED.
ALCOHOL.
YEAH. YOU DRINK IT.
I'M AWARE.

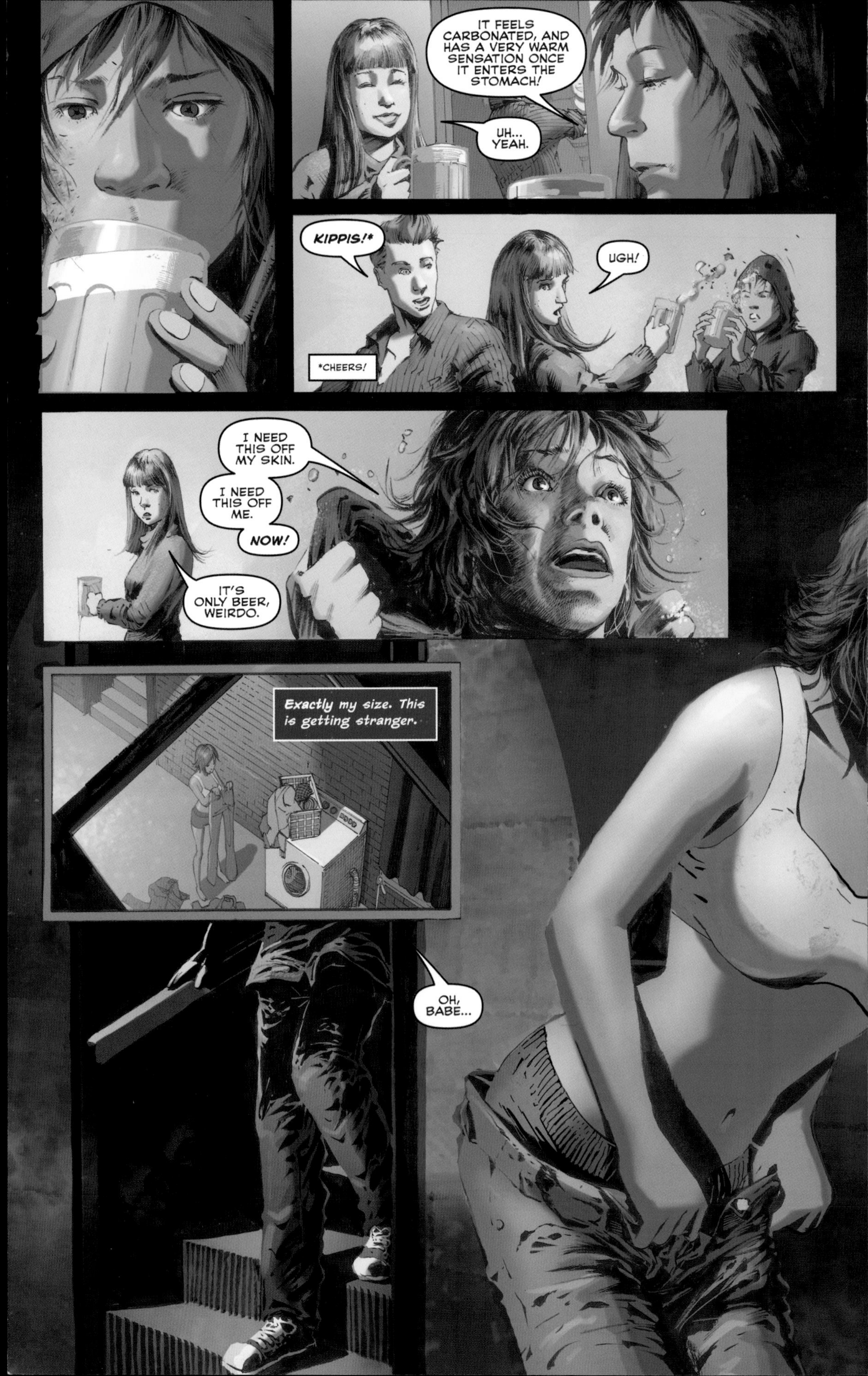
IT FEELS CARBONATED, AND HAS A VERY WARM SENSATION ONCE IT ENTERS THE STOMACH!
UH... YEAH.
KIPPIS!*
UGH!
*CHEERS!
I NEED THIS OFF MY SKIN.
I NEED THIS OFF ME.
NOW!
IT'S ONLY BEER, WEIRDO.
Exactly my size. This is getting stranger.
OH, BABE...

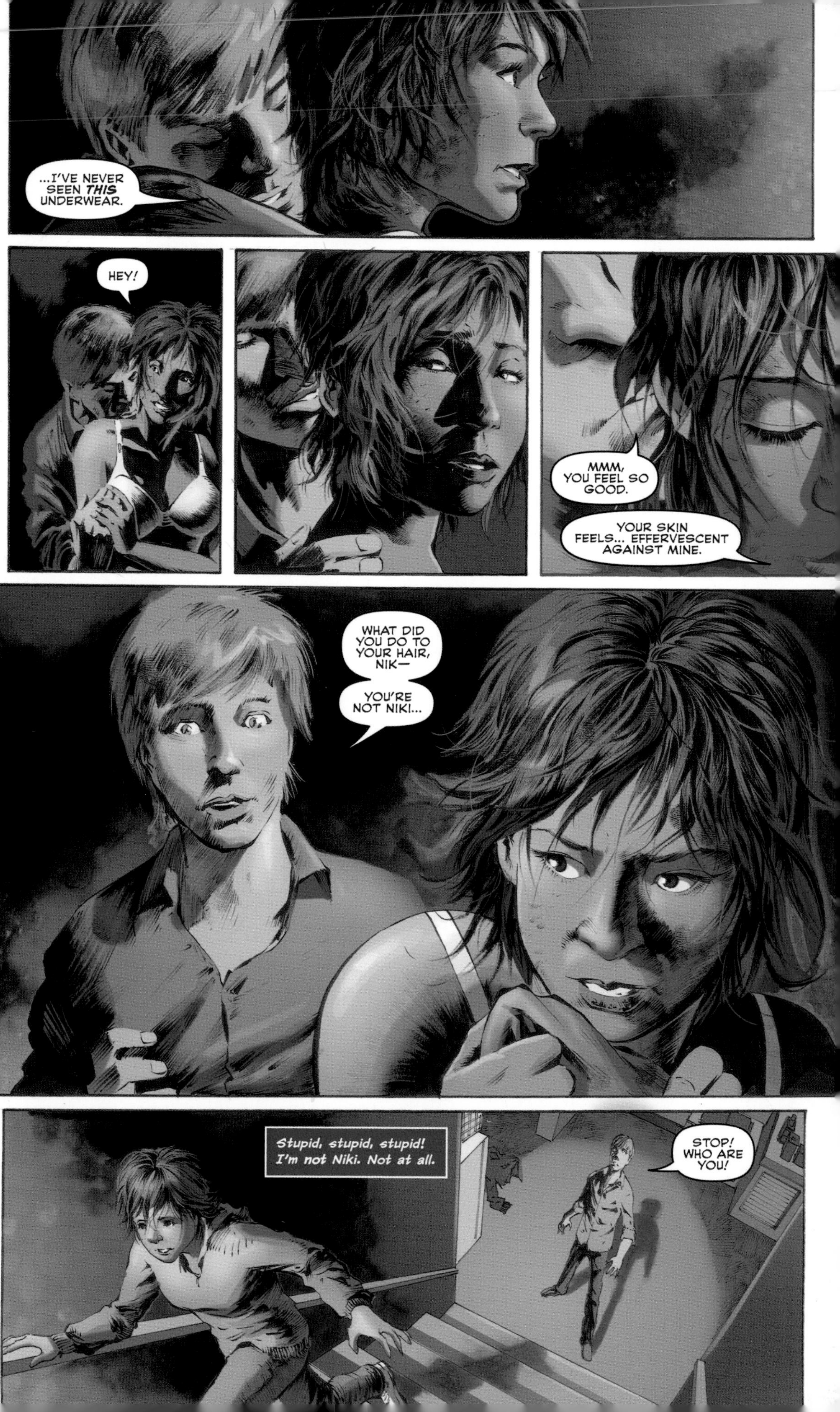
...I'VE NEVER SEEN *THIS* UNDERWEAR.
HEY!
MMM, YOU FEEL SO GOOD.
YOUR SKIN FEELS... EFFERVESCENT AGAINST MINE.
WHAT DID YOU DO TO YOUR HAIR, NIK—
YOU'RE NOT NIKI...
Stupid, stupid, stupid! I'm not Niki. Not at all.
STOP! WHO ARE YOU!

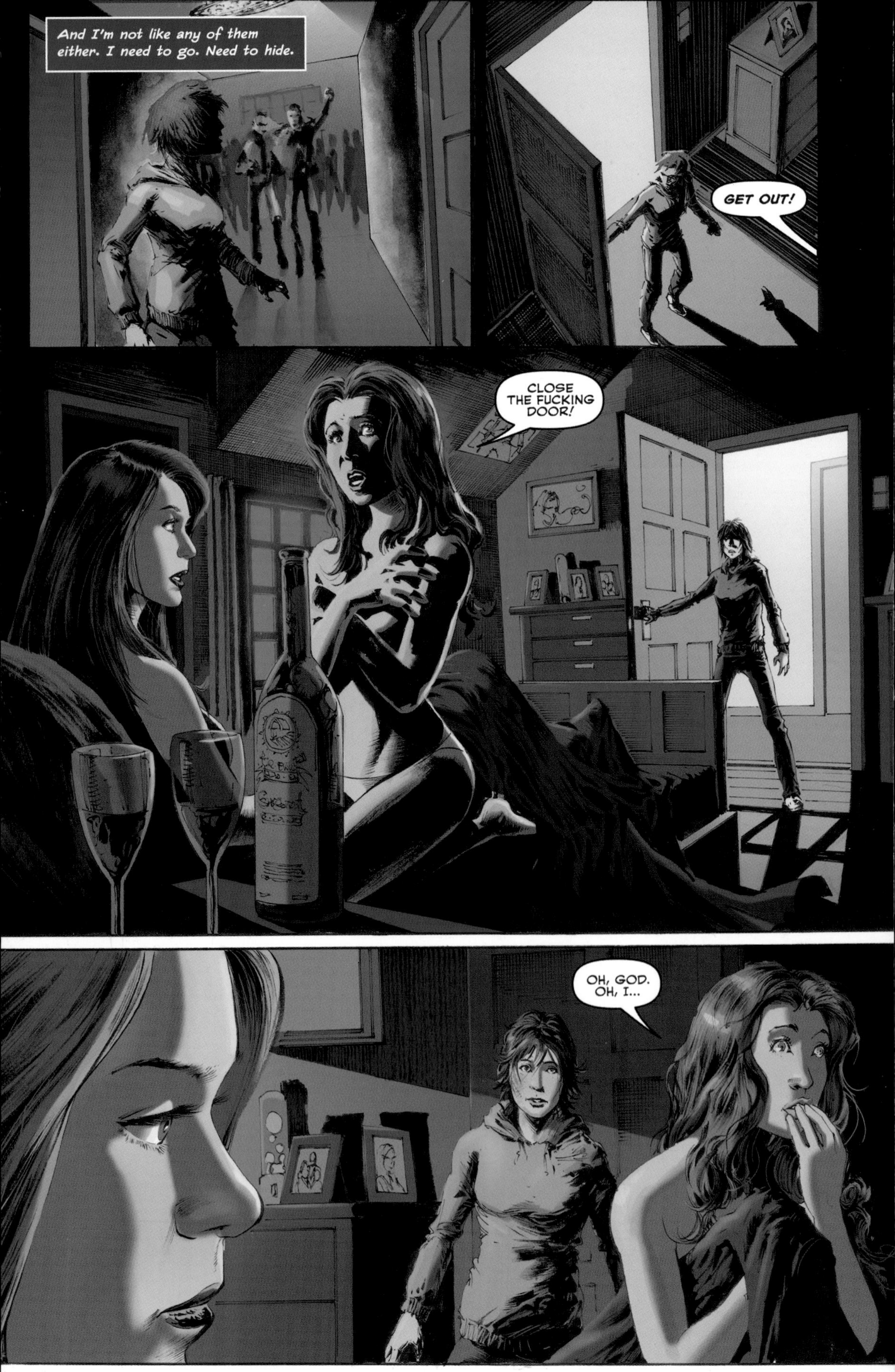
And I'm not like any of them either. I need to go. Need to hide.
GET OUT!
CLOSE THE FUCKING DOOR!
OH, GOD. OH, I...

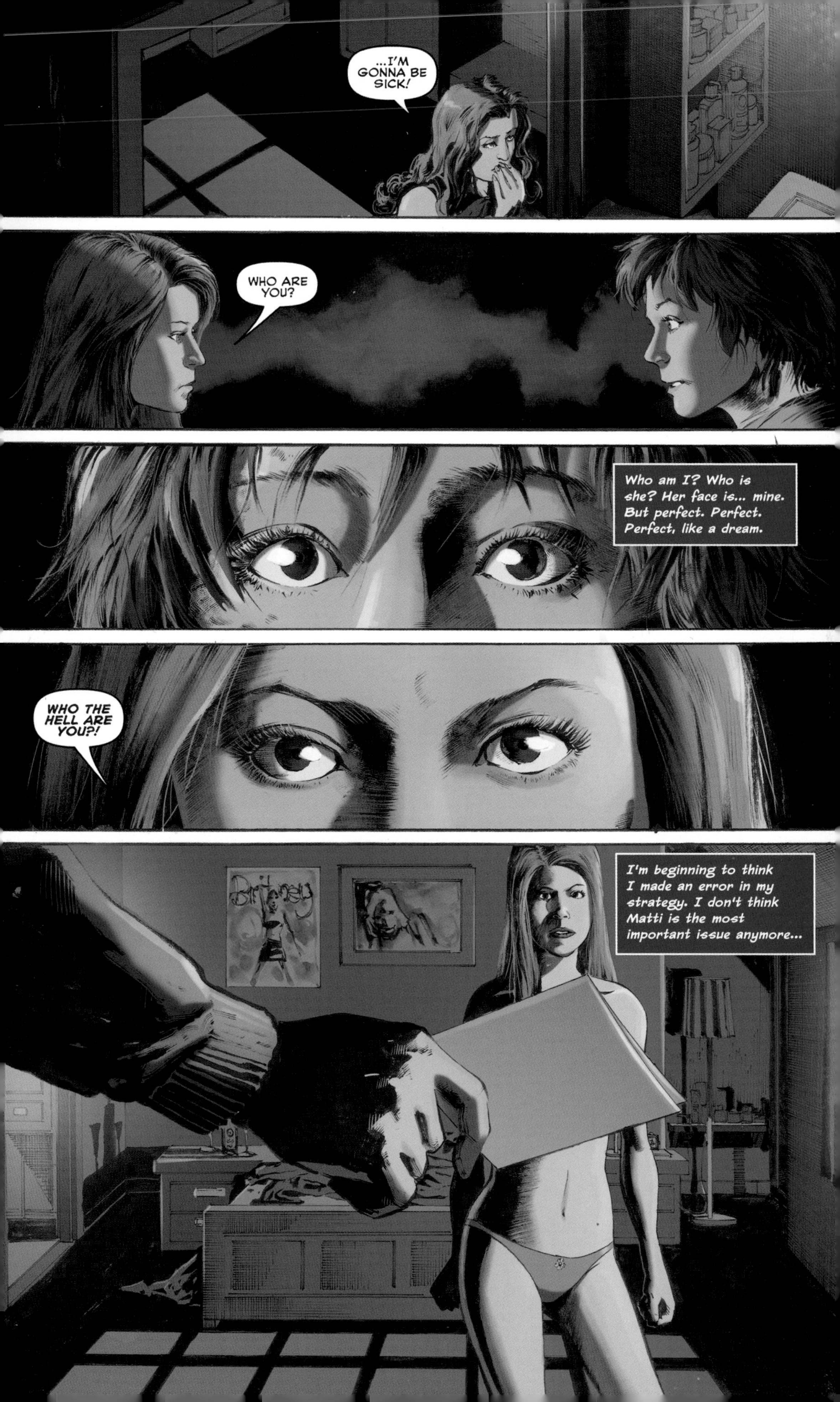

...I'M GONNA BE SICK!
WHO ARE YOU?
Who am I? Who is she? Her face is... mine. But perfect. Perfect. Perfect, like a dream.
WHO THE HELL ARE YOU?!
I'm beginning to think I made an error in my strategy. I don't think Matti is the most important issue anymore...

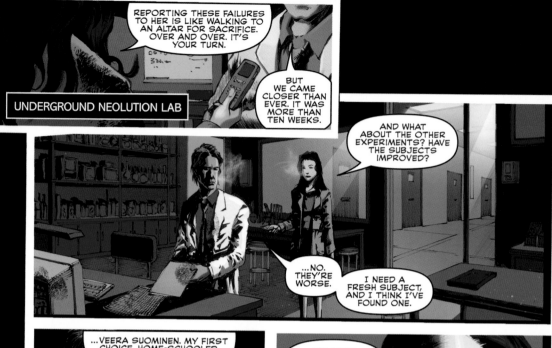

REPORTING THESE FAILURES TO HER IS LIKE WALKING TO AN ALTAR FOR SACRIFICE. OVER AND OVER. IT'S YOUR TURN.

UNDERGROUND NEOLUTION LAB

BUT WE CAME CLOSER THAN EVER. IT WAS MORE THAN TEN WEEKS.

AND WHAT ABOUT THE OTHER EXPERIMENTS? HAVE THE SUBJECTS IMPROVED?

...NO. THEY'RE WORSE.

I NEED A FRESH SUBJECT, AND I THINK I'VE FOUND ONE.

...VEERA SUOMINEN. MY FIRST CHOICE. HOME-SCHOOLED. ISOLATED. PRESENTS THE LEAST COLLATERAL.

VEERA SUOMINEN
LOCATION: HELSINKI, FINLAND
DOB: MARCH 3, 1984
3MK 29A

HER PSYCH EVALUATION SUGGESTS SHE WON'T BE COMPLIANT.

WE GAVE YOU NEARLY FREE REIGN, DMITRI. NOT AN INVITATION TO CREATE CHAOS.

CONSIDER THE ALTERNATIVE, MARION...

...FAILURE.

I HATE COMING UP HERE. ESPECIALLY FOR THAT...

WHERE IS THE NEW "SUBJECT" LOCATED?

NOT FAR— HELSINKI.

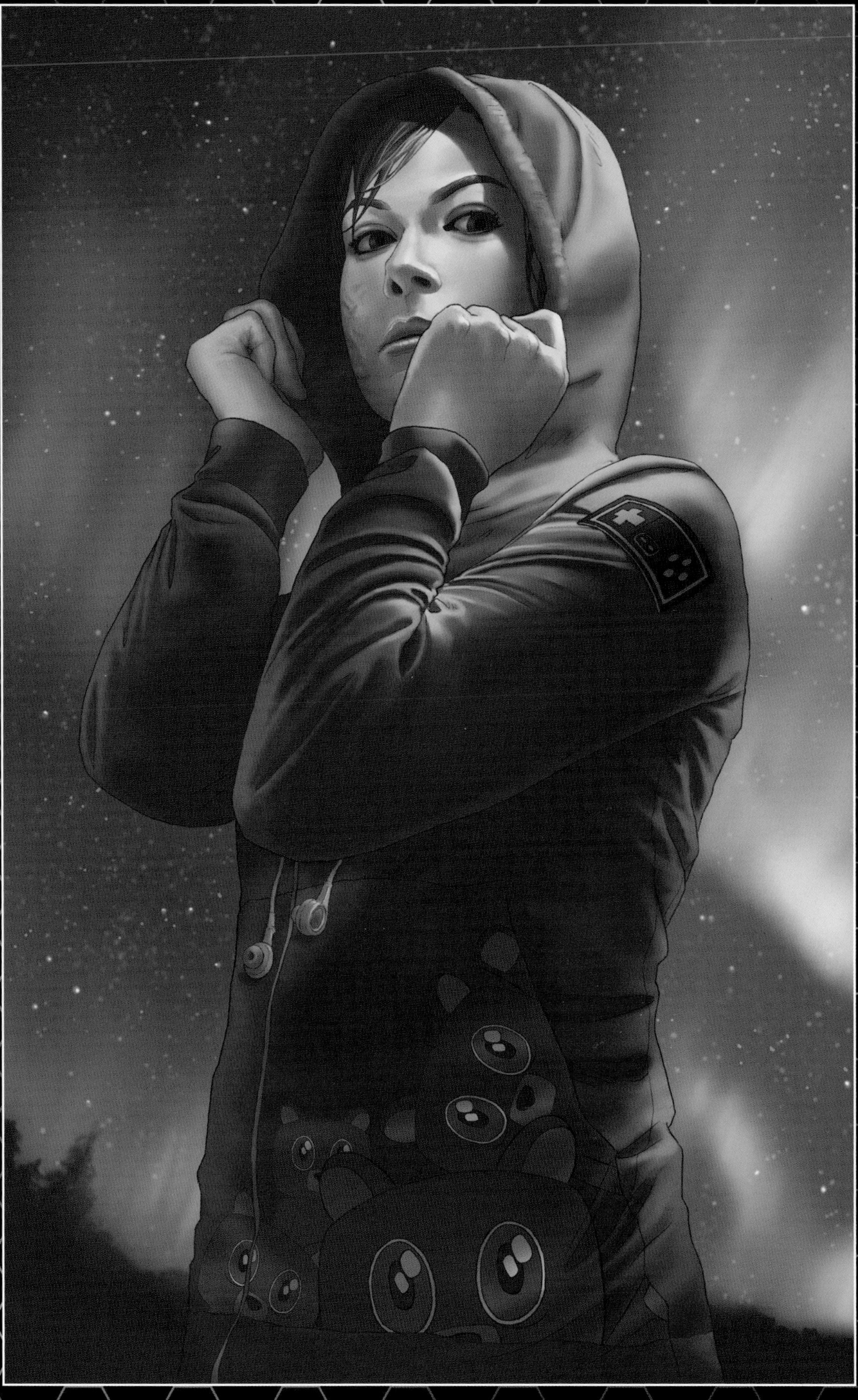

BY **RODIN ESQUEJO**

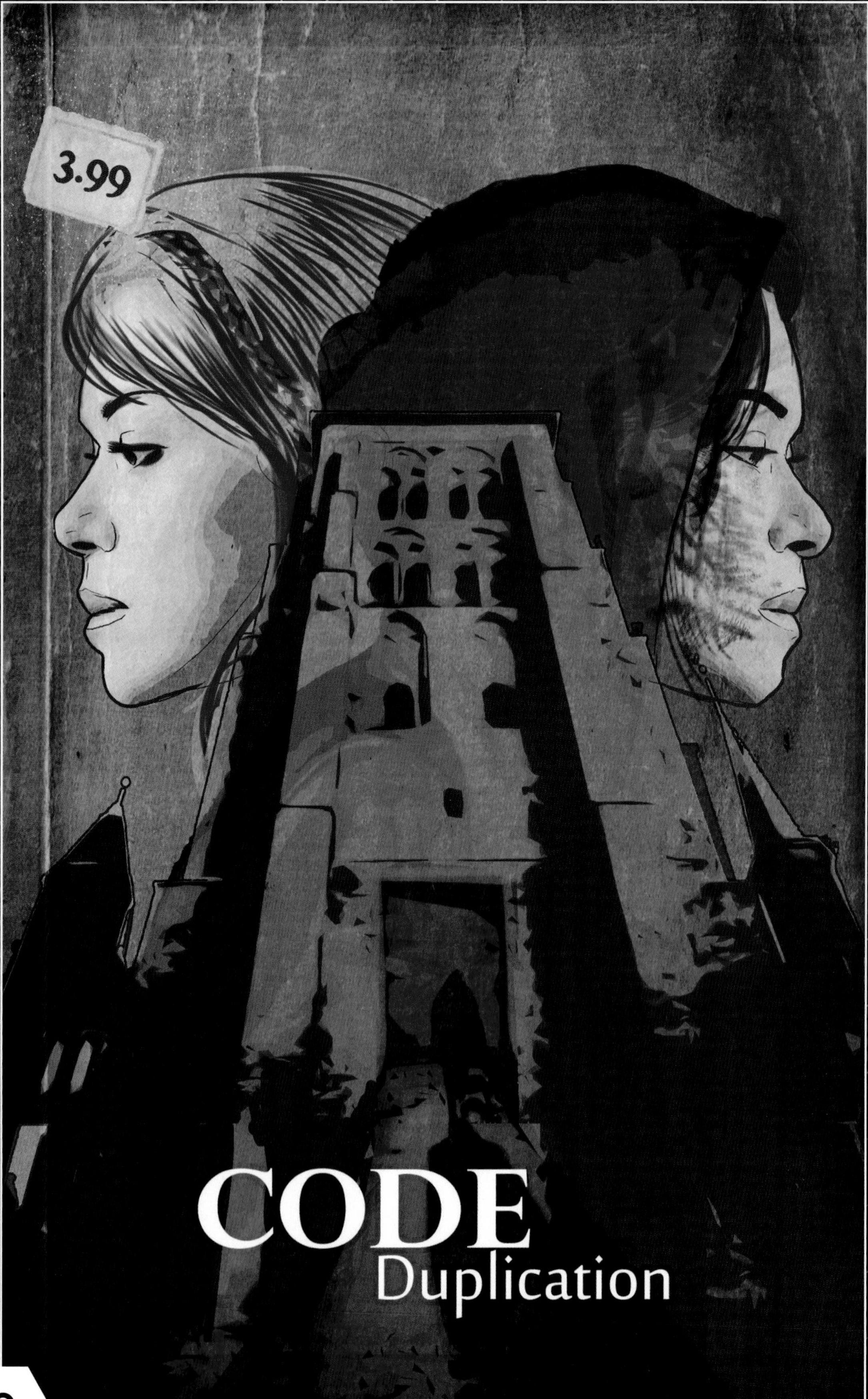
3.99
CODE
Duplication

BY CAT STAGGS

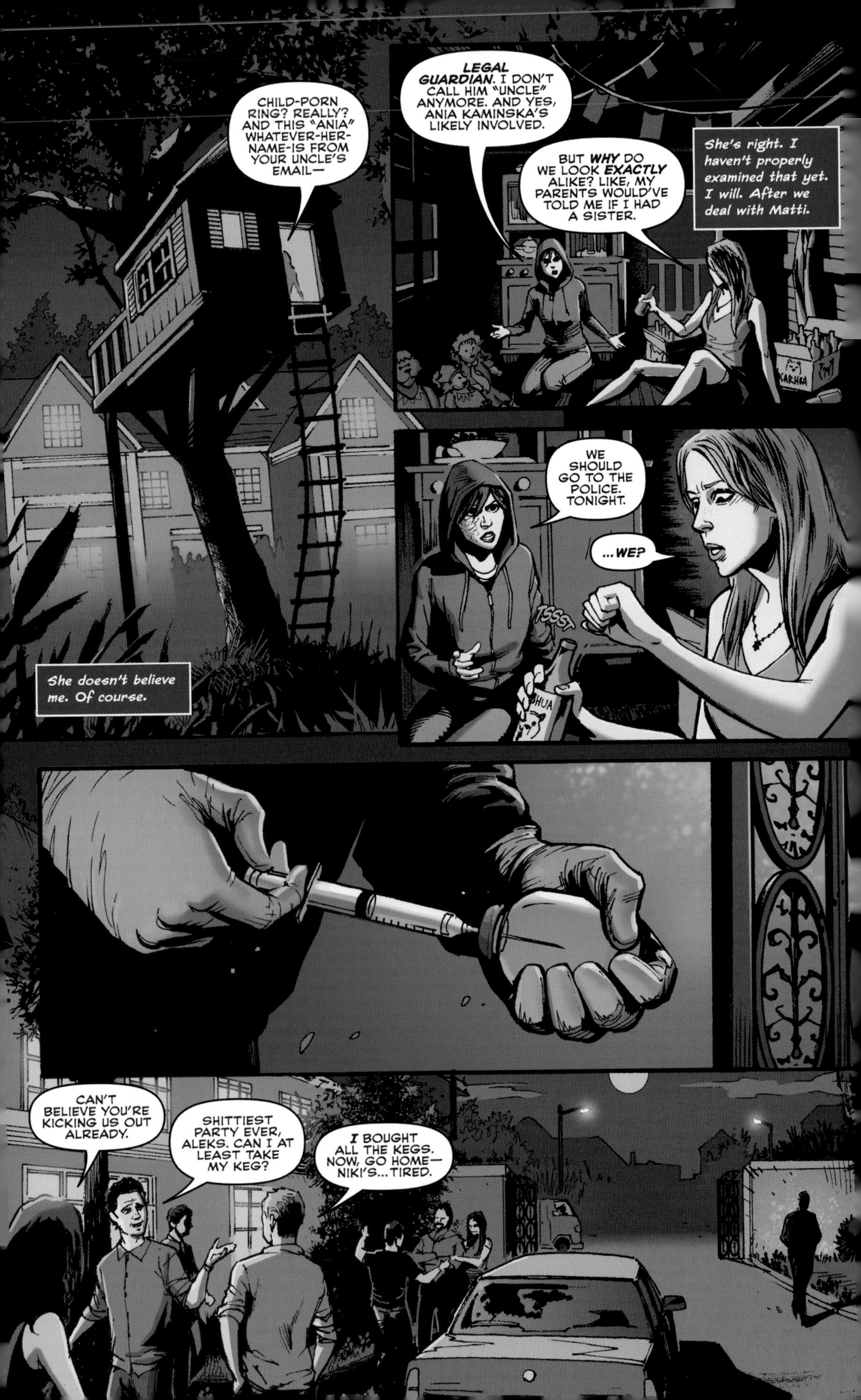
CHILD-PORN RING? REALLY? AND THIS "ANIA" WHATEVER-HER-NAME-IS FROM YOUR UNCLE'S EMAIL—
LEGAL GUARDIAN. I DON'T CALL HIM "UNCLE" ANYMORE. AND YES, ANIA KAMINSKA'S LIKELY INVOLVED.
BUT WHY DO WE LOOK EXACTLY ALIKE? LIKE, MY PARENTS WOULD'VE TOLD ME IF I HAD A SISTER.
She's right. I haven't properly examined that yet. I will. After we deal with Matti.
She doesn't believe me. Of course.
WE SHOULD GO TO THE POLICE. TONIGHT.
...WE?
TSSST
CAN'T BELIEVE YOU'RE KICKING US OUT ALREADY.
SHITTIEST PARTY EVER, ALEKS. CAN I AT LEAST TAKE MY KEG?
I BOUGHT ALL THE KEGS. NOW, GO HOME— NIKI'S...TIRED.

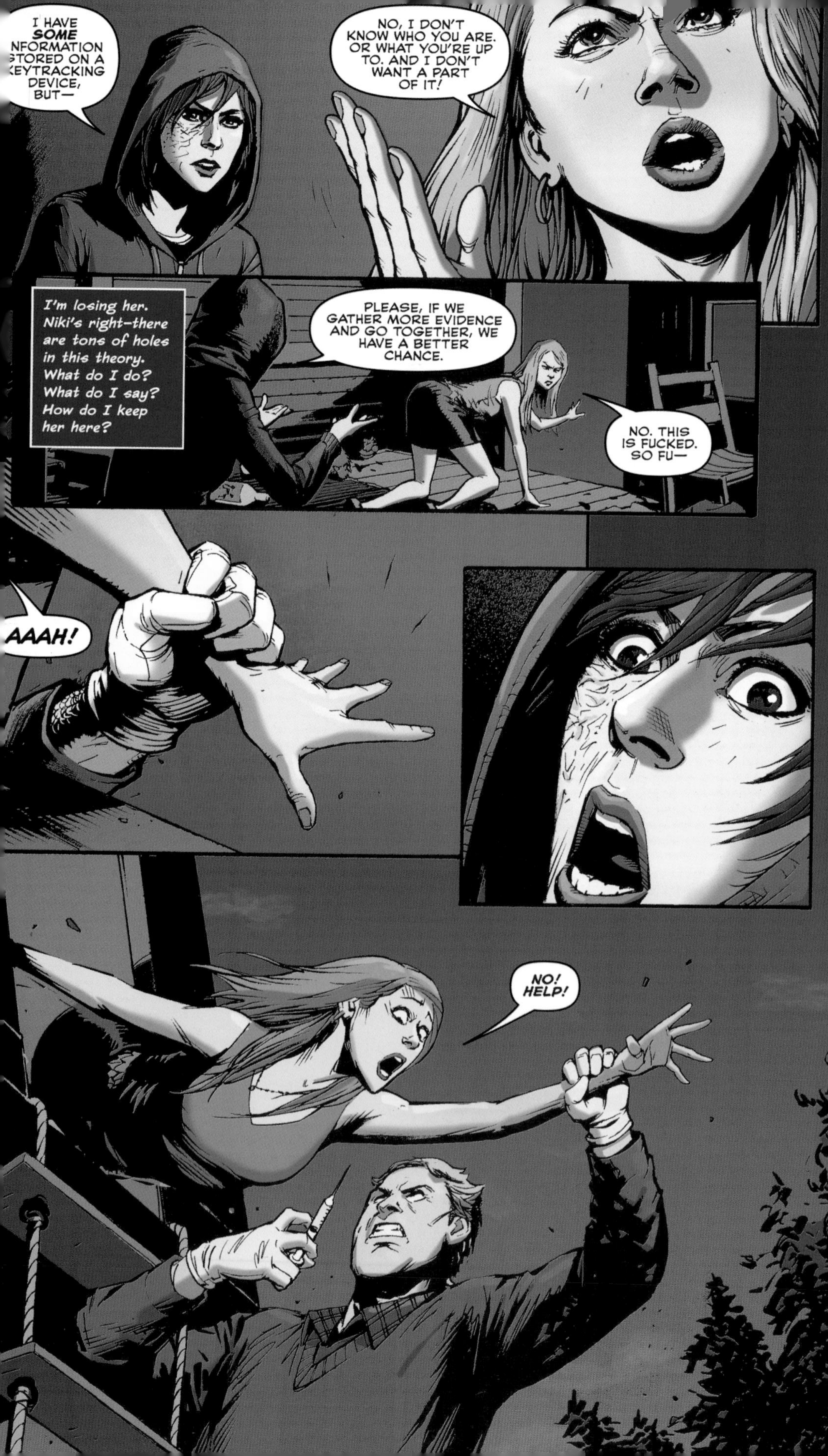
I HAVE SOME NFORMATION STORED ON A KEYTRACKING DEVICE, BUT—
NO, I DON'T KNOW WHO YOU ARE. OR WHAT YOU'RE UP TO. AND I DON'T WANT A PART OF IT!
I'm losing her. Niki's right—there are tons of holes in this theory. What do I do? What do I say? How do I keep her here?
PLEASE, IF WE GATHER MORE EVIDENCE AND GO TOGETHER, WE HAVE A BETTER CHANCE.
NO. THIS IS FUCKED. SO FU—
AAAH!
NO! HELP!

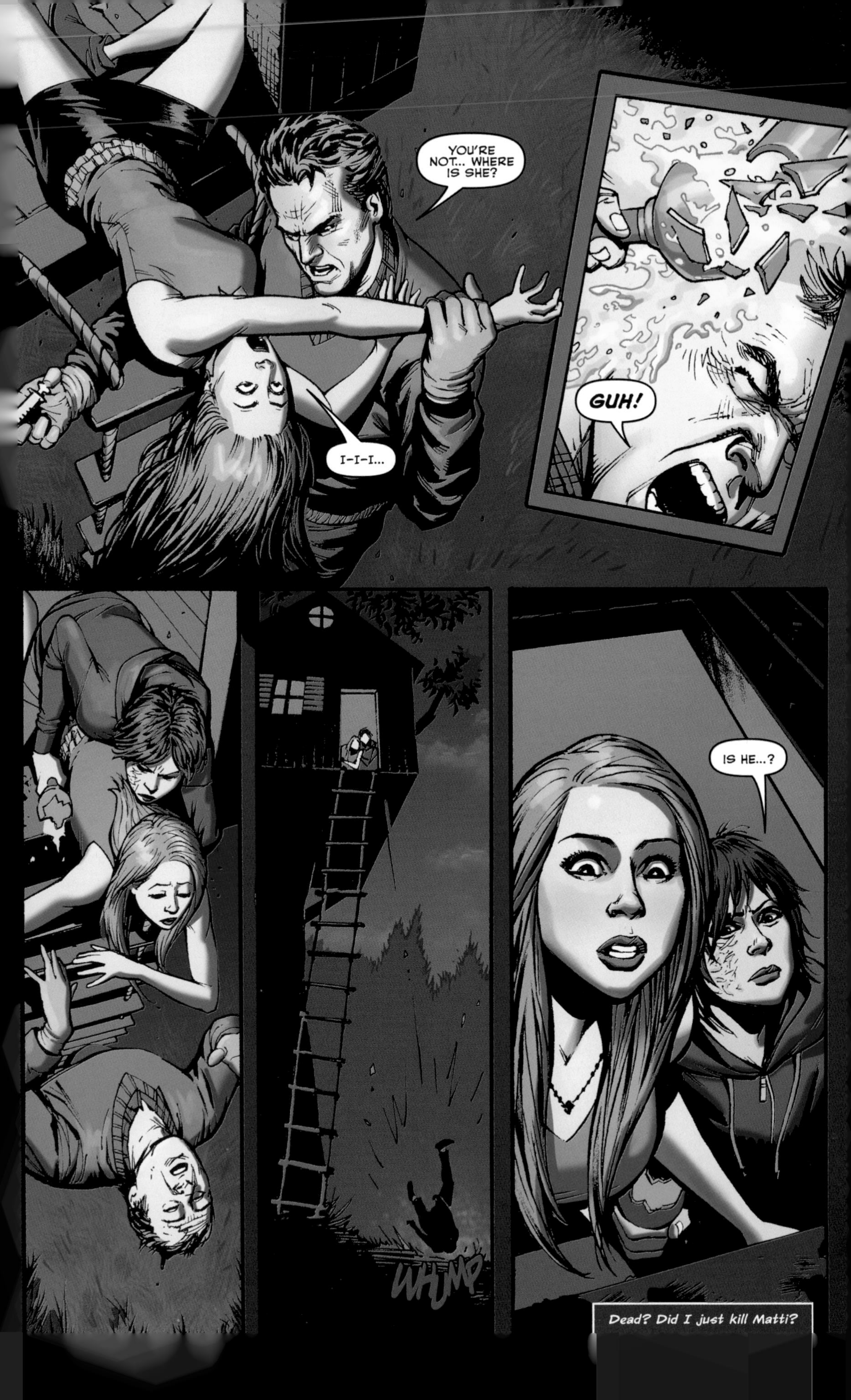
YOU'RE NOT... WHERE IS SHE?
I-I-I...
GUH!
WUMP
IS HE...?
Dead? Did I just kill Matti?

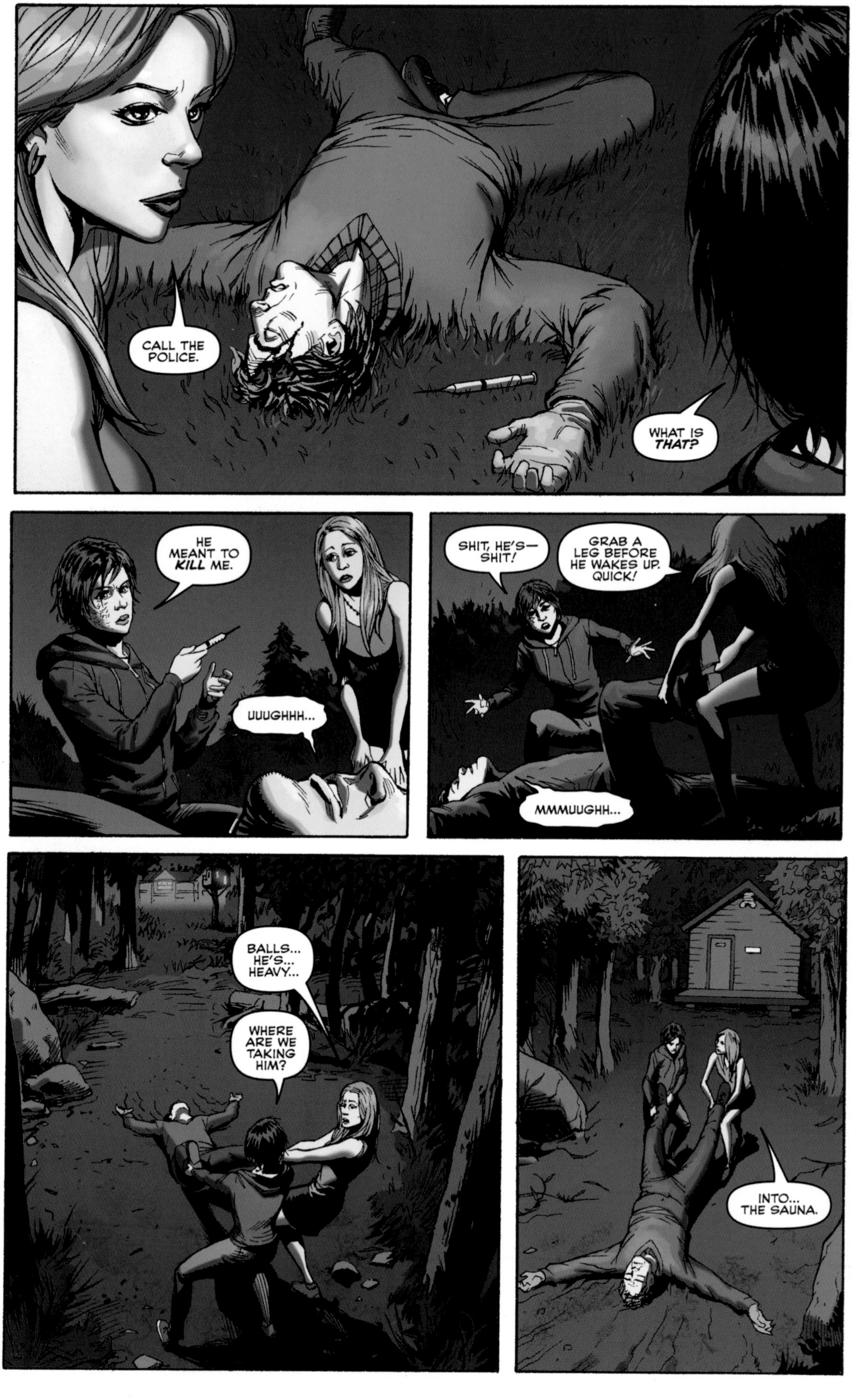
CALL THE POLICE.
WHAT IS *THAT?*
HE MEANT TO ***KILL*** ME.
UUUGHHH...
SHIT, HE'S— SHIT!
GRAB A LEG BEFORE HE WAKES UP. QUICK!
MMMUUGHH...
BALLS... HE'S... HEAVY...
WHERE ARE WE TAKING HIM?
INTO... THE SAUNA.

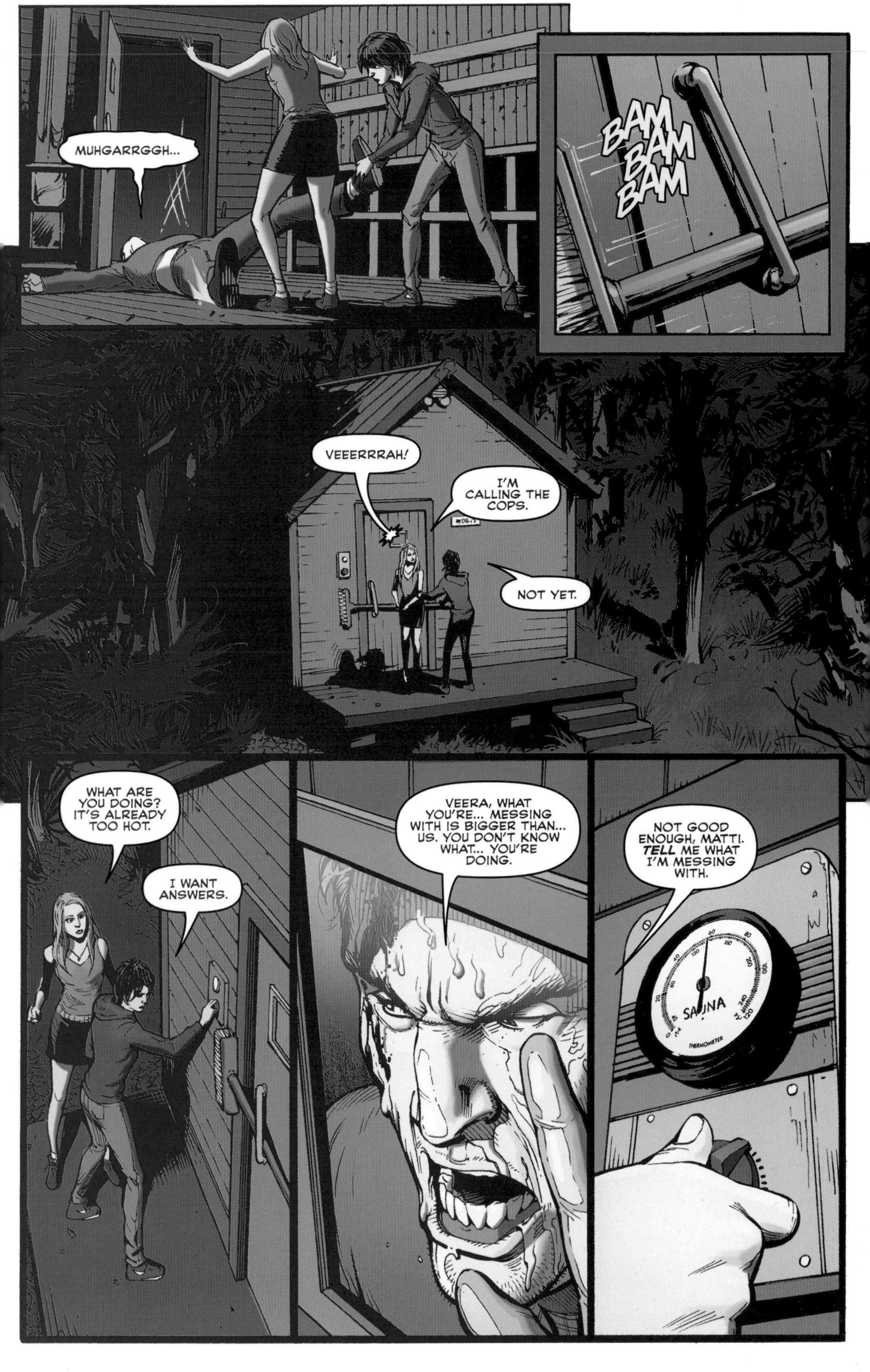
MUHGARRGGH...
BAM BAM BAM BAM
VEEERRRAH!
I'M CALLING THE COPS.
NOT YET.
WHAT ARE YOU DOING? IT'S ALREADY TOO HOT.
I WANT ANSWERS.
VEERA, WHAT YOU'RE... MESSING WITH IS BIGGER THAN... US. YOU DON'T KNOW WHAT... YOU'RE DOING.
NOT GOOD ENOUGH, MATTI. **TELL** ME WHAT I'M MESSING WITH.
SAUNA
THERMOMETER

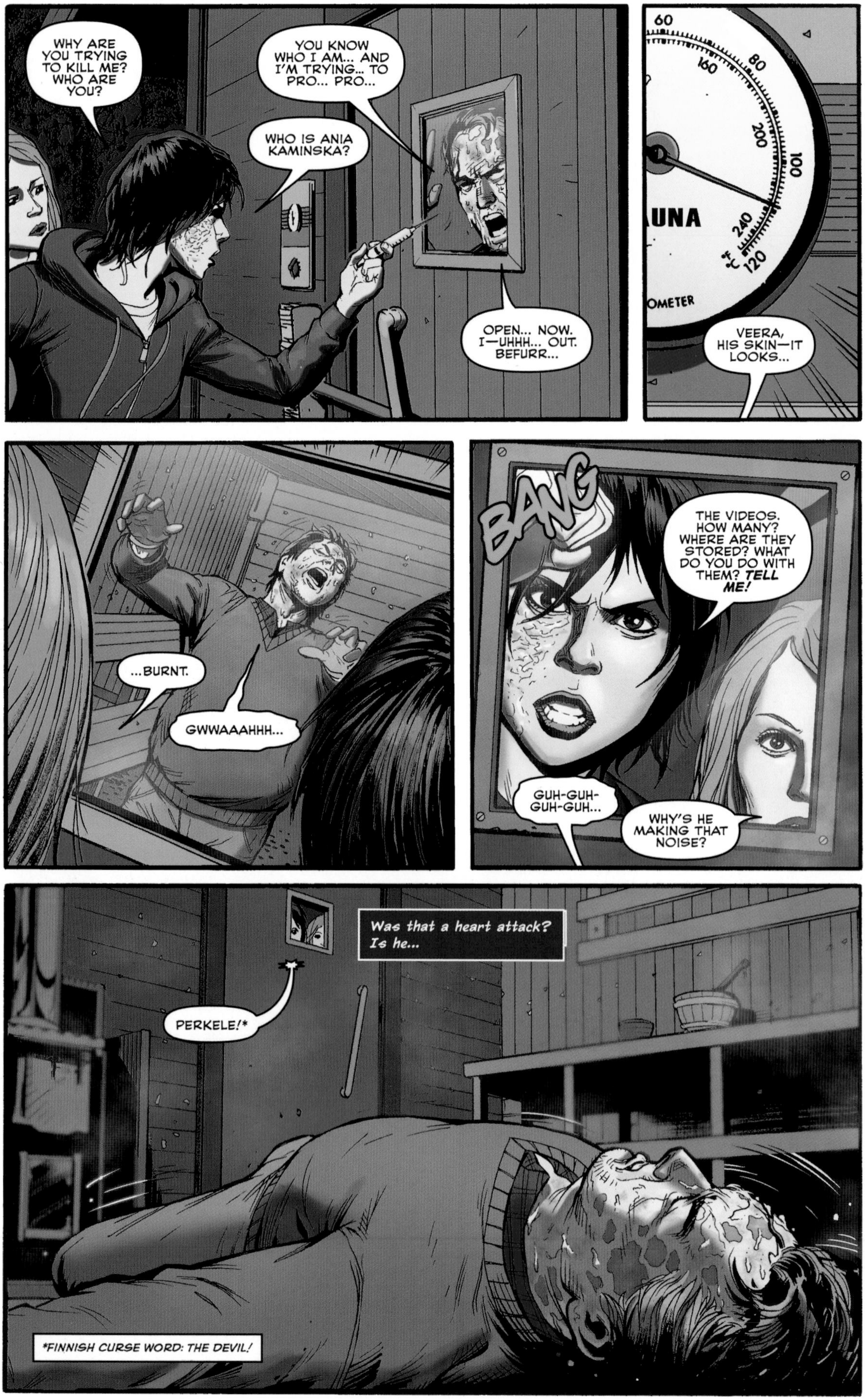
WHY ARE YOU TRYING TO KILL ME? WHO ARE YOU?
YOU KNOW WHO I AM... AND I'M TRYING... TO PRO... PRO...
WHO IS ANIA KAMINSKA?
OPEN... NOW. I—UHHH... OUT. BEFURR...
AUNA
OMETER
VEERA, HIS SKIN—IT LOOKS...
...BURNT.
GWWAAAHHH...
BANG
THE VIDEOS. HOW MANY? WHERE ARE THEY STORED? WHAT DO YOU DO WITH THEM? TELL ME!
GUH-GUH-GUH-GUH...
WHY'S HE MAKING THAT NOISE?
Was that a heart attack? Is he...
PERKELE!*
*FINNISH CURSE WORD: THE DEVIL!

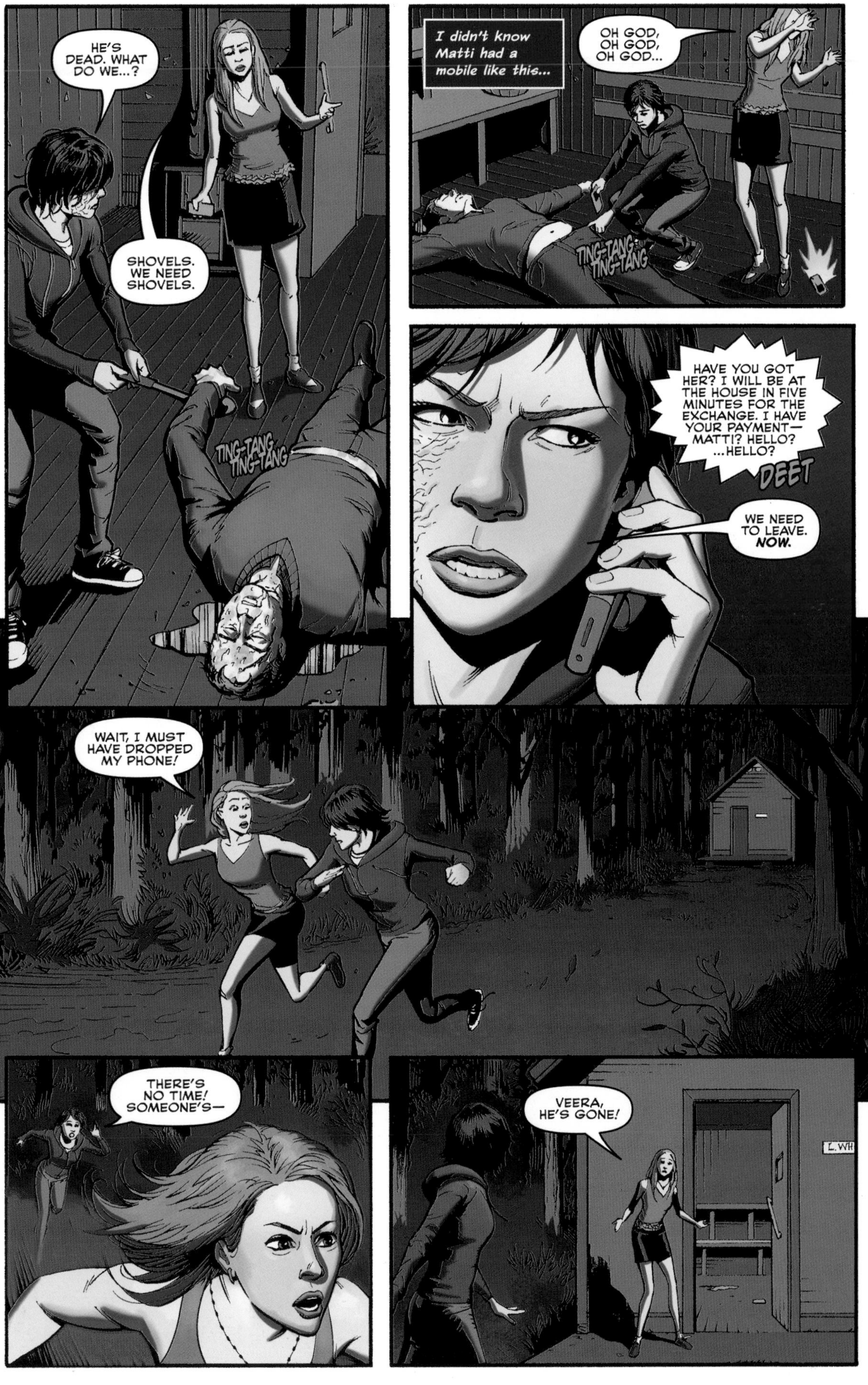
HE'S DEAD. WHAT DO WE...?
SHOVELS. WE NEED SHOVELS.
TING-TANG TING-TANG
I didn't know Matti had a mobile like this...
OH GOD, OH GOD, OH GOD...
TING-TANG TING-TANG
HAVE YOU GOT HER? I WILL BE AT THE HOUSE IN FIVE MINUTES FOR THE EXCHANGE. I HAVE YOUR PAYMENT— MATTI? HELLO? ...HELLO?
DEET
WE NEED TO LEAVE. NOW.
WAIT, I MUST HAVE DROPPED MY PHONE!
THERE'S NO TIME! SOMEONE'S—
VEERA, HE'S GONE!
L.WH

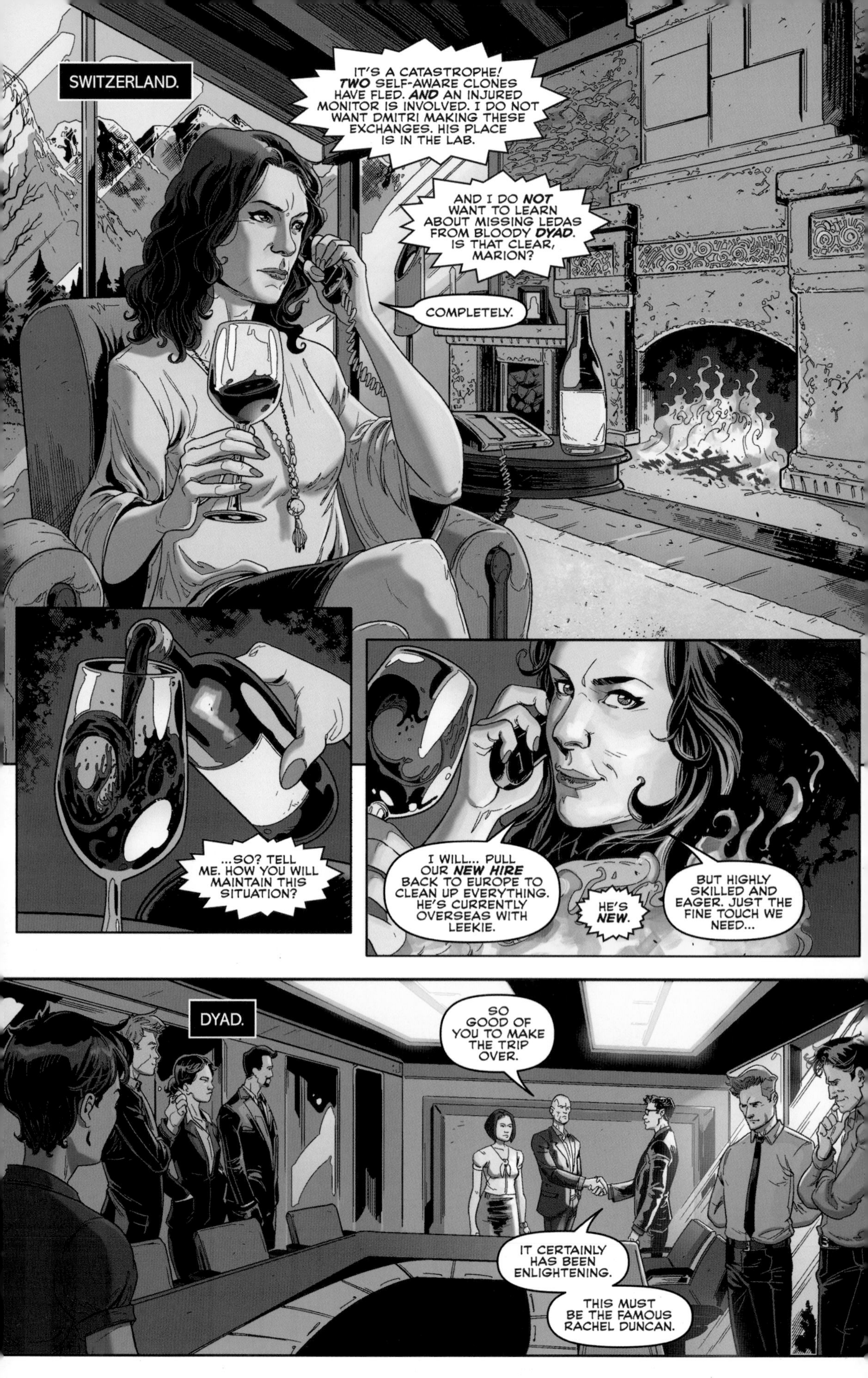
SWITZERLAND.
IT'S A CATASTROPHE! TWO SELF-AWARE CLONES HAVE FLED. AND AN INJURED MONITOR IS INVOLVED. I DO NOT WANT DMITRI MAKING THESE EXCHANGES. HIS PLACE IS IN THE LAB.
AND I DO NOT WANT TO LEARN ABOUT MISSING LEDAS FROM BLOODY DYAD. IS THAT CLEAR, MARION?
COMPLETELY.
...SO? TELL ME. HOW YOU WILL MAINTAIN THIS SITUATION?
I WILL... PULL OUR NEW HIRE BACK TO EUROPE TO CLEAN UP EVERYTHING. HE'S CURRENTLY OVERSEAS WITH LEEKIE.
HE'S NEW.
BUT HIGHLY SKILLED AND EAGER. JUST THE FINE TOUCH WE NEED...
DYAD.
SO GOOD OF YOU TO MAKE THE TRIP OVER.
IT CERTAINLY HAS BEEN ENLIGHTENING.
THIS MUST BE THE FAMOUS RACHEL DUNCAN.

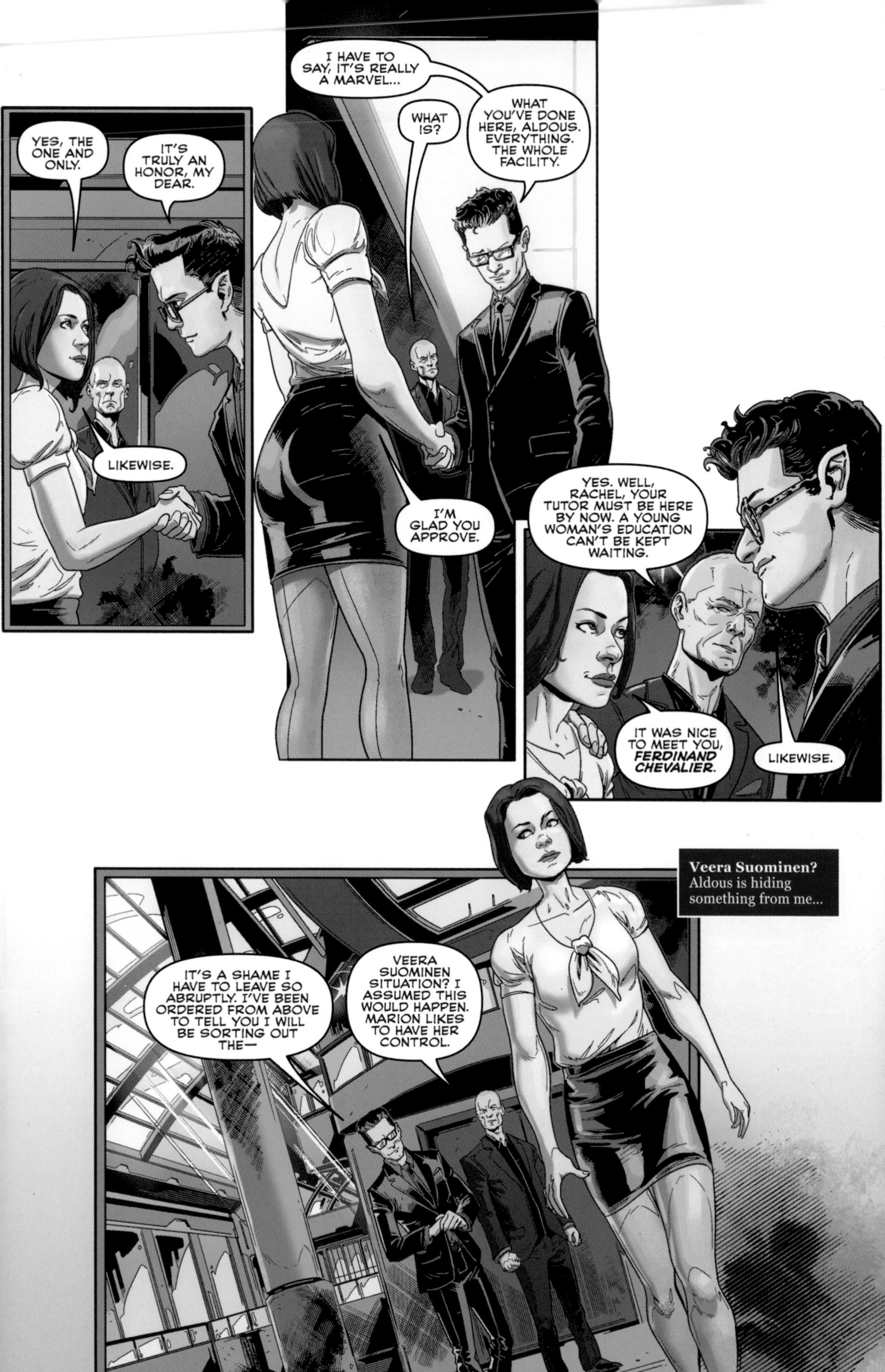
YES, THE ONE AND ONLY.
IT'S TRULY AN HONOR, MY DEAR.
LIKEWISE.
I HAVE TO SAY, IT'S REALLY A MARVEL...
WHAT IS?
WHAT YOU'VE DONE HERE, ALDOUS. EVERYTHING. THE WHOLE FACILITY.
I'M GLAD YOU APPROVE.
YES. WELL, RACHEL, YOUR TUTOR MUST BE HERE BY NOW. A YOUNG WOMAN'S EDUCATION CAN'T BE KEPT WAITING.
IT WAS NICE TO MEET YOU, ***FERDINAND CHEVALIER***.
LIKEWISE.
Veera Suominen? Aldous is hiding something from me...
IT'S A SHAME I HAVE TO LEAVE SO ABRUPTLY. I'VE BEEN ORDERED FROM ABOVE TO TELL YOU I WILL BE SORTING OUT THE—
VEERA SUOMINEN SITUATION? I ASSUMED THIS WOULD HAPPEN. MARION LIKES TO HAVE HER CONTROL.

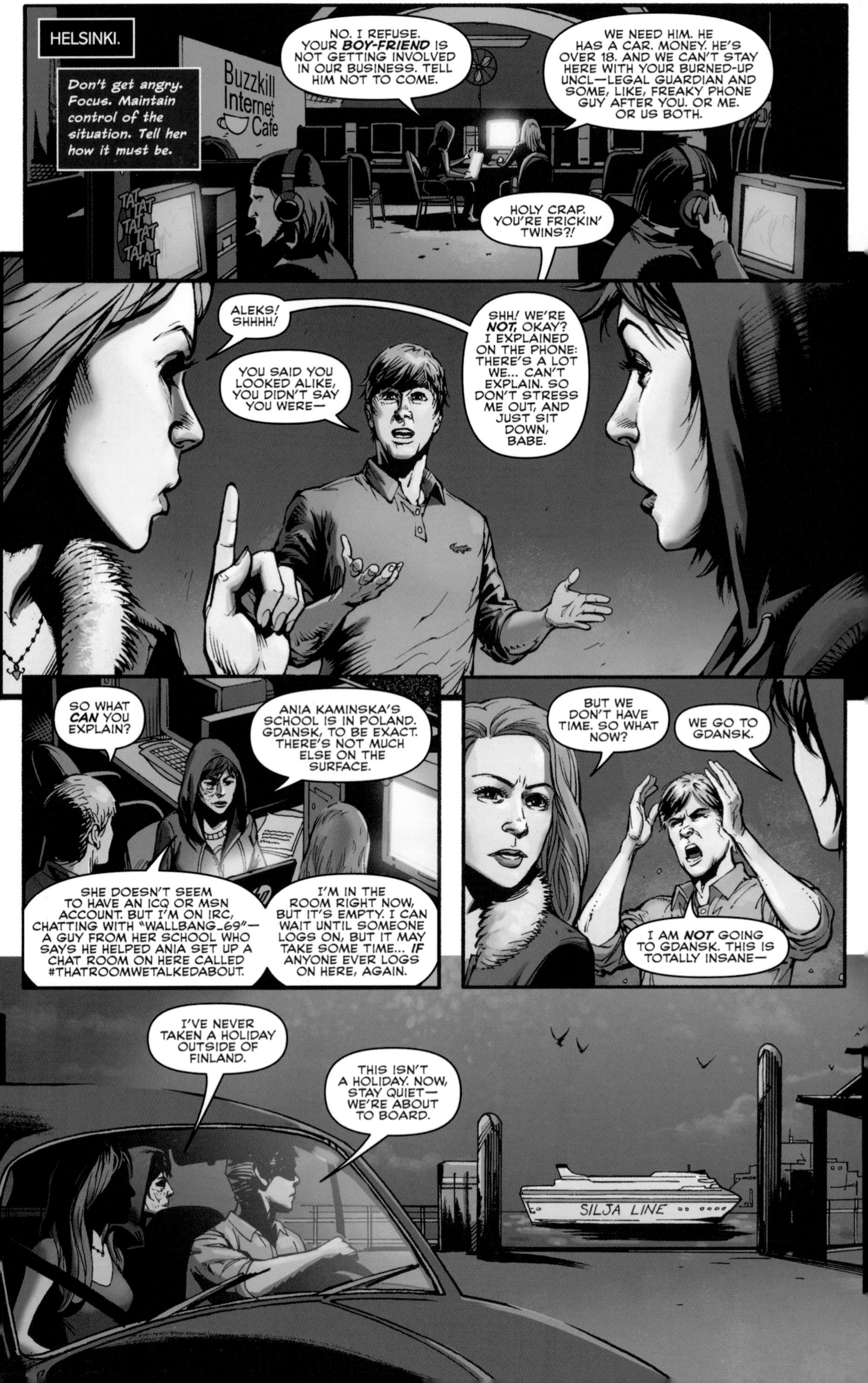
HELSINKI.
Don't get angry. Focus. Maintain control of the situation. Tell her how it must be.
Buzzkill Internet Cafe
TAT TAT TAT TAT TAT TAT
NO. I REFUSE. YOUR BOY-FRIEND IS NOT GETTING INVOLVED IN OUR BUSINESS. TELL HIM NOT TO COME.
WE NEED HIM. HE HAS A CAR. MONEY. HE'S OVER 18. AND WE CAN'T STAY HERE WITH YOUR BURNED-UP UNCL—LEGAL GUARDIAN AND SOME, LIKE, FREAKY PHONE GUY AFTER YOU. OR ME. OR US BOTH.
HOLY CRAP. YOU'RE FRICKIN' TWINS?!
ALEKS! SHHHH!
YOU SAID YOU LOOKED ALIKE, YOU DIDN'T SAY YOU WERE—
SHH! WE'RE NOT, OKAY? I EXPLAINED ON THE PHONE: THERE'S A LOT WE... CAN'T EXPLAIN. SO DON'T STRESS ME OUT, AND JUST SIT DOWN, BABE.
SO WHAT CAN YOU EXPLAIN?
ANIA KAMINSKA'S SCHOOL IS IN POLAND. GDANSK, TO BE EXACT. THERE'S NOT MUCH ELSE ON THE SURFACE.
SHE DOESN'T SEEM TO HAVE AN ICQ OR MSN ACCOUNT. BUT I'M ON IRC, CHATTING WITH "WALLBANG_69"—A GUY FROM HER SCHOOL WHO SAYS HE HELPED ANIA SET UP A CHAT ROOM ON HERE CALLED #THATROOMWETALKEDABOUT.
I'M IN THE ROOM RIGHT NOW, BUT IT'S EMPTY. I CAN WAIT UNTIL SOMEONE LOGS ON, BUT IT MAY TAKE SOME TIME... IF ANYONE EVER LOGS ON HERE, AGAIN.
BUT WE DON'T HAVE TIME. SO WHAT NOW?
WE GO TO GDANSK.
I AM NOT GOING TO GDANSK. THIS IS TOTALLY INSANE—
I'VE NEVER TAKEN A HOLIDAY OUTSIDE OF FINLAND.
THIS ISN'T A HOLIDAY. NOW, STAY QUIET—WE'RE ABOUT TO BOARD.
SILJA LINE

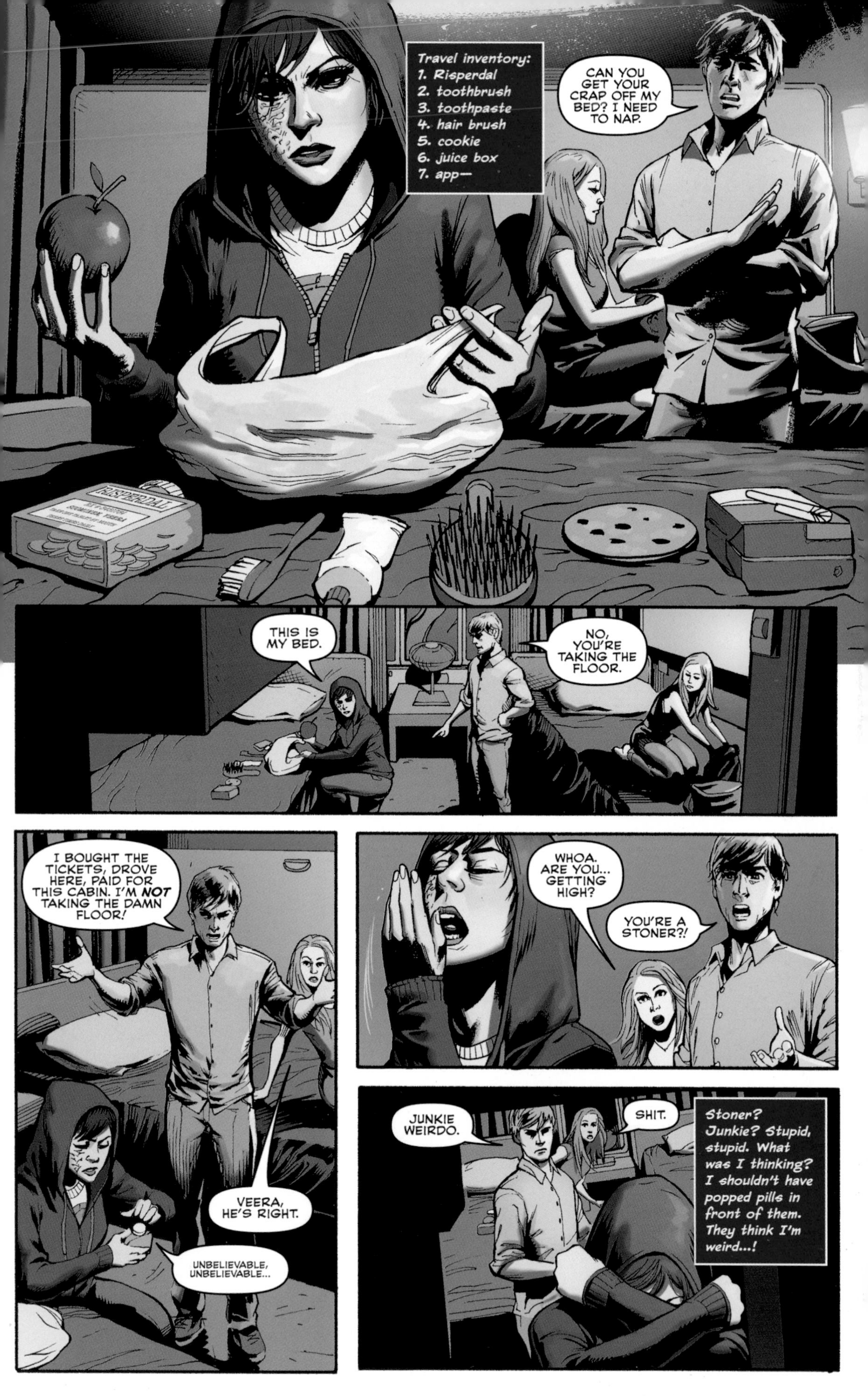
Travel inventory:
1. Risperdal
2. toothbrush
3. toothpaste
4. hair brush
5. cookie
6. juice box
7. app—
CAN YOU GET YOUR CRAP OFF MY BED? I NEED TO NAP.
RISPERDAL
THIS IS MY BED.
NO, YOU'RE TAKING THE FLOOR.
I BOUGHT THE TICKETS, DROVE HERE, PAID FOR THIS CABIN. I'M **NOT** TAKING THE DAMN FLOOR!
VEERA, HE'S RIGHT.
UNBELIEVABLE, UNBELIEVABLE...
WHOA. ARE YOU... GETTING HIGH?
YOU'RE A STONER?!
JUNKIE WEIRDO.
SHIT.
Stoner? Junkie? Stupid, stupid. What was I thinking? I shouldn't have popped pills in front of them. They think I'm weird...!

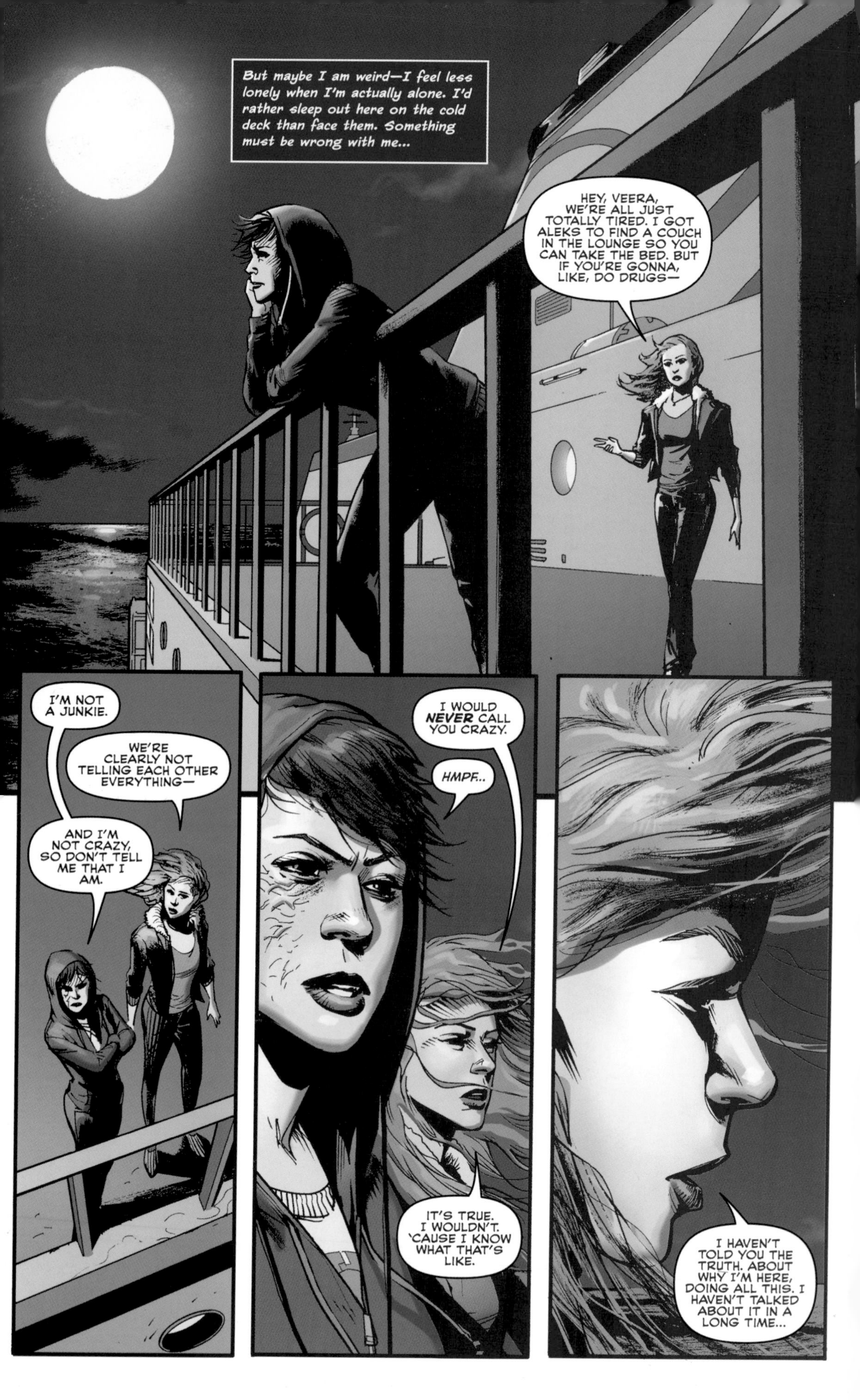

But maybe I am weird—I feel less lonely when I'm actually alone. I'd rather sleep out here on the cold deck than face them. Something must be wrong with me...
HEY, VEERA, WE'RE ALL JUST TOTALLY TIRED. I GOT ALEKS TO FIND A COUCH IN THE LOUNGE SO YOU CAN TAKE THE BED. BUT IF YOU'RE GONNA, LIKE, DO DRUGS—
I'M NOT A JUNKIE.
WE'RE CLEARLY NOT TELLING EACH OTHER EVERYTHING—
AND I'M NOT CRAZY, SO DON'T TELL ME THAT I AM.
I WOULD NEVER CALL YOU CRAZY.
HMPF..
IT'S TRUE. I WOULDN'T. 'CAUSE I KNOW WHAT THAT'S LIKE.
I HAVEN'T TOLD YOU THE TRUTH. ABOUT WHY I'M HERE, DOING ALL THIS. I HAVEN'T TALKED ABOUT IT IN A LONG TIME...

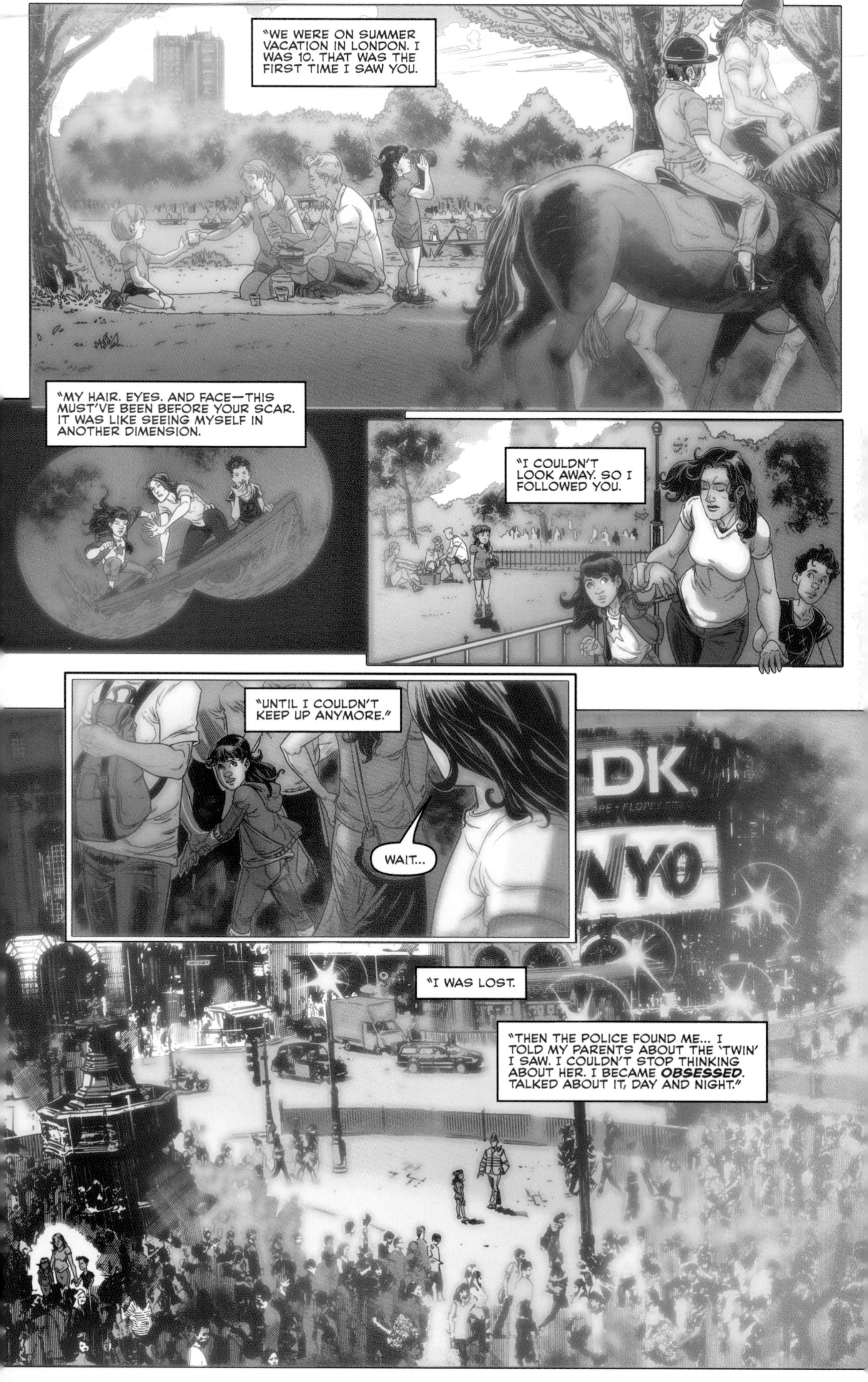
"WE WERE ON SUMMER VACATION IN LONDON. I WAS 10. THAT WAS THE FIRST TIME I SAW YOU.
"MY HAIR. EYES. AND FACE—THIS MUST'VE BEEN BEFORE YOUR SCAR. IT WAS LIKE SEEING MYSELF IN ANOTHER DIMENSION.
"I COULDN'T LOOK AWAY. SO I FOLLOWED YOU.
"UNTIL I COULDN'T KEEP UP ANYMORE."
WAIT...
DK
NYO
"I WAS LOST.
"THEN THE POLICE FOUND ME... I TOLD MY PARENTS ABOUT THE 'TWIN' I SAW. I COULDN'T STOP THINKING ABOUT HER. I BECAME *OBSESSED*. TALKED ABOUT IT, DAY AND NIGHT."

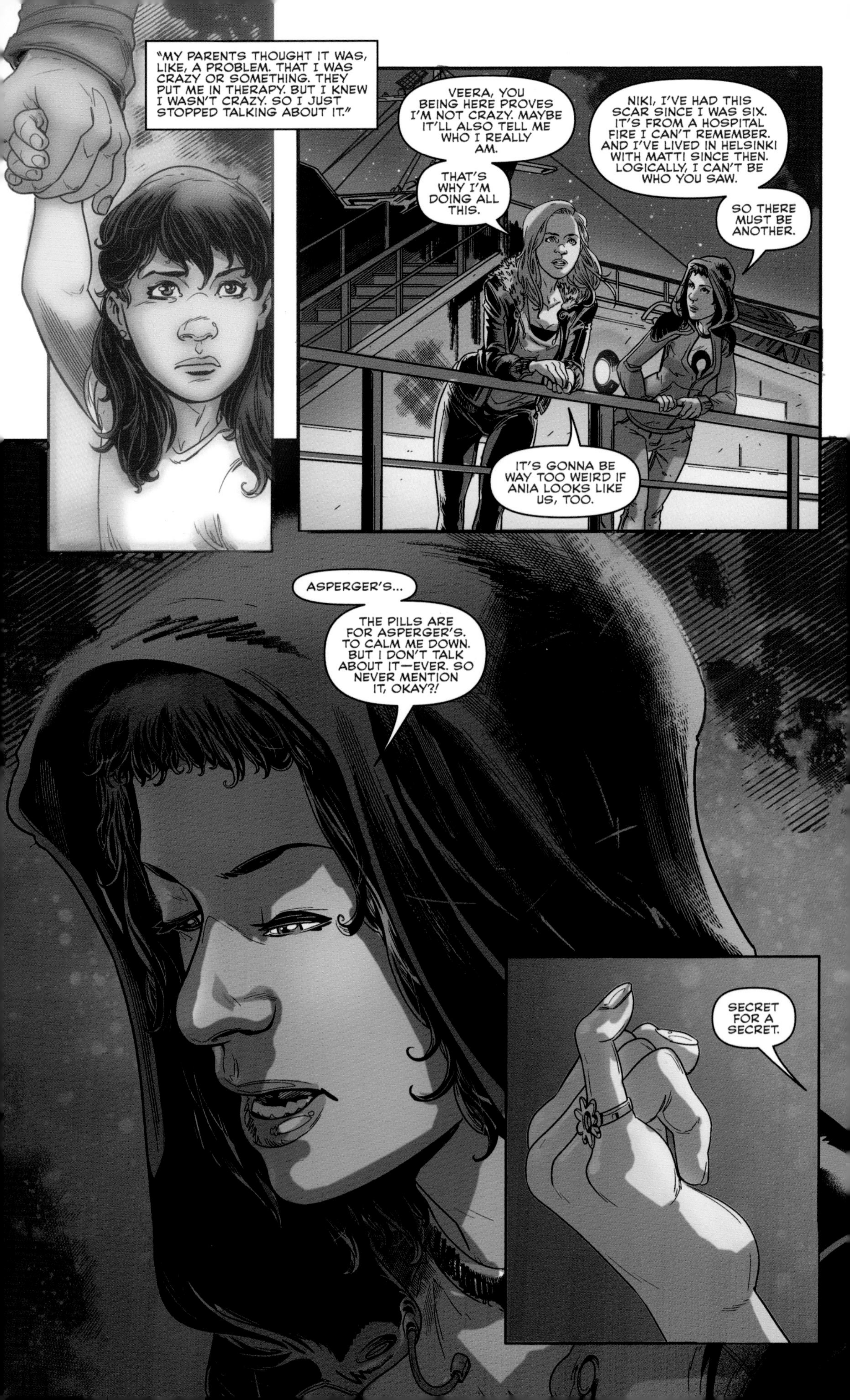
"MY PARENTS THOUGHT IT WAS, LIKE, A PROBLEM. THAT I WAS CRAZY OR SOMETHING. THEY PUT ME IN THERAPY. BUT I KNEW I WASN'T CRAZY. SO I JUST STOPPED TALKING ABOUT IT."
VEERA, YOU BEING HERE PROVES I'M NOT CRAZY. MAYBE IT'LL ALSO TELL ME WHO I REALLY AM.
THAT'S WHY I'M DOING ALL THIS.
NIKI, I'VE HAD THIS SCAR SINCE I WAS SIX. IT'S FROM A HOSPITAL FIRE I CAN'T REMEMBER. AND I'VE LIVED IN HELSINKI WITH MATTI SINCE THEN. LOGICALLY, I CAN'T BE WHO YOU SAW.
SO THERE MUST BE ANOTHER.
IT'S GONNA BE WAY TOO WEIRD IF ANIA LOOKS LIKE US, TOO.
ASPERGER'S...
THE PILLS ARE FOR ASPERGER'S. TO CALM ME DOWN. BUT I DON'T TALK ABOUT IT—EVER. SO NEVER MENTION IT, OKAY?!
SECRET FOR A SECRET.

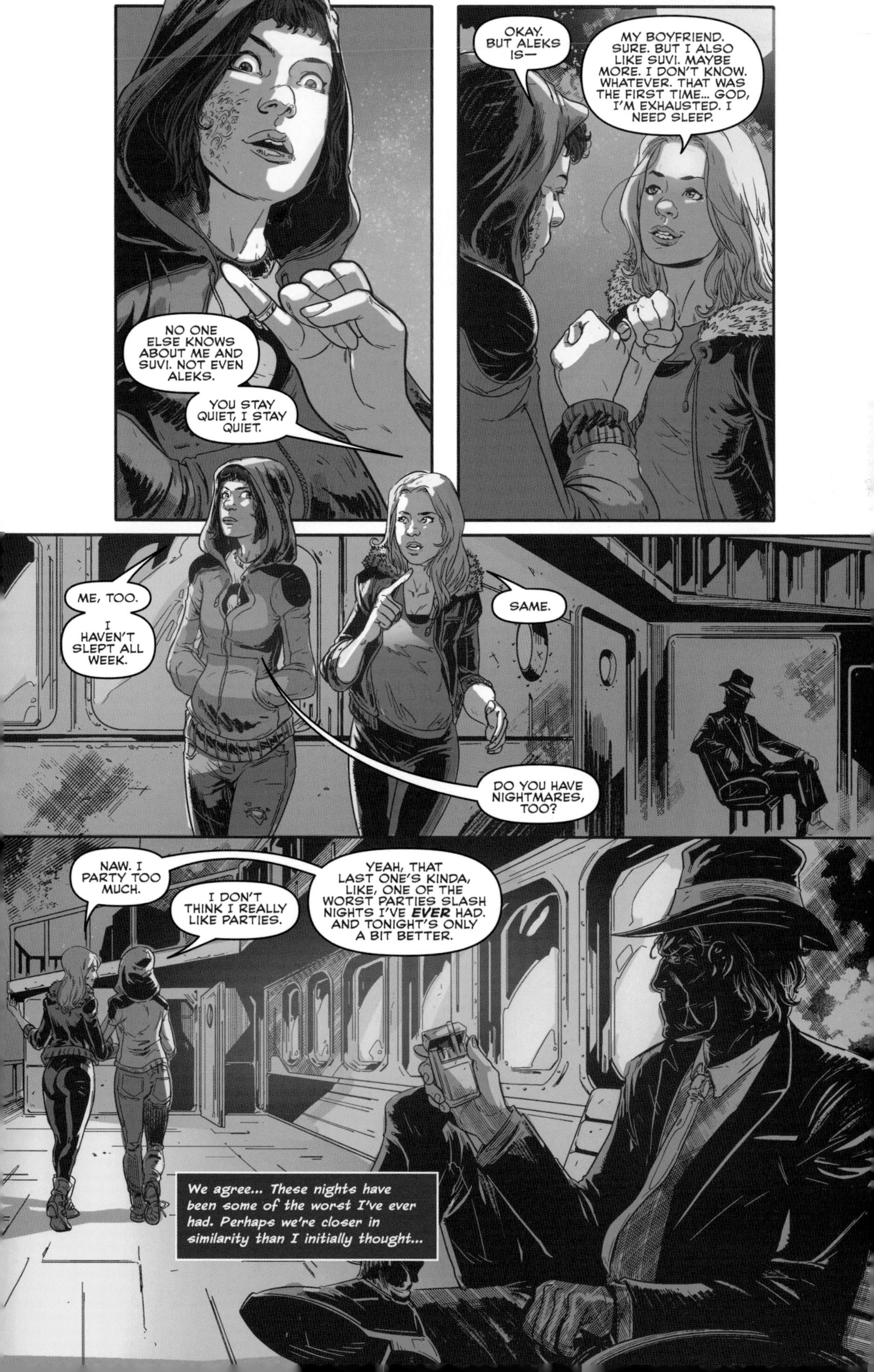
NO ONE ELSE KNOWS ABOUT ME AND SUVI. NOT EVEN ALEKS.
YOU STAY QUIET, I STAY QUIET.
OKAY. BUT ALEKS IS—
MY BOYFRIEND. SURE. BUT I ALSO LIKE SUVI. MAYBE MORE. I DON'T KNOW. WHATEVER. THAT WAS THE FIRST TIME... GOD, I'M EXHAUSTED. I NEED SLEEP.
ME, TOO.
I HAVEN'T SLEPT ALL WEEK.
SAME.
DO YOU HAVE NIGHTMARES, TOO?
NAW. I PARTY TOO MUCH.
I DON'T THINK I REALLY LIKE PARTIES.
YEAH, THAT LAST ONE'S KINDA, LIKE, ONE OF THE WORST PARTIES SLASH NIGHTS I'VE EVER HAD. AND TONIGHT'S ONLY A BIT BETTER.
We agree... These nights have been some of the worst I've ever had. Perhaps we're closer in similarity than I initially thought...

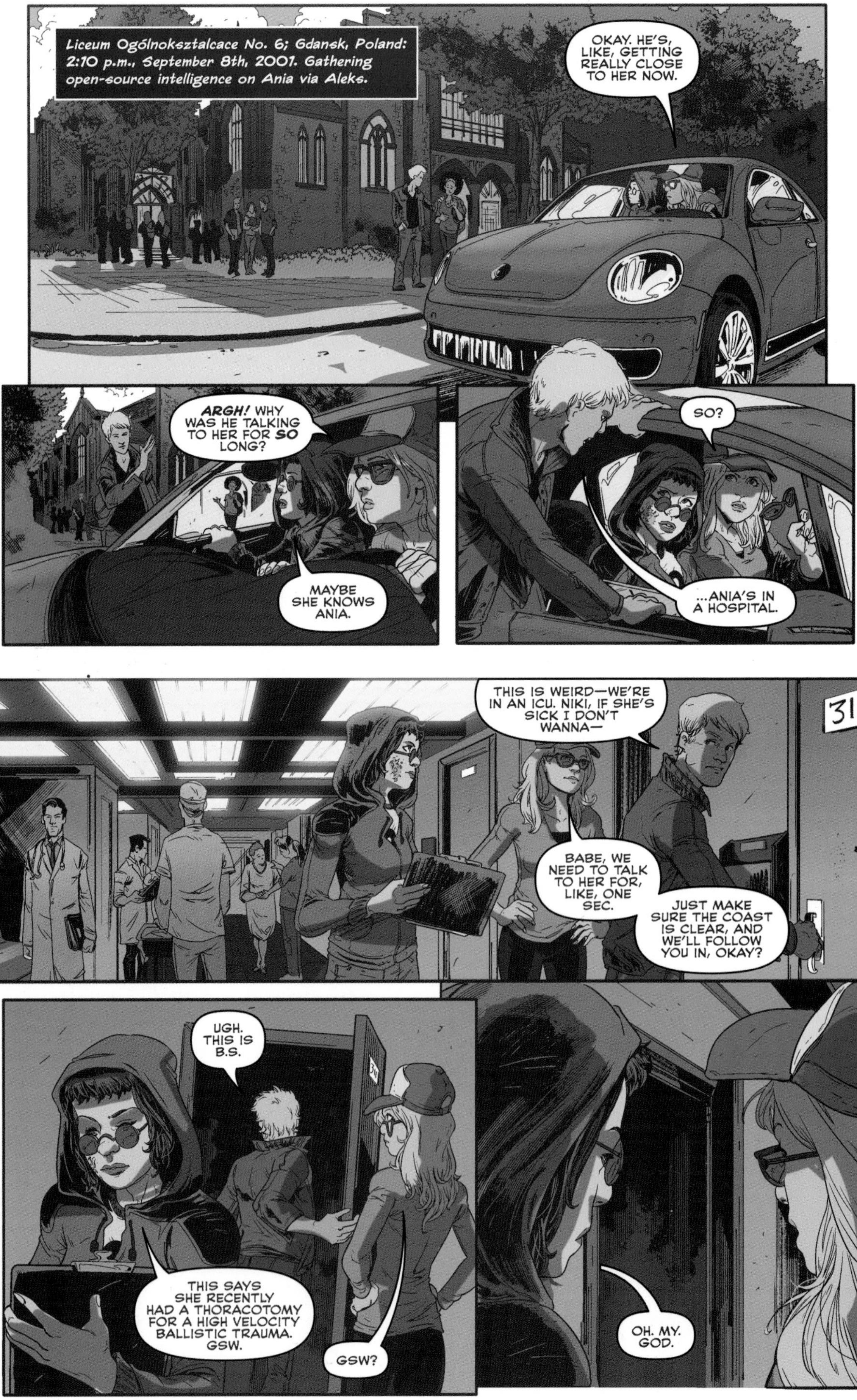

Liceum Ogólnokształcace No. 6; Gdansk, Poland: 2:10 p.m., September 8th, 2001. Gathering open-source intelligence on Ania via Aleks.
OKAY. HE'S, LIKE, GETTING REALLY CLOSE TO HER NOW.
ARGH! WHY WAS HE TALKING TO HER FOR SO LONG?
MAYBE SHE KNOWS ANIA.
SO?
...ANIA'S IN A HOSPITAL.
THIS IS WEIRD—WE'RE IN AN ICU. NIKI, IF SHE'S SICK I DON'T WANNA—
311
BABE, WE NEED TO TALK TO HER FOR, LIKE, ONE SEC.
JUST MAKE SURE THE COAST IS CLEAR, AND WE'LL FOLLOW YOU IN, OKAY?
UGH. THIS IS B.S.
THIS SAYS SHE RECENTLY HAD A THORACOTOMY FOR A HIGH VELOCITY BALLISTIC TRAUMA. GSW.
GSW?
OH. MY. GOD.

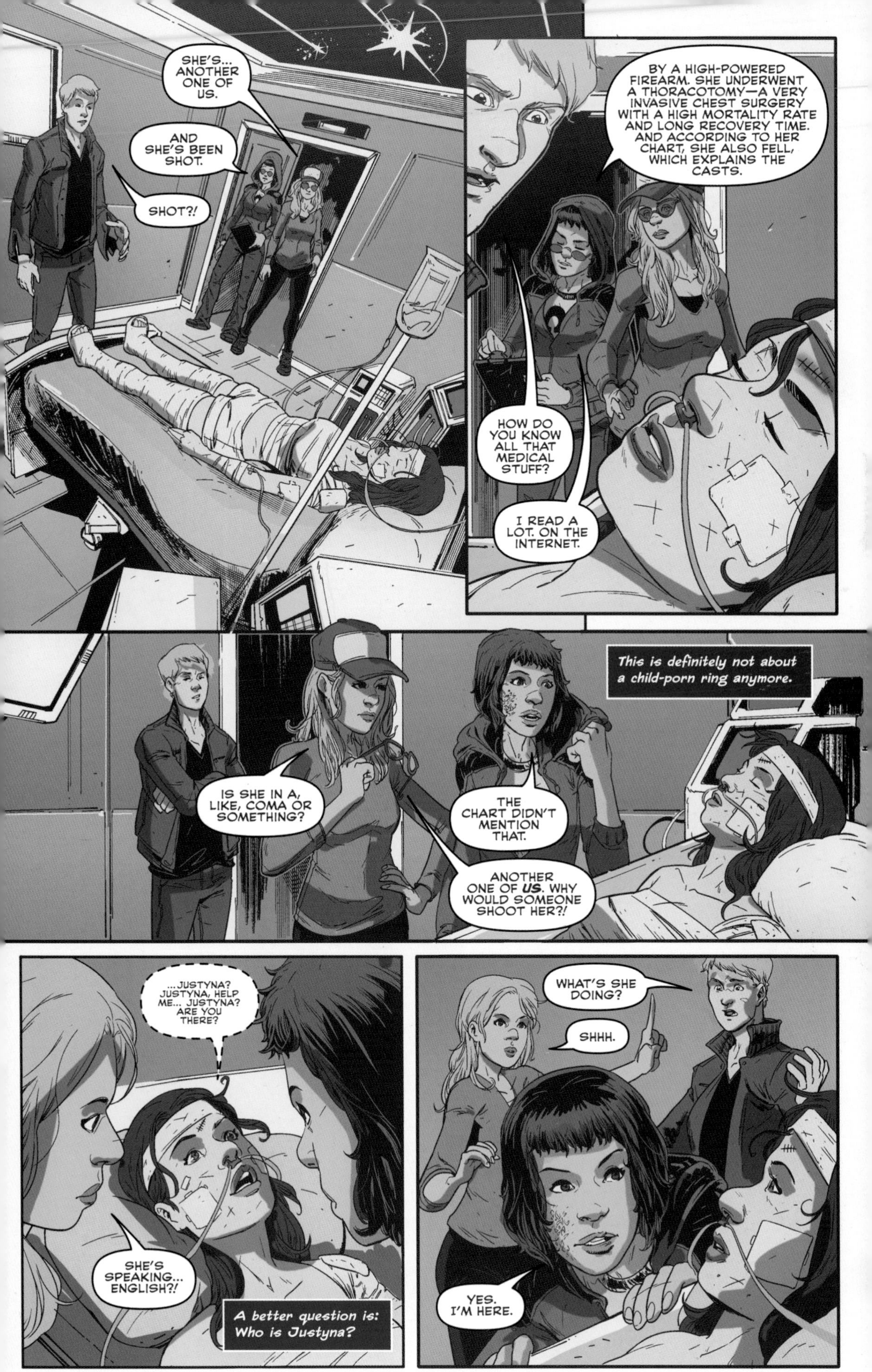
SHE'S... ANOTHER ONE OF US.
AND SHE'S BEEN SHOT.
SHOT?!
BY A HIGH-POWERED FIREARM. SHE UNDERWENT A THORACOTOMY—A VERY INVASIVE CHEST SURGERY WITH A HIGH MORTALITY RATE AND LONG RECOVERY TIME. AND ACCORDING TO HER CHART, SHE ALSO FELL, WHICH EXPLAINS THE CASTS.
HOW DO YOU KNOW ALL THAT MEDICAL STUFF?
I READ A LOT. ON THE INTERNET.
This is definitely not about a child-porn ring anymore.
IS SHE IN A, LIKE, COMA OR SOMETHING?
THE CHART DIDN'T MENTION THAT.
ANOTHER ONE OF US. WHY WOULD SOMEONE SHOOT HER?!
...JUSTYNA? JUSTYNA, HELP ME... JUSTYNA? ARE YOU THERE?
SHE'S SPEAKING... ENGLISH?!
A better question is: Who is Justyna?
WHAT'S SHE DOING?
SHHH.
YES. I'M HERE.

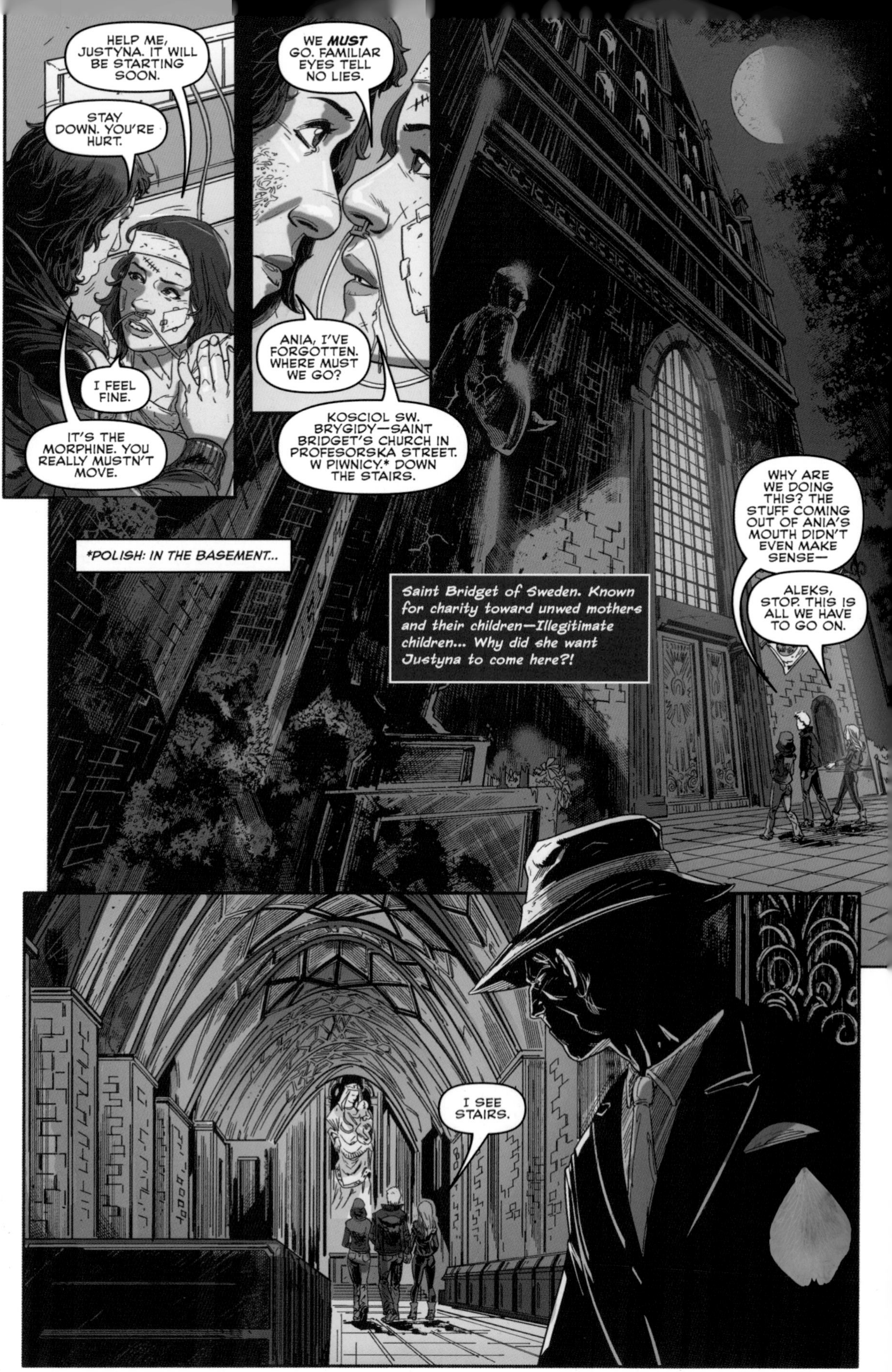
HELP ME, JUSTYNA. IT WILL BE STARTING SOON.
STAY DOWN. YOU'RE HURT.
I FEEL FINE.
IT'S THE MORPHINE. YOU REALLY MUSTN'T MOVE.
WE ***MUST*** GO. FAMILIAR EYES TELL NO LIES.
ANIA, I'VE FORGOTTEN. WHERE MUST WE GO?
KOSCIOL SW. BRYGIDY—SAINT BRIDGET'S CHURCH IN PROFESORSKA STREET. W PIWNICY.* DOWN THE STAIRS.
*POLISH: IN THE BASEMENT...
Saint Bridget of Sweden. Known for charity toward unwed mothers and their children—Illegitimate children... Why did she want Justyna to come here?!
WHY ARE WE DOING THIS? THE STUFF COMING OUT OF ANIA'S MOUTH DIDN'T EVEN MAKE SENSE—
ALEKS, STOP. THIS IS ALL WE HAVE TO GO ON.
I SEE STAIRS.

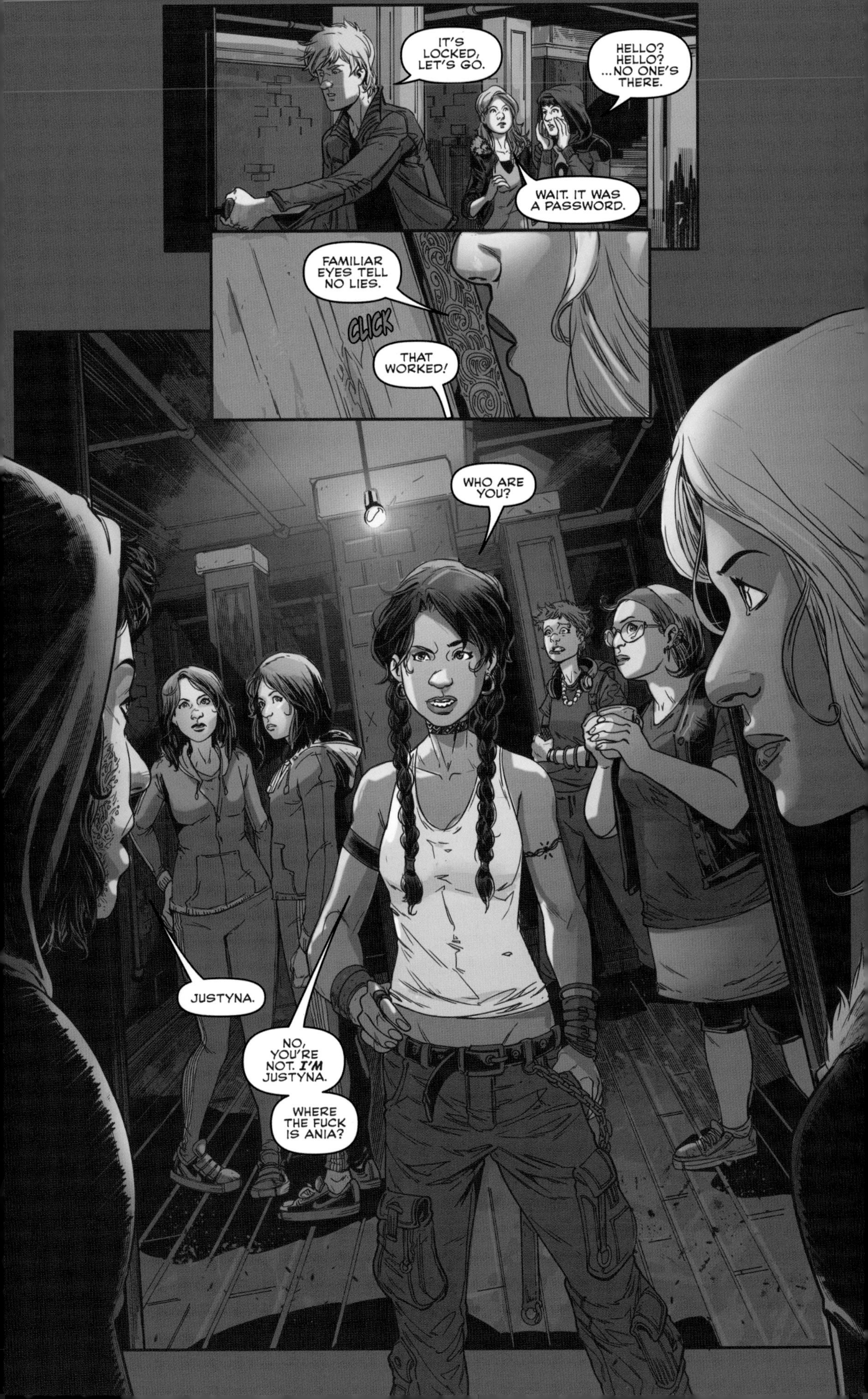
IT'S LOCKED, LET'S GO.
HELLO? HELLO? ...NO ONE'S THERE.
WAIT. IT WAS A PASSWORD.
FAMILIAR EYES TELL NO LIES.
CLICK
THAT WORKED!
WHO ARE YOU?
JUSTYNA.
NO, YOU'RE NOT. I'M JUSTYNA.
WHERE THE FUCK IS ANIA?

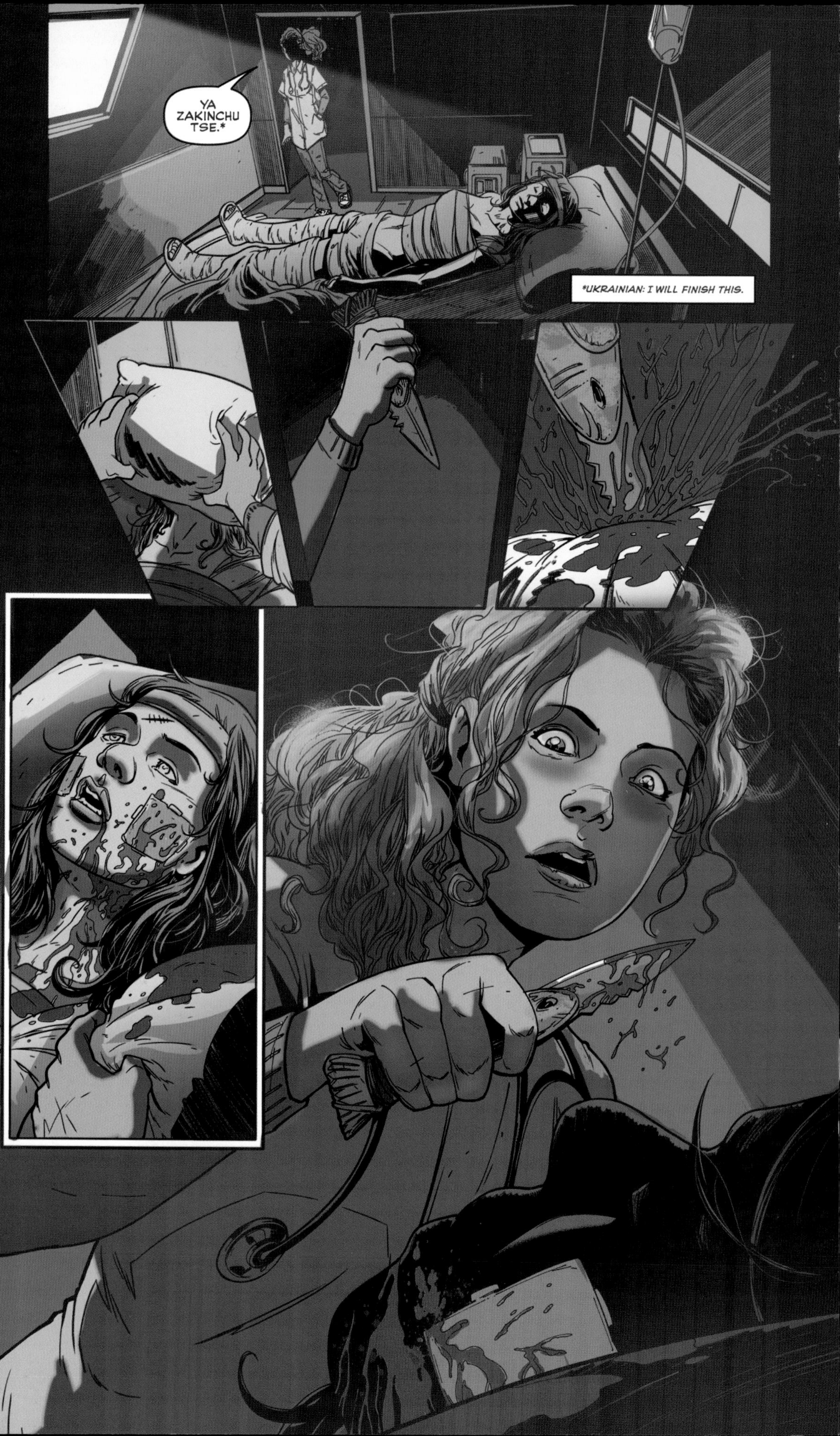
YA ZAKINCHU TSE.*
*UKRAINIAN: I WILL FINISH THIS.

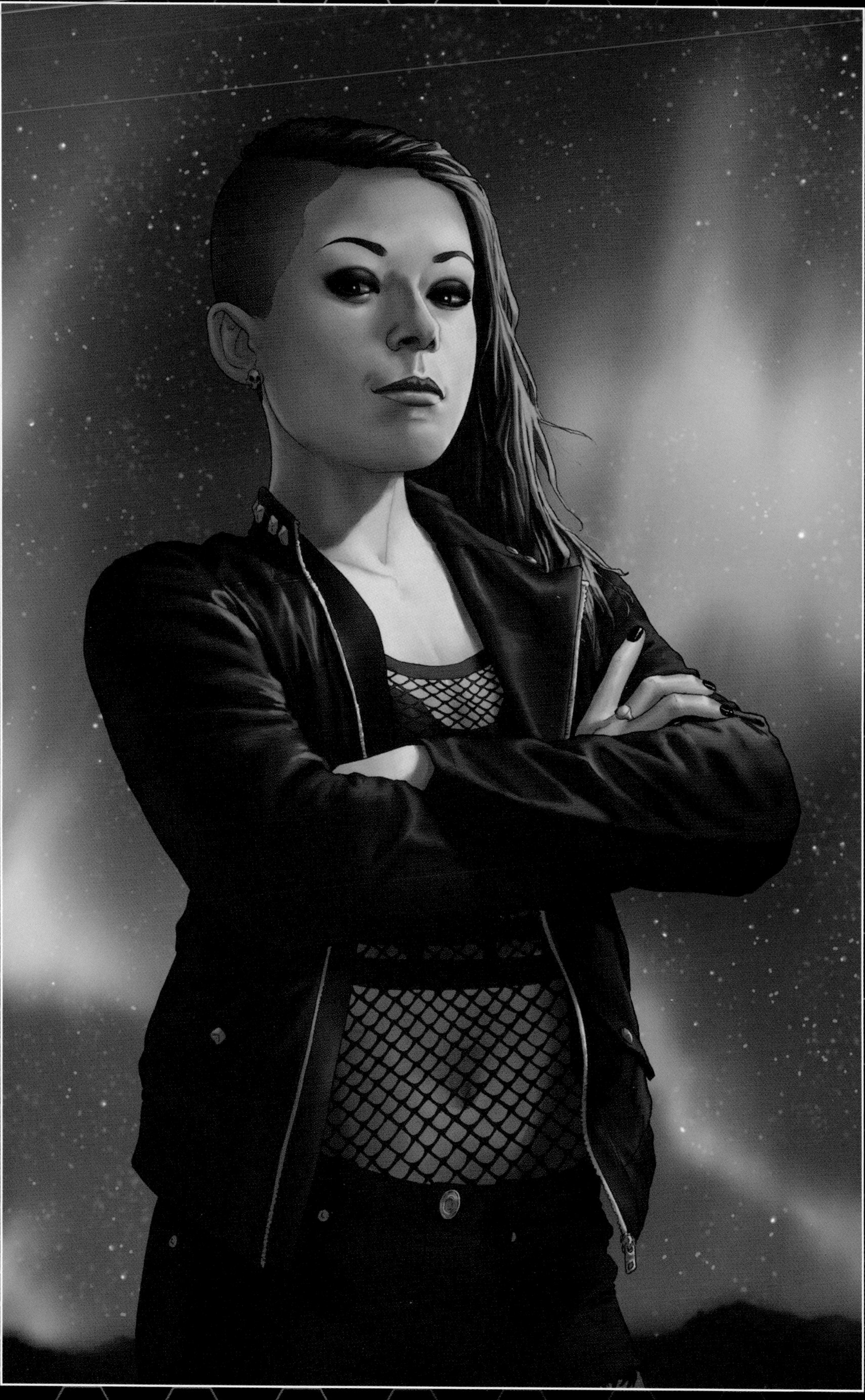

BY **RODIN ESQUEJO**

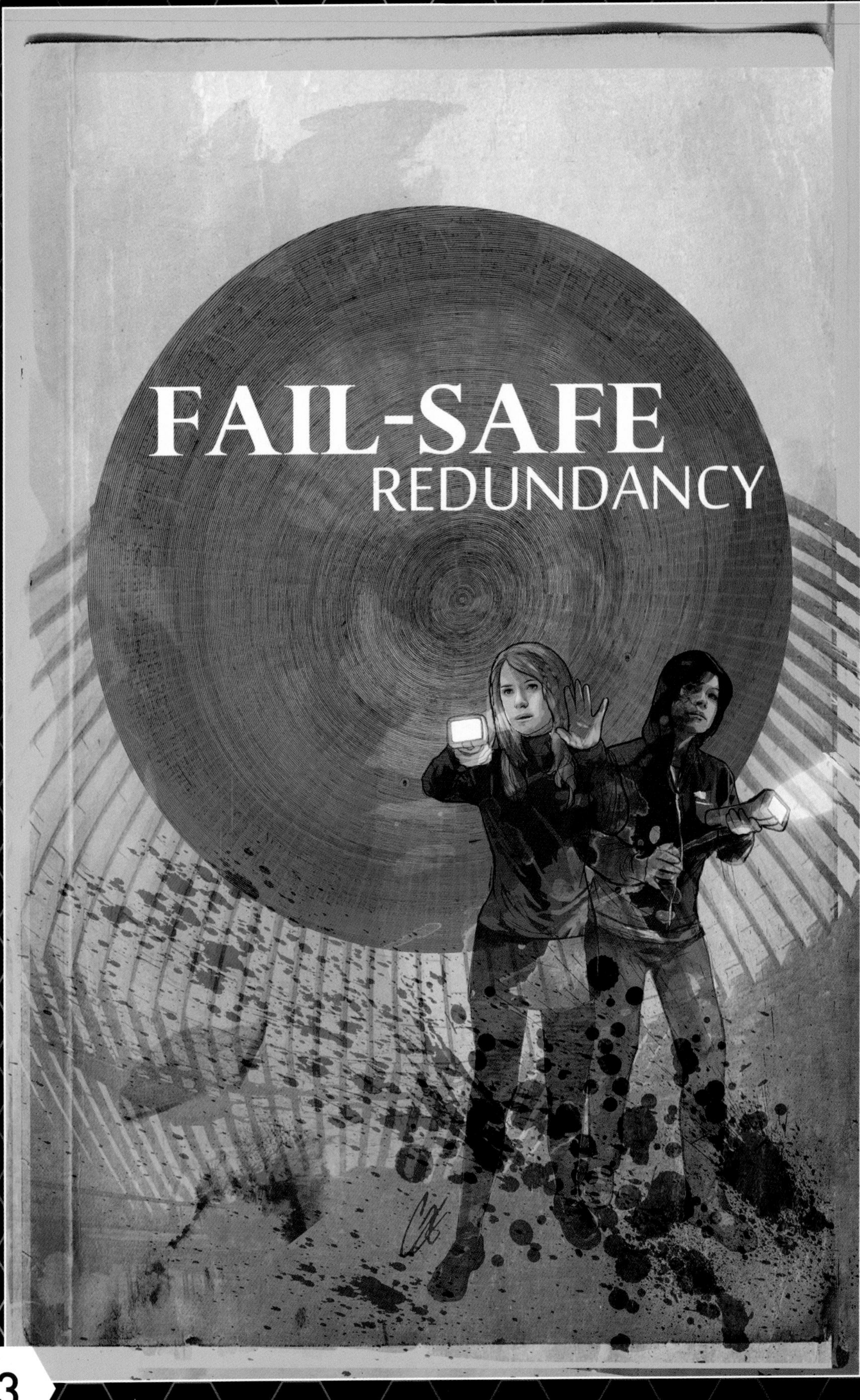
FAIL-SAFE
REDUNDANCY

BY CAT STAGGS

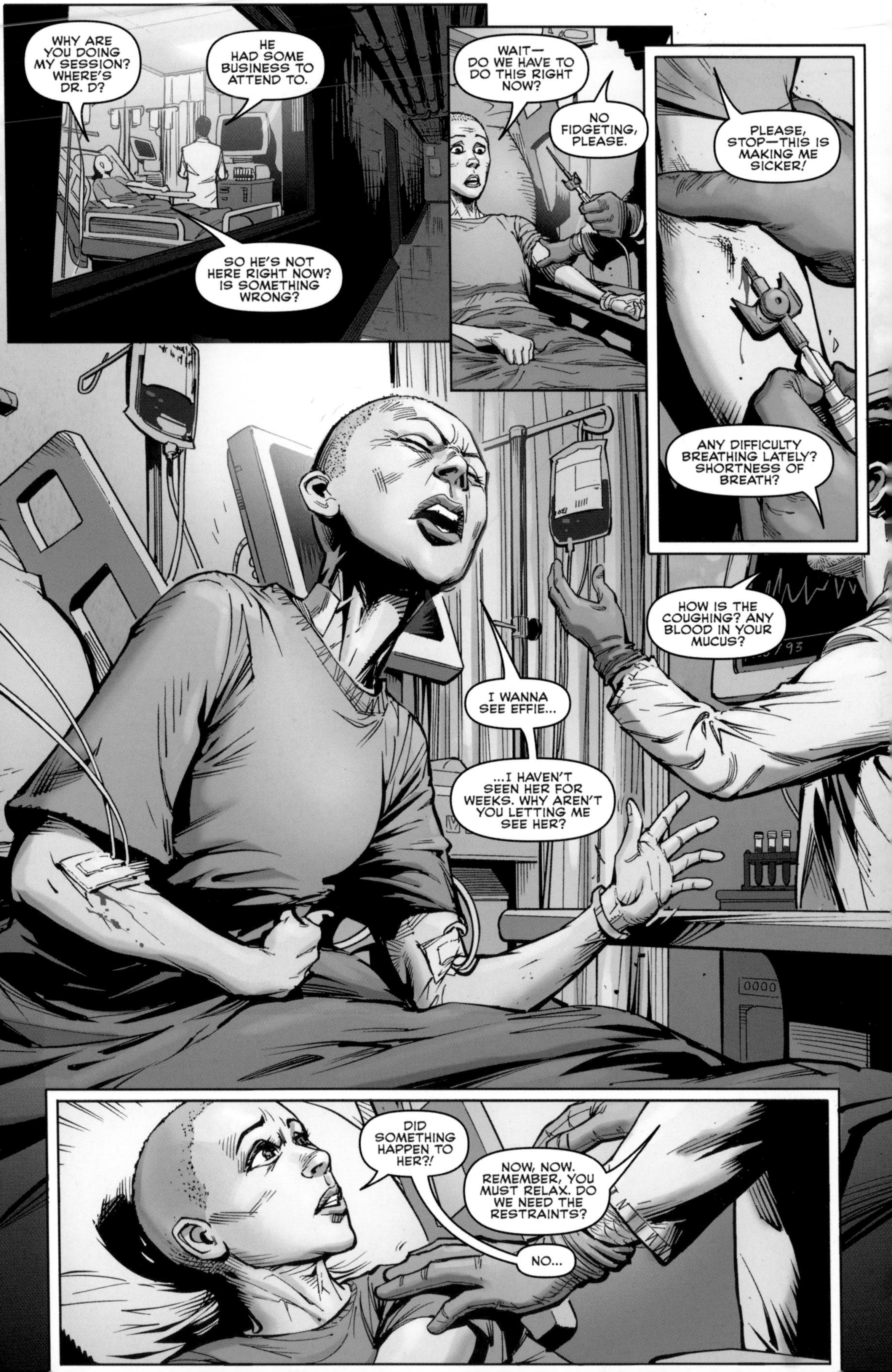
WHY ARE YOU DOING MY SESSION? WHERE'S DR. D?
HE HAD SOME BUSINESS TO ATTEND TO.
SO HE'S NOT HERE RIGHT NOW? IS SOMETHING WRONG?
WAIT— DO WE HAVE TO DO THIS RIGHT NOW?
NO FIDGETING, PLEASE.
PLEASE, STOP—THIS IS MAKING ME SICKER!
ANY DIFFICULTY BREATHING LATELY? SHORTNESS OF BREATH?
HOW IS THE COUGHING? ANY BLOOD IN YOUR MUCUS?
I WANNA SEE EFFIE...
...I HAVEN'T SEEN HER FOR WEEKS. WHY AREN'T YOU LETTING ME SEE HER?
DID SOMETHING HAPPEN TO HER?!
NOW, NOW. REMEMBER, YOU MUST RELAX. DO WE NEED THE RESTRAINTS?
NO...

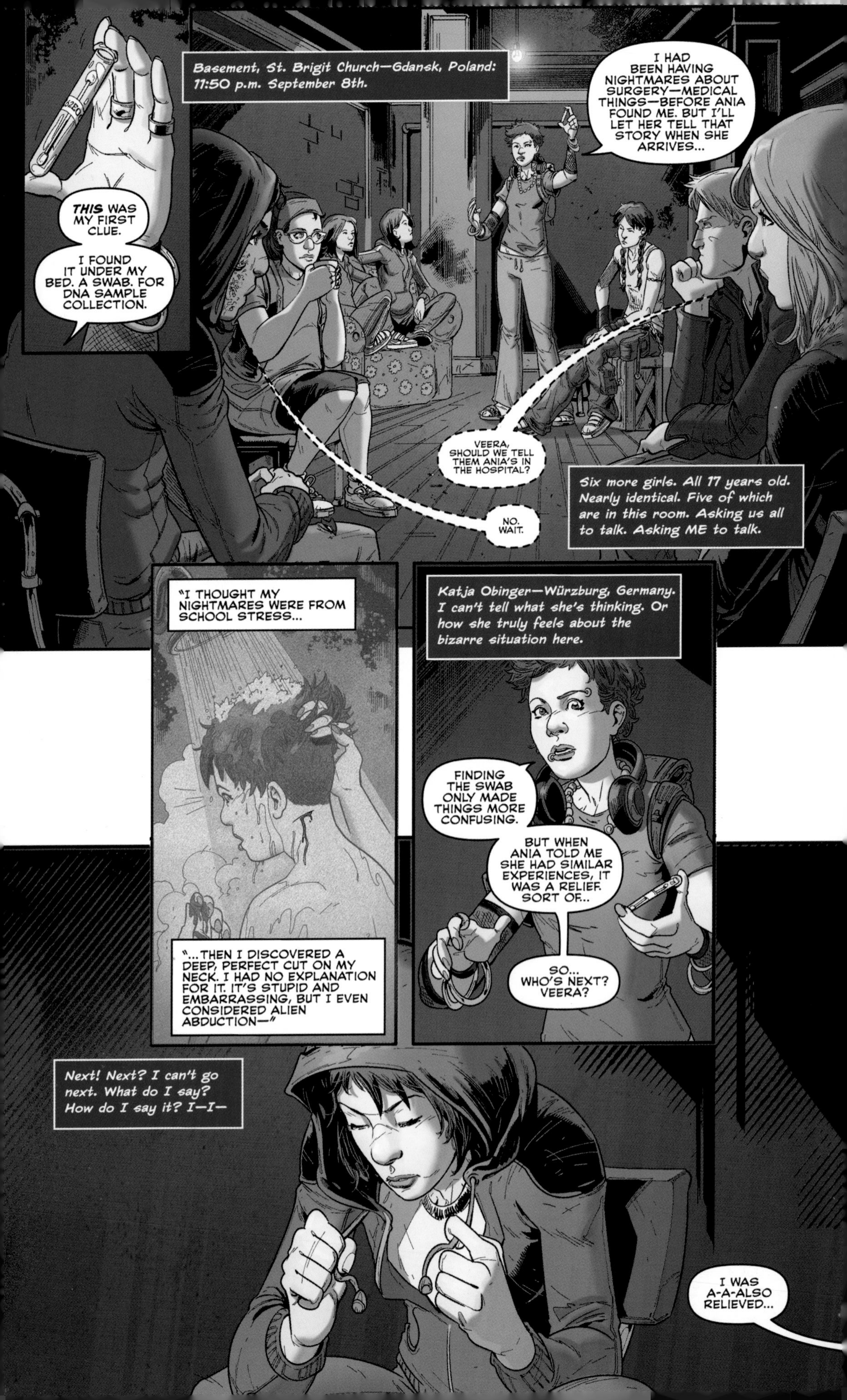
THIS WAS MY FIRST CLUE.
I FOUND IT UNDER MY BED. A SWAB. FOR DNA SAMPLE COLLECTION.
Basement, St. Brigit Church—Gdansk, Poland: 11:50 p.m. September 8th.
I HAD BEEN HAVING NIGHTMARES ABOUT SURGERY—MEDICAL THINGS—BEFORE ANIA FOUND ME. BUT I'LL LET HER TELL THAT STORY WHEN SHE ARRIVES...
VEERA, SHOULD WE TELL THEM ANIA'S IN THE HOSPITAL?
NO. WAIT.
Six more girls. All 17 years old. Nearly identical. Five of which are in this room. Asking us all to talk. Asking ME to talk.
"I THOUGHT MY NIGHTMARES WERE FROM SCHOOL STRESS...
"...THEN I DISCOVERED A DEEP, PERFECT CUT ON MY NECK. I HAD NO EXPLANATION FOR IT. IT'S STUPID AND EMBARRASSING, BUT I EVEN CONSIDERED ALIEN ABDUCTION—"
Katja Obinger—Würzburg, Germany. I can't tell what she's thinking. Or how she truly feels about the bizarre situation here.
FINDING THE SWAB ONLY MADE THINGS MORE CONFUSING.
BUT WHEN ANIA TOLD ME SHE HAD SIMILAR EXPERIENCES, IT WAS A RELIEF. SORT OF...
SO... WHO'S NEXT? VEERA?
Next! Next? I can't go next. What do I say? How do I say it? I—I—
I WAS A-A-ALSO RELIEVED...

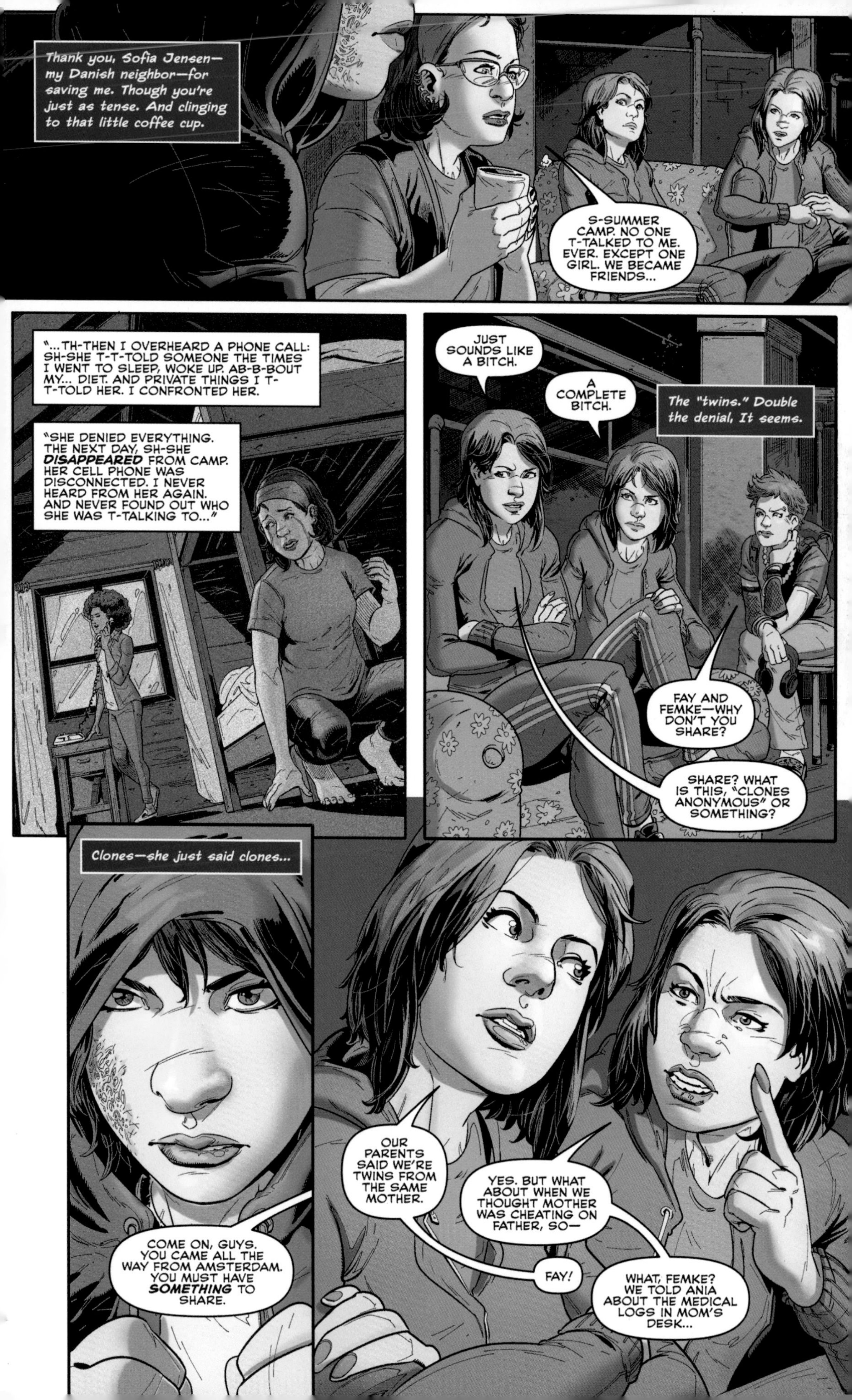
Thank you, Sofia Jensen—my Danish neighbor—for saving me. Though you're just as tense. And clinging to that little coffee cup.
S-SUMMER CAMP. NO ONE T-TALKED TO ME. EVER. EXCEPT ONE GIRL. WE BECAME FRIENDS...
"...TH-THEN I OVERHEARD A PHONE CALL: SH-SHE T-T-TOLD SOMEONE THE TIMES I WENT TO SLEEP, WOKE UP. AB-B-BOUT MY... DIET. AND PRIVATE THINGS I T-T-TOLD HER. I CONFRONTED HER.
"SHE DENIED EVERYTHING. THE NEXT DAY, SH-SHE DISAPPEARED FROM CAMP. HER CELL PHONE WAS DISCONNECTED. I NEVER HEARD FROM HER AGAIN. AND NEVER FOUND OUT WHO SHE WAS T-TALKING TO..."
JUST SOUNDS LIKE A BITCH.
A COMPLETE BITCH.
The "twins." Double the denial, It seems.
FAY AND FEMKE—WHY DON'T YOU SHARE?
SHARE? WHAT IS THIS, "CLONES ANONYMOUS" OR SOMETHING?
Clones—she just said clones...
COME ON, GUYS. YOU CAME ALL THE WAY FROM AMSTERDAM. YOU MUST HAVE SOMETHING TO SHARE.
OUR PARENTS SAID WE'RE TWINS FROM THE SAME MOTHER.
YES. BUT WHAT ABOUT WHEN WE THOUGHT MOTHER WAS CHEATING ON FATHER, SO—
FAY!
WHAT, FEMKE? WE TOLD ANIA ABOUT THE MEDICAL LOGS IN MOM'S DESK...

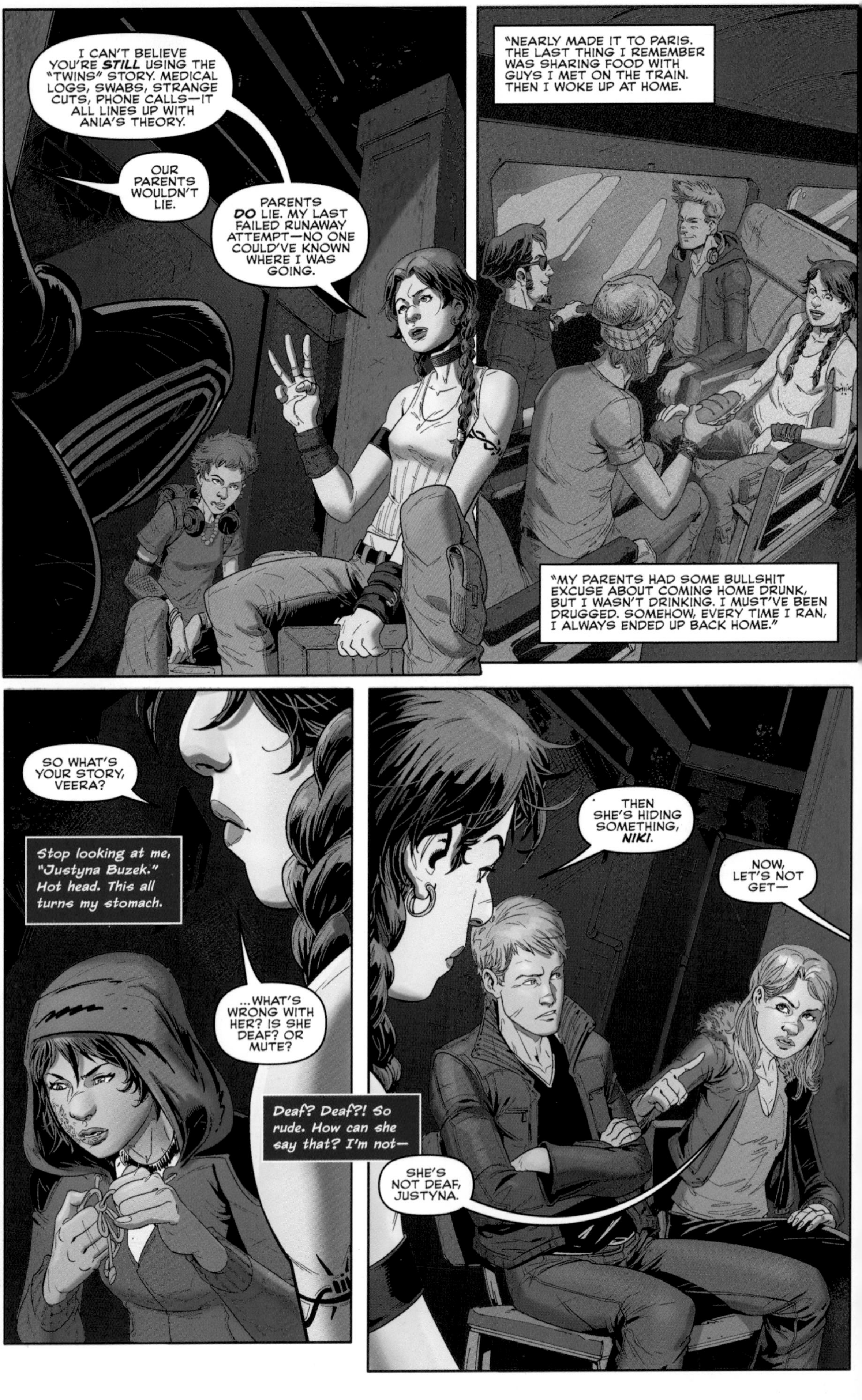
I CAN'T BELIEVE YOU'RE **STILL** USING THE "TWINS" STORY. MEDICAL LOGS, SWABS, STRANGE CUTS, PHONE CALLS—IT ALL LINES UP WITH ANIA'S THEORY.
OUR PARENTS WOULDN'T LIE.
PARENTS **DO** LIE. MY LAST FAILED RUNAWAY ATTEMPT—NO ONE COULD'VE KNOWN WHERE I WAS GOING.
"NEARLY MADE IT TO PARIS. THE LAST THING I REMEMBER WAS SHARING FOOD WITH GUYS I MET ON THE TRAIN. THEN I WOKE UP AT HOME.
"MY PARENTS HAD SOME BULLSHIT EXCUSE ABOUT COMING HOME DRUNK, BUT I WASN'T DRINKING. I MUST'VE BEEN DRUGGED. SOMEHOW, EVERY TIME I RAN, I ALWAYS ENDED UP BACK HOME."
SO WHAT'S YOUR STORY, VEERA?
Stop looking at me, "Justyna Buzek." Hot head. This all turns my stomach.
...WHAT'S WRONG WITH HER? IS SHE DEAF? OR MUTE?
Deaf? Deaf?! So rude. How can she say that? I'm not—
SHE'S NOT DEAF, JUSTYNA.
THEN SHE'S HIDING SOMETHING, **NIKI**.
NOW, LET'S NOT GET—

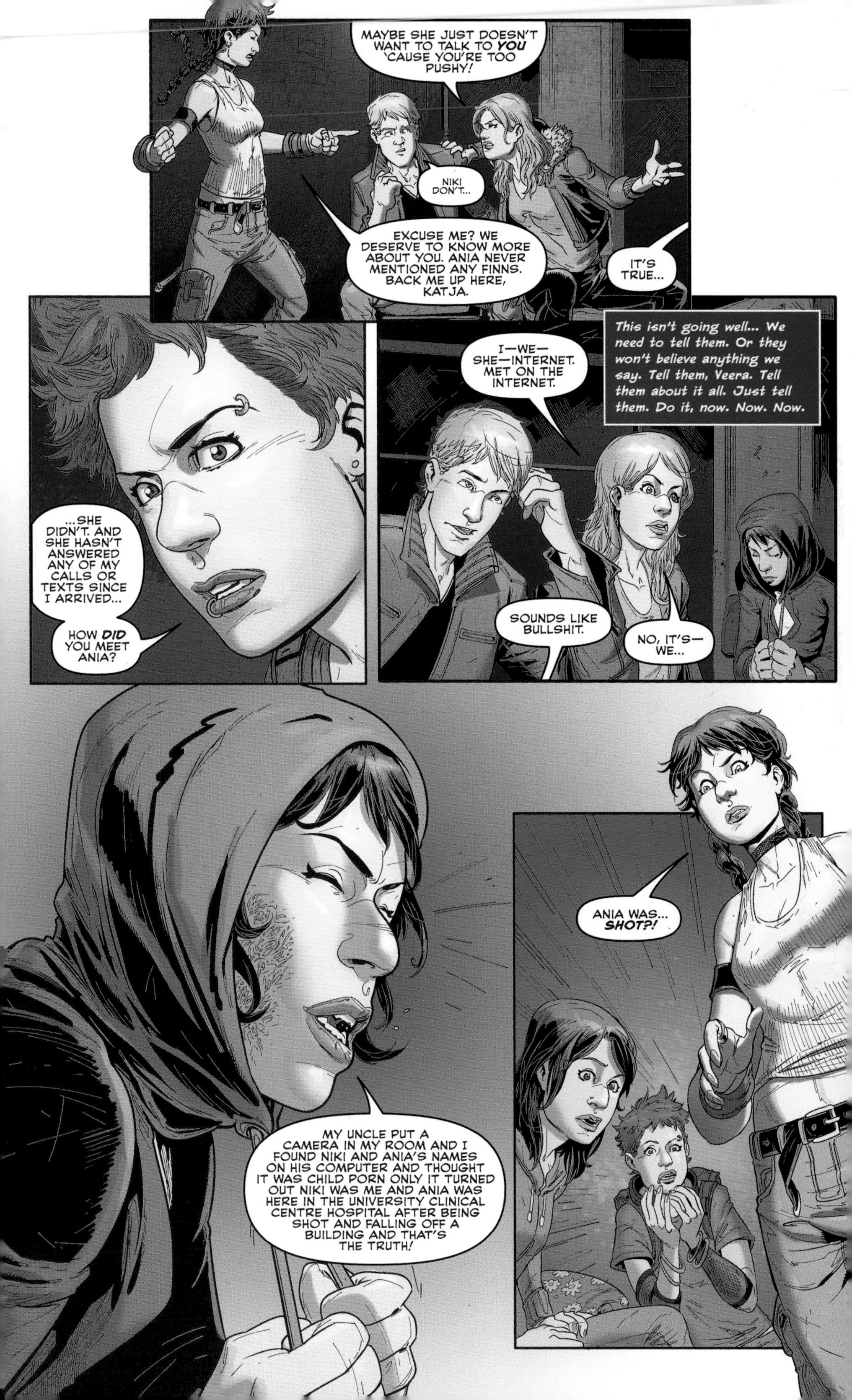

MAYBE SHE JUST DOESN'T WANT TO TALK TO ***YOU*** 'CAUSE YOU'RE TOO PUSHY!
NIKI DON'T...
EXCUSE ME? WE DESERVE TO KNOW MORE ABOUT YOU. ANIA NEVER MENTIONED ANY FINNS. BACK ME UP HERE, KATJA.
IT'S TRUE...
...SHE DIDN'T. AND SHE HASN'T ANSWERED ANY OF MY CALLS OR TEXTS SINCE I ARRIVED...
HOW ***DID*** YOU MEET ANIA?
I—WE— SHE—INTERNET. MET ON THE INTERNET.
This isn't going well... We need to tell them. Or they won't believe anything we say. Tell them, Veera. Tell them about it all. Just tell them. Do it, now. Now. Now.
SOUNDS LIKE BULLSHIT.
NO, IT'S— WE...
MY UNCLE PUT A CAMERA IN MY ROOM AND I FOUND NIKI AND ANIA'S NAMES ON HIS COMPUTER AND THOUGHT IT WAS CHILD PORN ONLY IT TURNED OUT NIKI WAS ME AND ANIA WAS HERE IN THE UNIVERSITY CLINICAL CENTRE HOSPITAL AFTER BEING SHOT AND FALLING OFF A BUILDING AND THAT'S THE TRUTH!
ANIA WAS... ***SHOT?!***

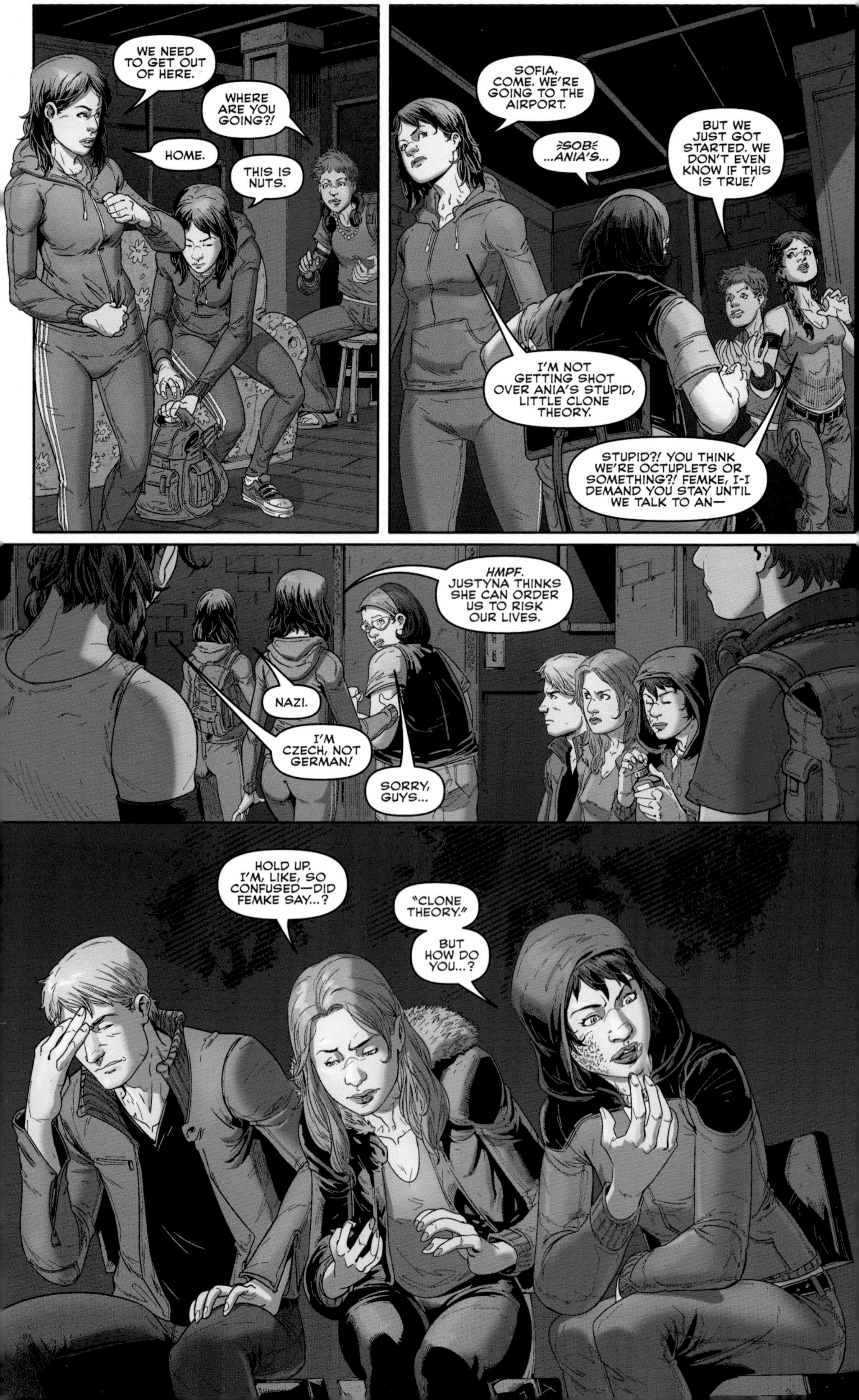

WE NEED TO GET OUT OF HERE.
WHERE ARE YOU GOING?!
HOME.
THIS IS NUTS.
SOFIA, COME. WE'RE GOING TO THE AIRPORT.
SOB ...ANIA'S...
BUT WE JUST GOT STARTED. WE DON'T EVEN KNOW IF THIS IS TRUE!
I'M NOT GETTING SHOT OVER ANIA'S STUPID, LITTLE CLONE THEORY.
STUPID?! YOU THINK WE'RE OCTUPLETS OR SOMETHING?! FEMKE, I-I DEMAND YOU STAY UNTIL WE TALK TO AN—
HMPF. JUSTYNA THINKS SHE CAN ORDER US TO RISK OUR LIVES.
NAZI.
I'M CZECH, NOT GERMAN!
SORRY, GUYS...
HOLD UP. I'M, LIKE, SO CONFUSED—DID FEMKE SAY...?
"CLONE THEORY."
BUT HOW DO YOU...?

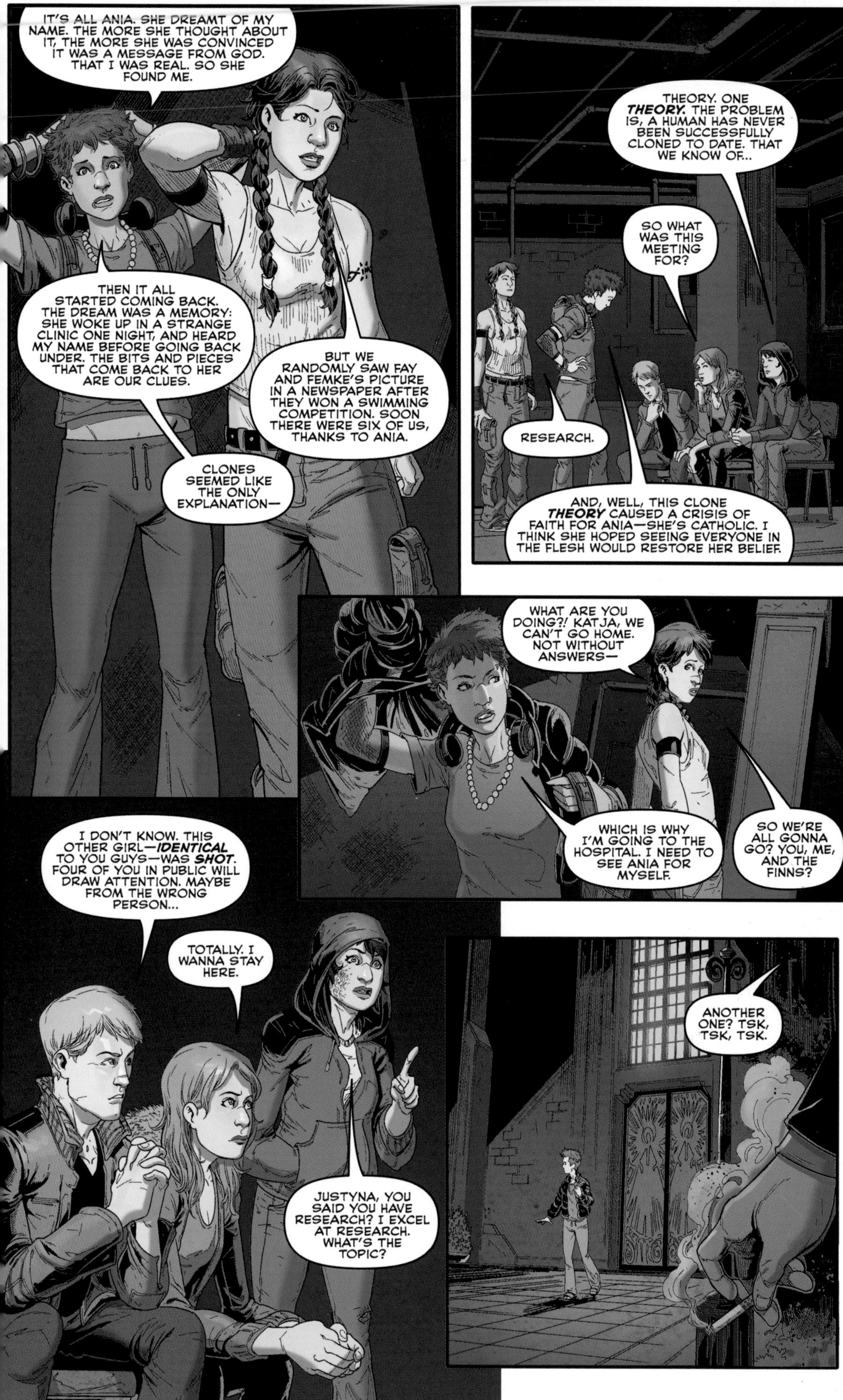
IT'S ALL ANIA. SHE DREAMT OF MY NAME. THE MORE SHE THOUGHT ABOUT IT, THE MORE SHE WAS CONVINCED IT WAS A MESSAGE FROM GOD. THAT I WAS REAL. SO SHE FOUND ME.
THEN IT ALL STARTED COMING BACK. THE DREAM WAS A MEMORY: SHE WOKE UP IN A STRANGE CLINIC ONE NIGHT, AND HEARD MY NAME BEFORE GOING BACK UNDER. THE BITS AND PIECES THAT COME BACK TO HER ARE OUR CLUES.
BUT WE RANDOMLY SAW FAY AND FEMKE'S PICTURE IN A NEWSPAPER AFTER THEY WON A SWIMMING COMPETITION. SOON THERE WERE SIX OF US, THANKS TO ANIA.
CLONES SEEMED LIKE THE ONLY EXPLANATION—
THEORY. ONE THEORY. THE PROBLEM IS, A HUMAN HAS NEVER BEEN SUCCESSFULLY CLONED TO DATE. THAT WE KNOW OF...
SO WHAT WAS THIS MEETING FOR?
RESEARCH.
AND, WELL, THIS CLONE THEORY CAUSED A CRISIS OF FAITH FOR ANIA—SHE'S CATHOLIC. I THINK SHE HOPED SEEING EVERYONE IN THE FLESH WOULD RESTORE HER BELIEF.
WHAT ARE YOU DOING?! KATJA, WE CAN'T GO HOME. NOT WITHOUT ANSWERS—
WHICH IS WHY I'M GOING TO THE HOSPITAL. I NEED TO SEE ANIA FOR MYSELF.
SO WE'RE ALL GONNA GO? YOU, ME, AND THE FINNS?
I DON'T KNOW. THIS OTHER GIRL—IDENTICAL TO YOU GUYS—WAS SHOT. FOUR OF YOU IN PUBLIC WILL DRAW ATTENTION. MAYBE FROM THE WRONG PERSON...
TOTALLY. I WANNA STAY HERE.
JUSTYNA, YOU SAID YOU HAVE RESEARCH? I EXCEL AT RESEARCH. WHAT'S THE TOPIC?
ANOTHER ONE? TSK, TSK, TSK.

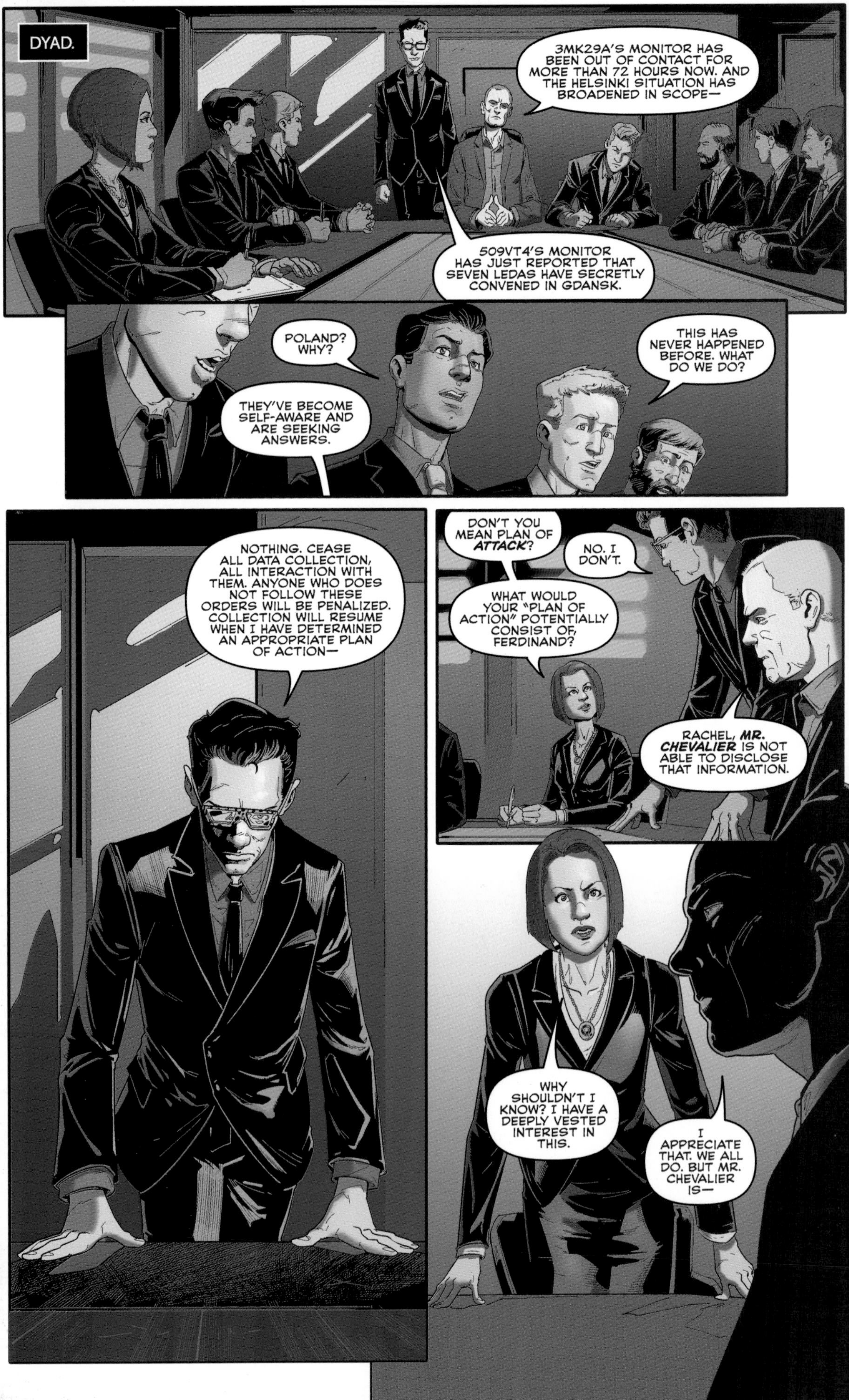
DYAD.
3MK29A'S MONITOR HAS BEEN OUT OF CONTACT FOR MORE THAN 72 HOURS NOW. AND THE HELSINKI SITUATION HAS BROADENED IN SCOPE—
509VT4'S MONITOR HAS JUST REPORTED THAT SEVEN LEDAS HAVE SECRETLY CONVENED IN GDANSK.
POLAND? WHY?
THEY'VE BECOME SELF-AWARE AND ARE SEEKING ANSWERS.
THIS HAS NEVER HAPPENED BEFORE. WHAT DO WE DO?
NOTHING. CEASE ALL DATA COLLECTION, ALL INTERACTION WITH THEM. ANYONE WHO DOES NOT FOLLOW THESE ORDERS WILL BE PENALIZED. COLLECTION WILL RESUME WHEN I HAVE DETERMINED AN APPROPRIATE PLAN OF ACTION—
DON'T YOU MEAN PLAN OF ***ATTACK***?
NO. I DON'T.
WHAT WOULD YOUR "PLAN OF ACTION" POTENTIALLY CONSIST OF, FERDINAND?
RACHEL, ***MR. CHEVALIER*** IS NOT ABLE TO DISCLOSE THAT INFORMATION.
WHY SHOULDN'T I KNOW? I HAVE A DEEPLY VESTED INTEREST IN THIS.
I APPRECIATE THAT. WE ALL DO. BUT MR. CHEVALIER IS—

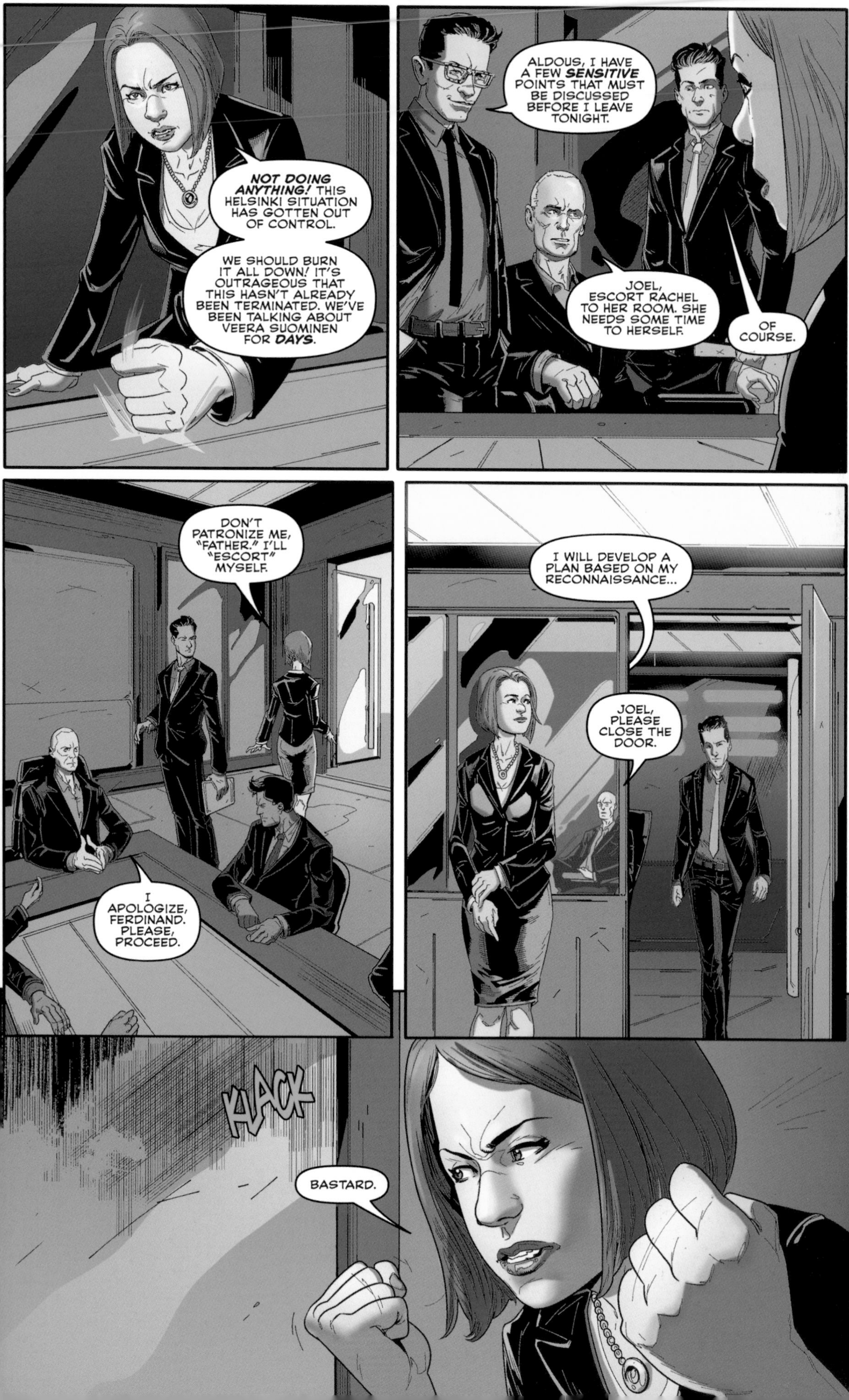
NOT DOING ANYTHING! THIS HELSINKI SITUATION HAS GOTTEN OUT OF CONTROL.
WE SHOULD BURN IT ALL DOWN! IT'S OUTRAGEOUS THAT THIS HASN'T ALREADY BEEN TERMINATED. WE'VE BEEN TALKING ABOUT VEERA SUOMINEN FOR DAYS.
ALDOUS, I HAVE A FEW SENSITIVE POINTS THAT MUST BE DISCUSSED BEFORE I LEAVE TONIGHT.
JOEL, ESCORT RACHEL TO HER ROOM. SHE NEEDS SOME TIME TO HERSELF.
OF COURSE.
DON'T PATRONIZE ME, "FATHER." I'LL "ESCORT" MYSELF.
I APOLOGIZE, FERDINAND. PLEASE, PROCEED.
I WILL DEVELOP A PLAN BASED ON MY RECONNAISSANCE...
JOEL, PLEASE CLOSE THE DOOR.
KLACK
BASTARD.

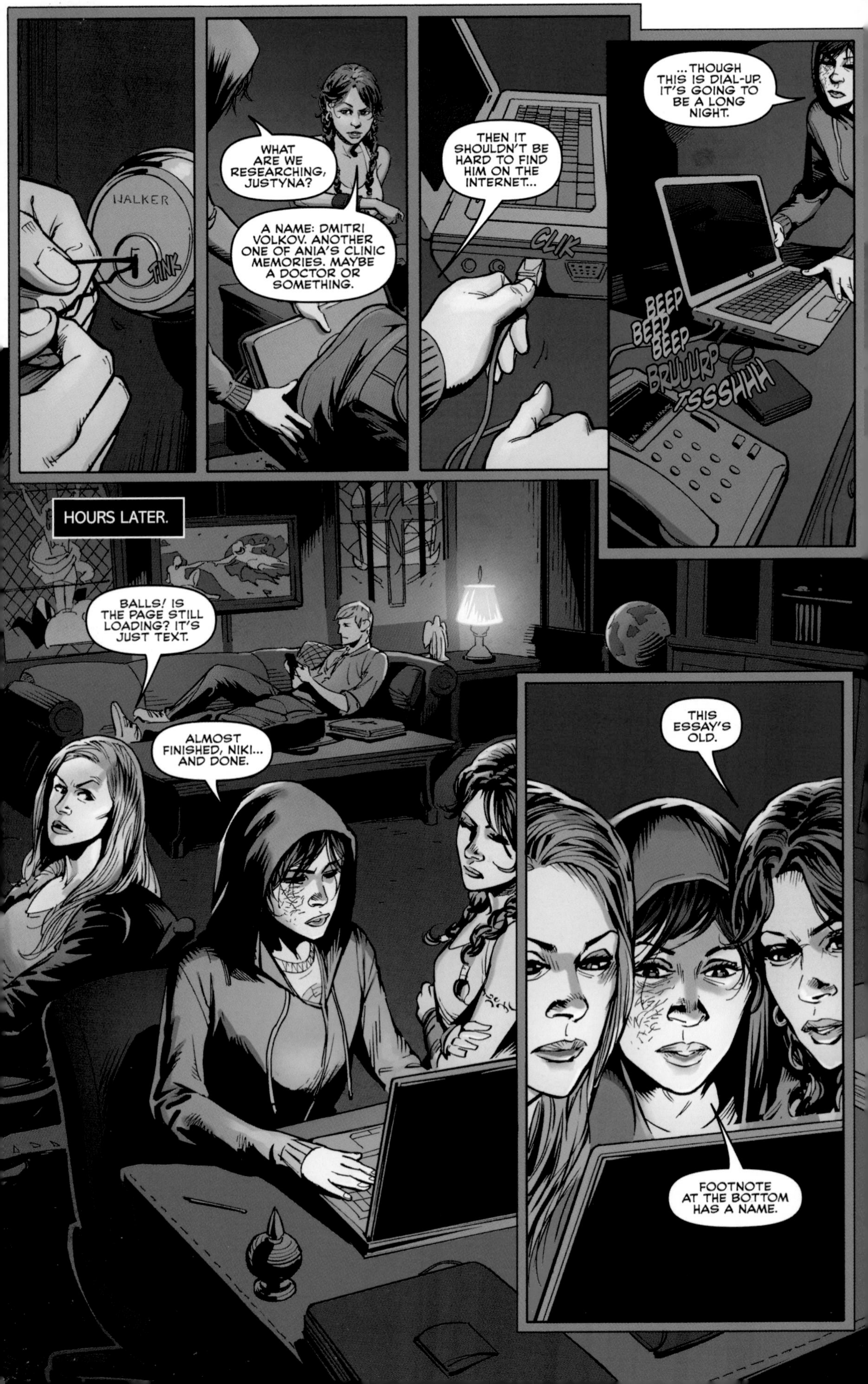
WALKER
TINK
WHAT ARE WE RESEARCHING, JUSTYNA?
A NAME: DMITRI VOLKOV. ANOTHER ONE OF ANIA'S CLINIC MEMORIES. MAYBE A DOCTOR OR SOMETHING.
THEN IT SHOULDN'T BE HARD TO FIND HIM ON THE INTERNET...
CLIK
...THOUGH THIS IS DIAL-UP. IT'S GOING TO BE A LONG NIGHT.
BEEP BEEP BEEP BRUUURP TSSSHHH
HOURS LATER.
BALLS! IS THE PAGE STILL LOADING? IT'S JUST TEXT.
ALMOST FINISHED, NIKI... AND DONE.
THIS ESSAY'S OLD.
FOOTNOTE AT THE BOTTOM HAS A NAME.

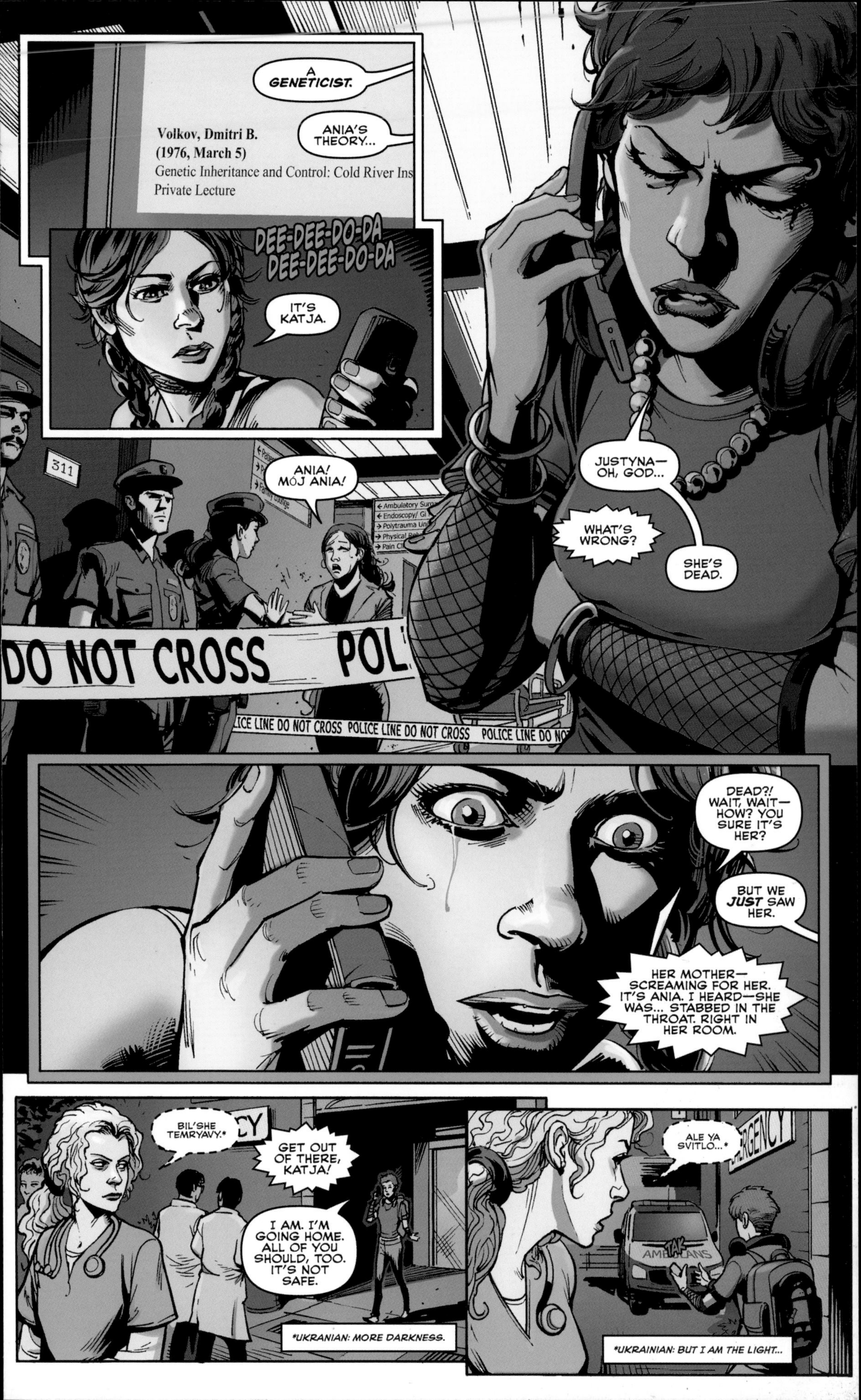

A GENETICIST.
ANIA'S THEORY...
Volkov, Dmitri B.
(1976, March 5)
Genetic Inheritance and Control: Cold River Ins
Private Lecture
DEE-DEE-DO-DA DEE-DEE-DO-DA
IT'S KATJA.
JUSTYNA— OH, GOD...
WHAT'S WRONG?
SHE'S DEAD.
311
ANIA! MÓJ ANIA!
DO NOT CROSS
POL
POLICE LINE DO NOT CROSS POLICE LINE DO NOT CROSS POLICE LINE DO NO
DEAD?! WAIT, WAIT— HOW? YOU SURE IT'S HER?
BUT WE *JUST* SAW HER.
HER MOTHER— SCREAMING FOR HER. IT'S ANIA. I HEARD—SHE WAS... STABBED IN THE THROAT. RIGHT IN HER ROOM.
BIL'SHE TEMRYAVY.*
GET OUT OF THERE, KATJA!
I AM. I'M GOING HOME. ALL OF YOU SHOULD, TOO. IT'S NOT SAFE.
*UKRANIAN: MORE DARKNESS.
ALE YA SVITLO...*
TAK
*UKRAINIAN: BUT I AM THE LIGHT...

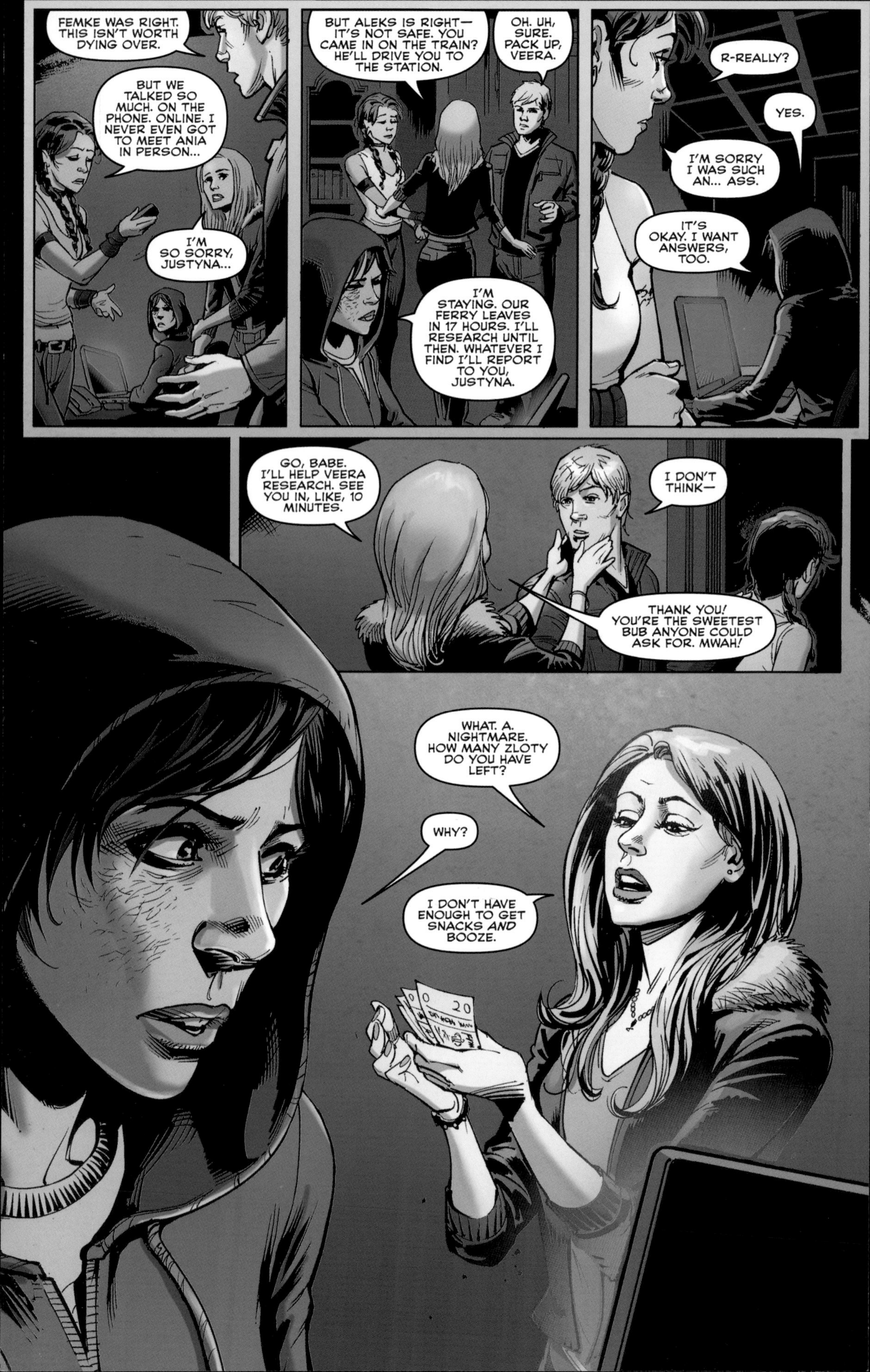
FEMKE WAS RIGHT. THIS ISN'T WORTH DYING OVER.
BUT WE TALKED SO MUCH. ON THE PHONE. ONLINE. I NEVER EVEN GOT TO MEET ANIA IN PERSON...
I'M SO SORRY, JUSTYNA...
BUT ALEKS IS RIGHT— IT'S NOT SAFE. YOU CAME IN ON THE TRAIN? HE'LL DRIVE YOU TO THE STATION.
OH. UH, SURE. PACK UP, VEERA.
I'M STAYING. OUR FERRY LEAVES IN 17 HOURS. I'LL RESEARCH UNTIL THEN. WHATEVER I FIND I'LL REPORT TO YOU, JUSTYNA.
R-REALLY?
YES.
I'M SORRY I WAS SUCH AN... ASS.
IT'S OKAY. I WANT ANSWERS, TOO.
GO, BABE. I'LL HELP VEERA RESEARCH. SEE YOU IN, LIKE, 10 MINUTES.
I DON'T THINK—
THANK YOU! YOU'RE THE SWEETEST BUB ANYONE COULD ASK FOR. MWAH!
WHAT. A. NIGHTMARE. HOW MANY ZLOTY DO YOU HAVE LEFT?
WHY?
I DON'T HAVE ENOUGH TO GET SNACKS *AND* BOOZE.

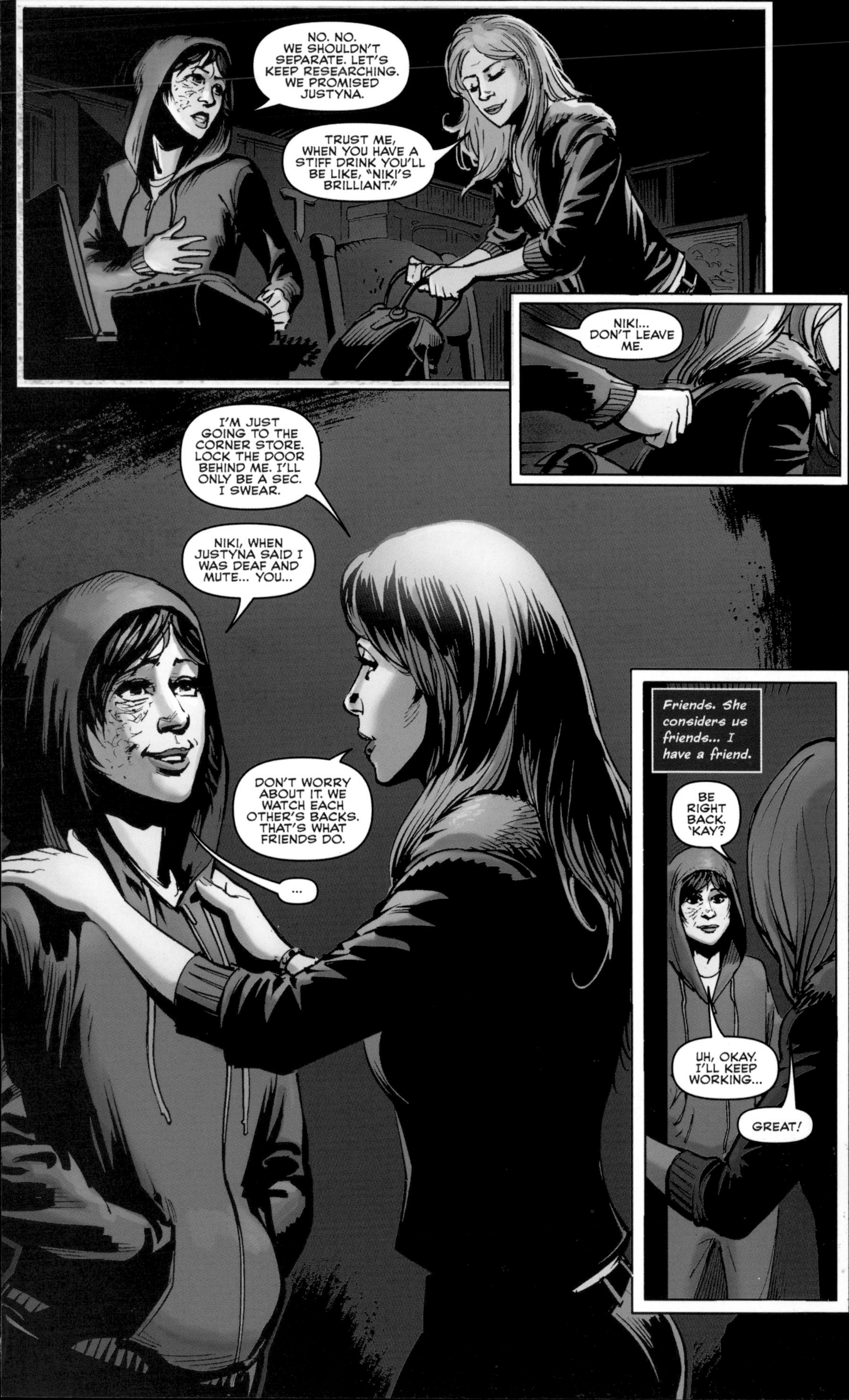
NO. NO. WE SHOULDN'T SEPARATE. LET'S KEEP RESEARCHING. WE PROMISED JUSTYNA.
TRUST ME, WHEN YOU HAVE A STIFF DRINK YOU'LL BE LIKE, "NIKI'S BRILLIANT."
NIKI... DON'T LEAVE ME.
I'M JUST GOING TO THE CORNER STORE. LOCK THE DOOR BEHIND ME. I'LL ONLY BE A SEC. I SWEAR.
NIKI, WHEN JUSTYNA SAID I WAS DEAF AND MUTE... YOU...
DON'T WORRY ABOUT IT. WE WATCH EACH OTHER'S BACKS. THAT'S WHAT FRIENDS DO.
...
Friends. She considers us friends... I have a friend.
BE RIGHT BACK. 'KAY?
UH, OKAY. I'LL KEEP WORKING...
GREAT!

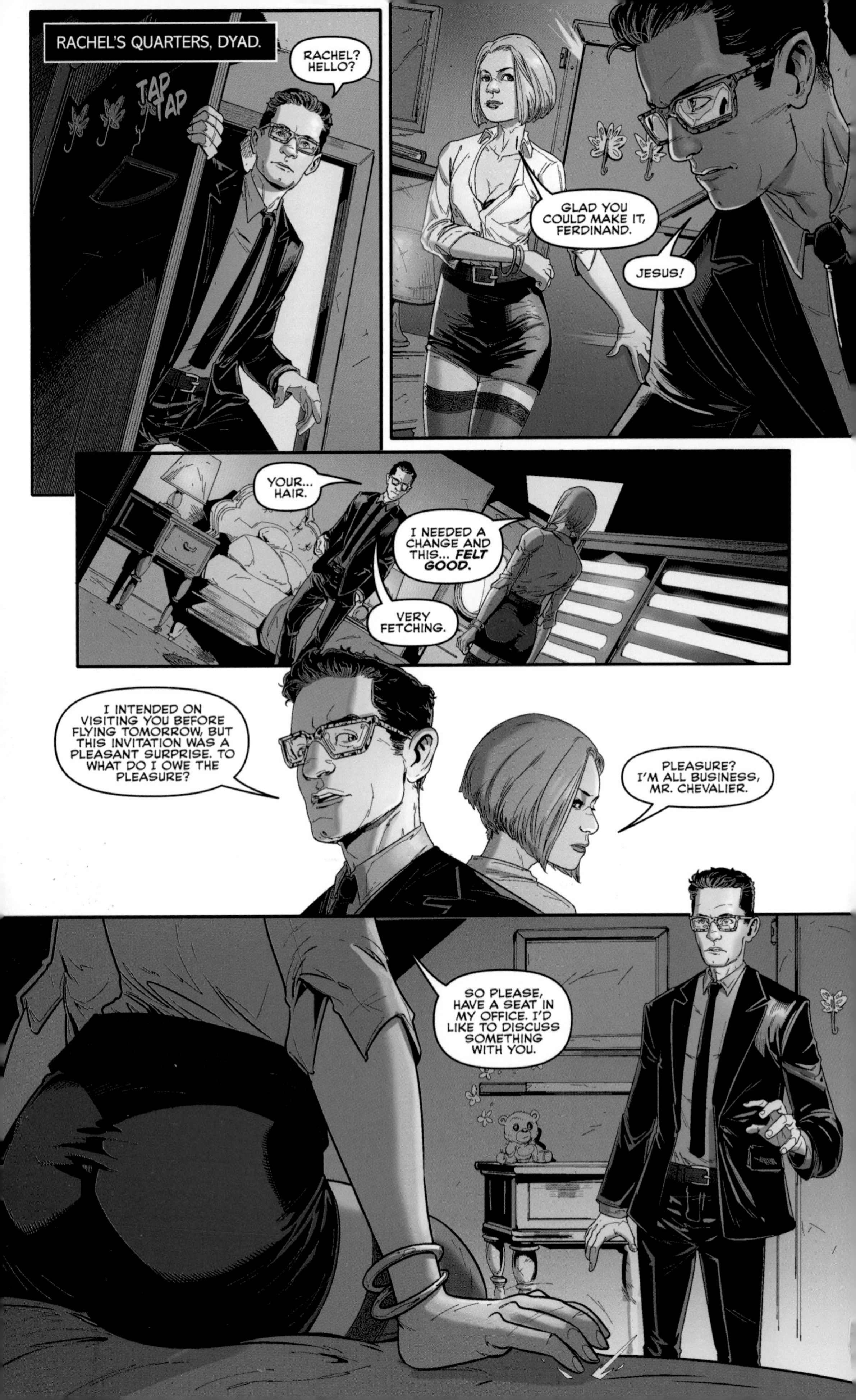
RACHEL'S QUARTERS, DYAD.
TAP TAP
RACHEL? HELLO?
GLAD YOU COULD MAKE IT, FERDINAND.
JESUS!
YOUR... HAIR.
I NEEDED A CHANGE AND THIS... FELT GOOD.
VERY FETCHING.
I INTENDED ON VISITING YOU BEFORE FLYING TOMORROW, BUT THIS INVITATION WAS A PLEASANT SURPRISE. TO WHAT DO I OWE THE PLEASURE?
PLEASURE? I'M ALL BUSINESS, MR. CHEVALIER.
SO PLEASE, HAVE A SEAT IN MY OFFICE. I'D LIKE TO DISCUSS SOMETHING WITH YOU.

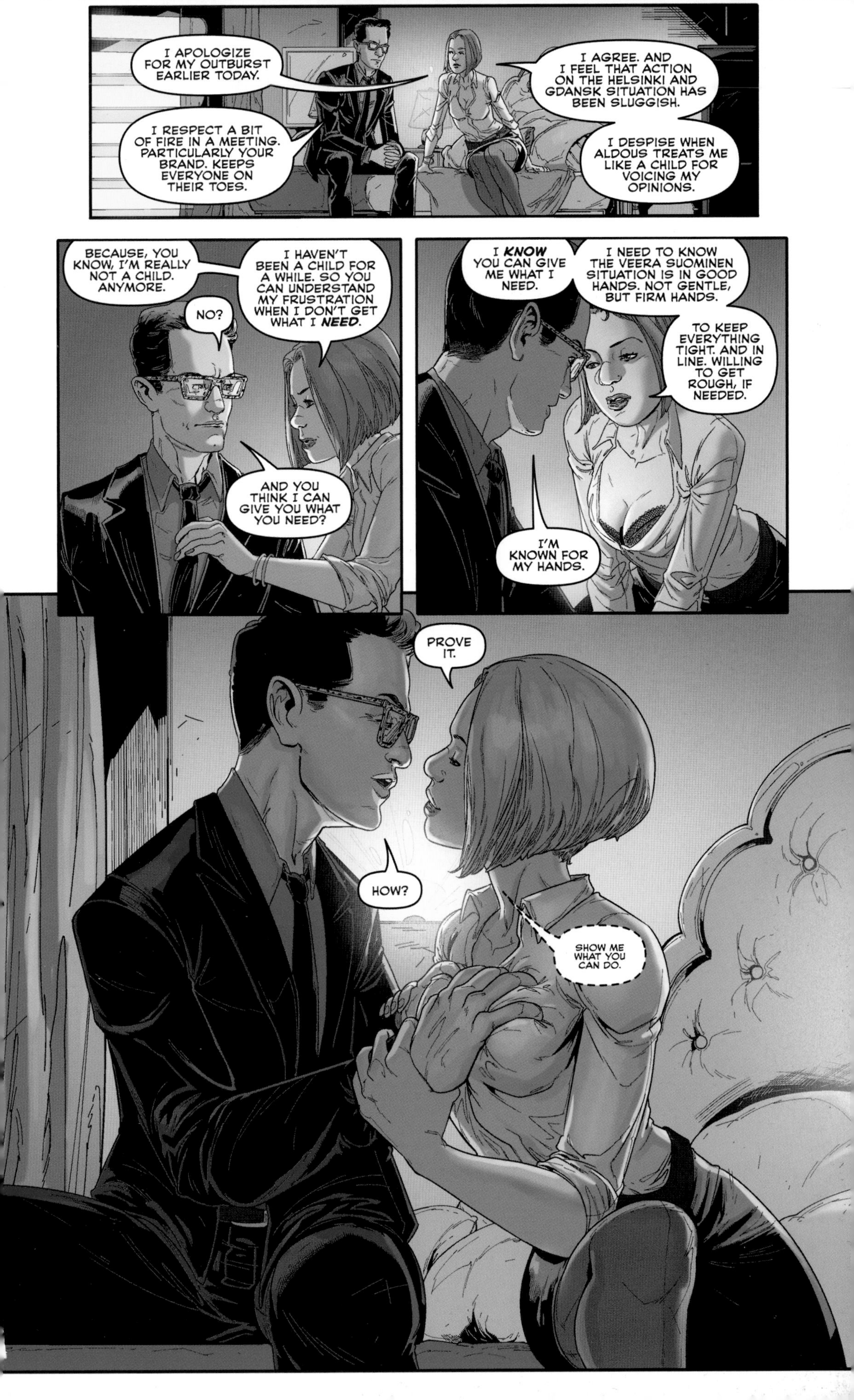
I APOLOGIZE FOR MY OUTBURST EARLIER TODAY.
I RESPECT A BIT OF FIRE IN A MEETING. PARTICULARLY YOUR BRAND. KEEPS EVERYONE ON THEIR TOES.
I AGREE. AND I FEEL THAT ACTION ON THE HELSINKI AND GDANSK SITUATION HAS BEEN SLUGGISH.
I DESPISE WHEN ALDOUS TREATS ME LIKE A CHILD FOR VOICING MY OPINIONS.
BECAUSE, YOU KNOW, I'M REALLY NOT A CHILD. ANYMORE.
NO?
I HAVEN'T BEEN A CHILD FOR A WHILE. SO YOU CAN UNDERSTAND MY FRUSTRATION WHEN I DON'T GET WHAT I ***NEED***.
AND YOU THINK I CAN GIVE YOU WHAT YOU NEED?
I ***KNOW*** YOU CAN GIVE ME WHAT I NEED.
I NEED TO KNOW THE VEERA SUOMINEN SITUATION IS IN GOOD HANDS. NOT GENTLE, BUT FIRM HANDS.
TO KEEP EVERYTHING TIGHT. AND IN LINE. WILLING TO GET ROUGH, IF NEEDED.
I'M KNOWN FOR MY HANDS.
PROVE IT.
HOW?
SHOW ME WHAT YOU CAN DO.

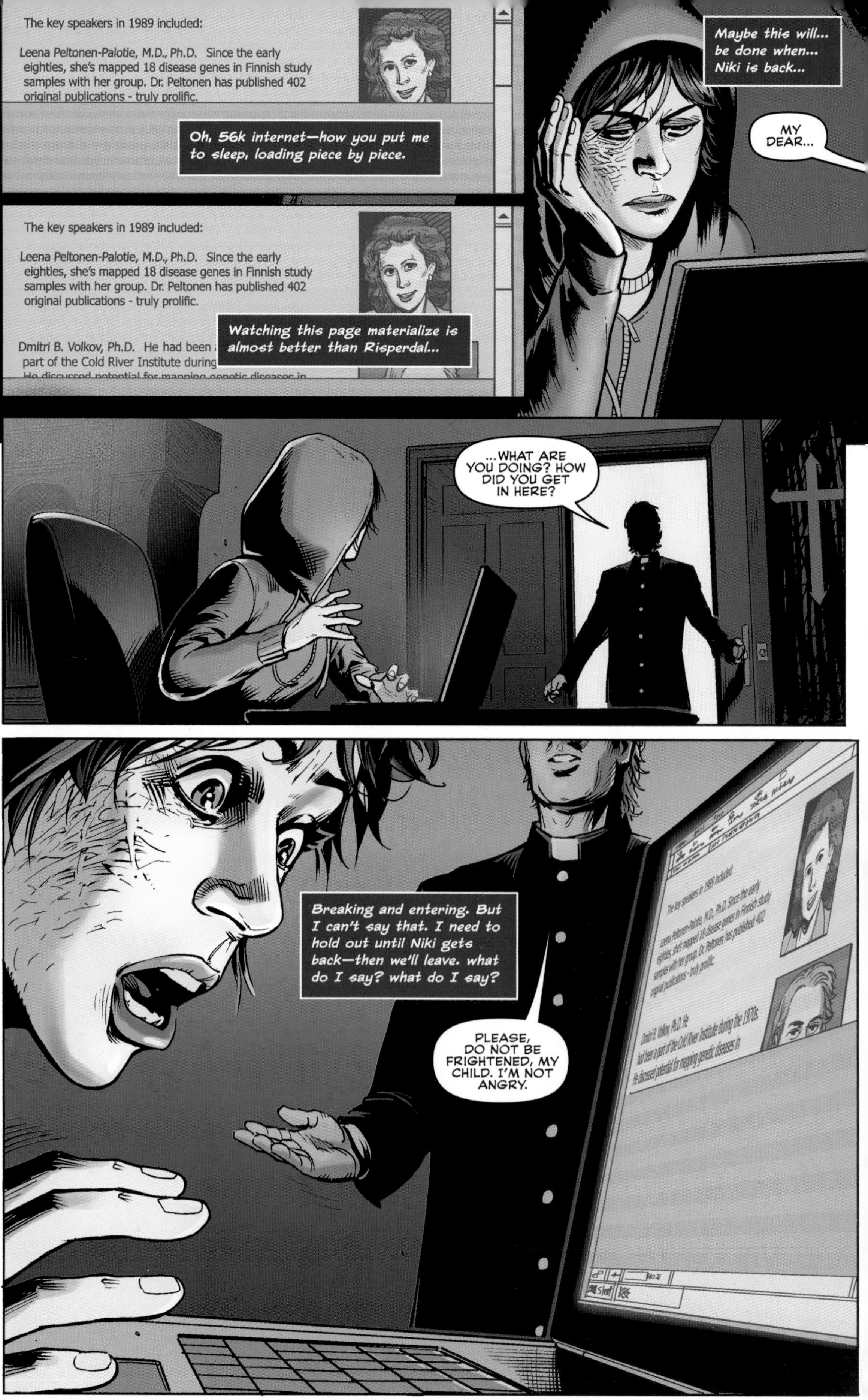
The key speakers in 1989 included:
Leena Peltonen-Palotie, M.D., Ph.D. Since the early eighties, she's mapped 18 disease genes in Finnish study samples with her group. Dr. Peltonen has published 402 original publications - truly prolific.
Oh, 56k internet—how you put me to sleep, loading piece by piece.
The key speakers in 1989 included:
Leena Peltonen-Palotie, M.D., Ph.D. Since the early eighties, she's mapped 18 disease genes in Finnish study samples with her group. Dr. Peltonen has published 402 original publications - truly prolific.
Dmitri B. Volkov, Ph.D. He had been
part of the Cold River Institute during
Watching this page materialize is almost better than Risperdal...
Maybe this will... be done when... Niki is back...
MY DEAR...
...WHAT ARE YOU DOING? HOW DID YOU GET IN HERE?
Breaking and entering. But I can't say that. I need to hold out until Niki gets back—then we'll leave. what do I say? what do I say?
PLEASE, DO NOT BE FRIGHTENED, MY CHILD. I'M NOT ANGRY.

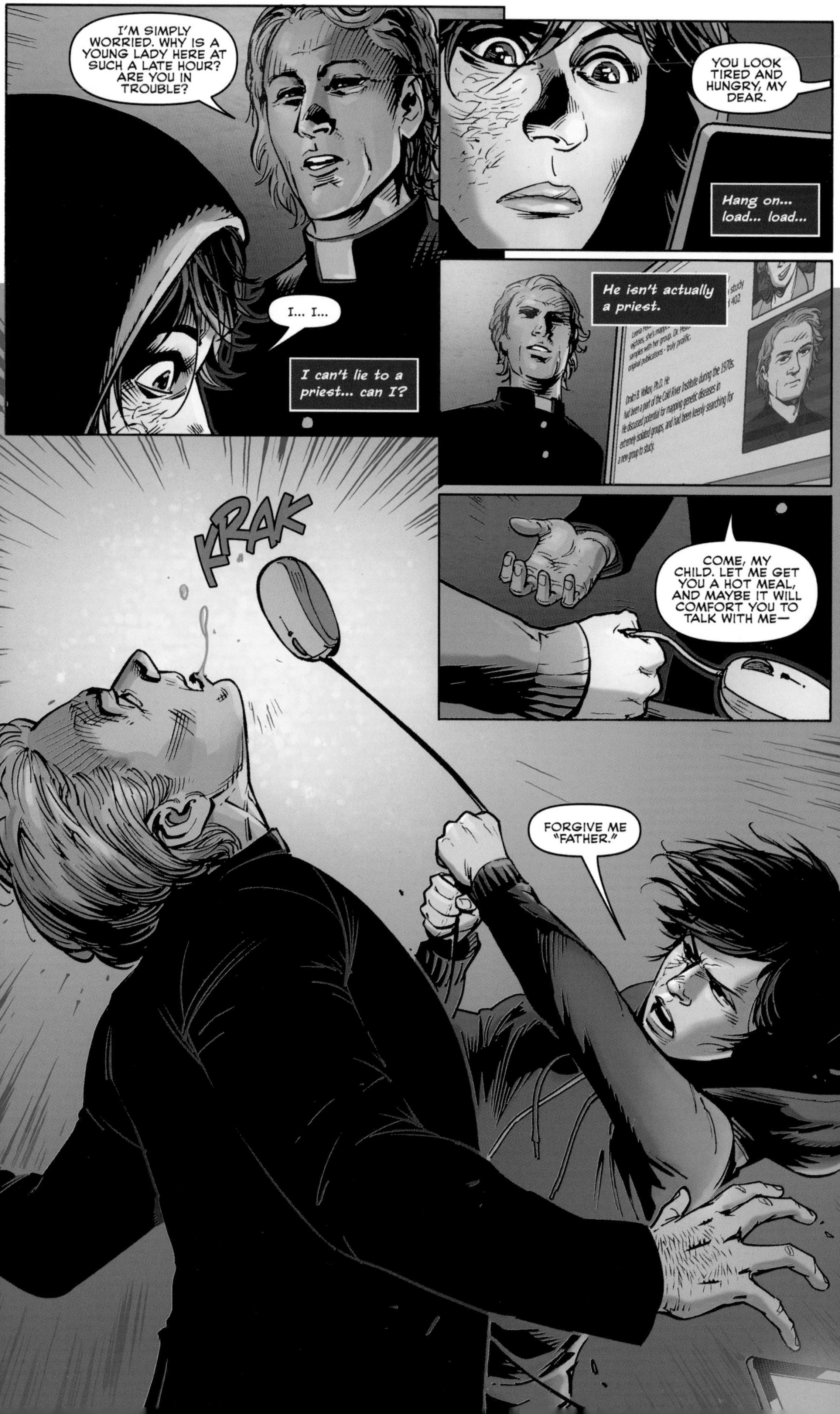
I'M SIMPLY WORRIED. WHY IS A YOUNG LADY HERE AT SUCH A LATE HOUR? ARE YOU IN TROUBLE?
I... I...
I can't lie to a priest... can I?
YOU LOOK TIRED AND HUNGRY, MY DEAR.
Hang on... load... load...
He isn't actually a priest.
COME, MY CHILD. LET ME GET YOU A HOT MEAL, AND MAYBE IT WILL COMFORT YOU TO TALK WITH ME—
KRAK
FORGIVE ME "FATHER."

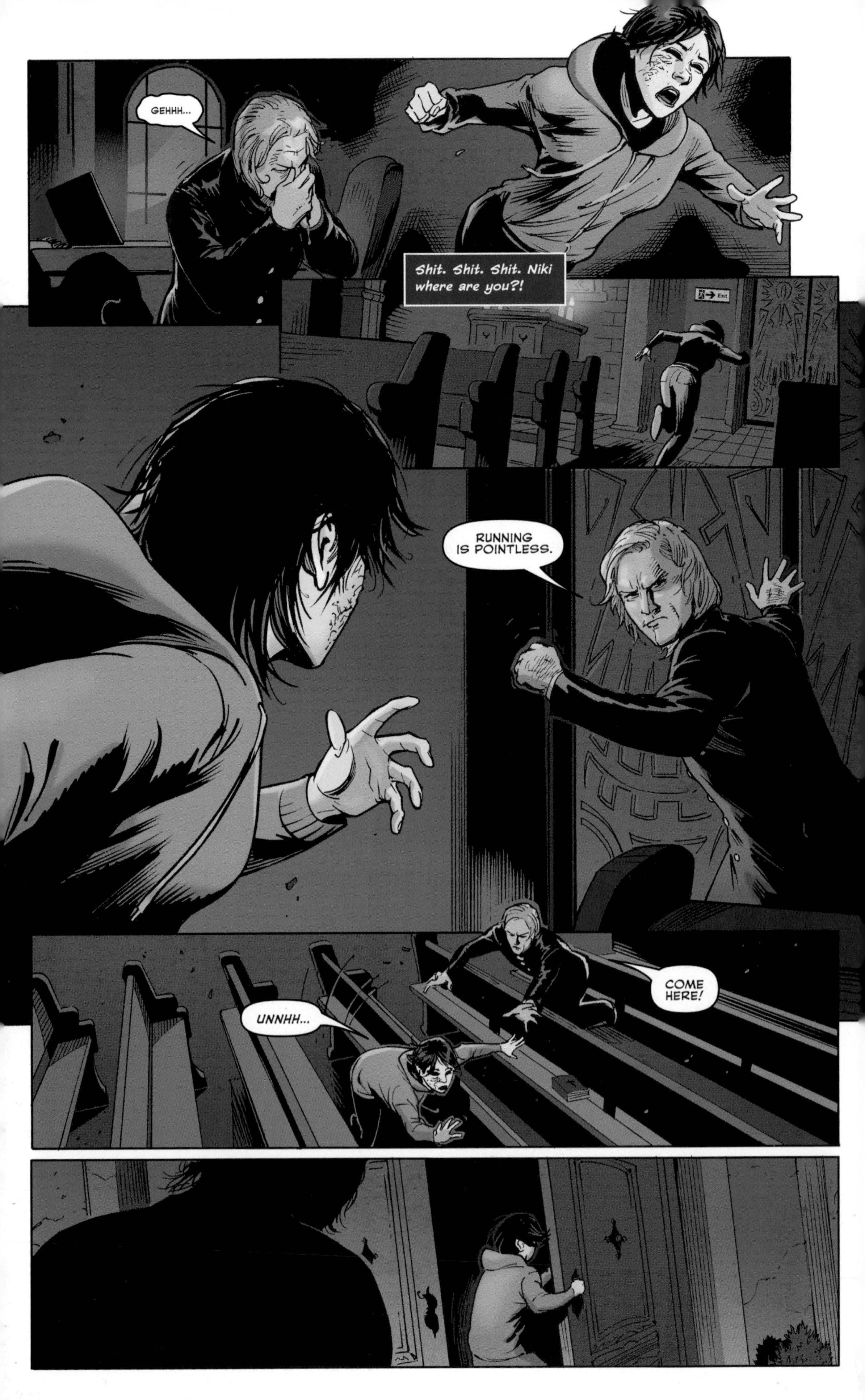
GEHHH...
Shit. Shit. Shit. Niki where are you?!
Exit
RUNNING IS POINTLESS.
UNNHH...
COME HERE!

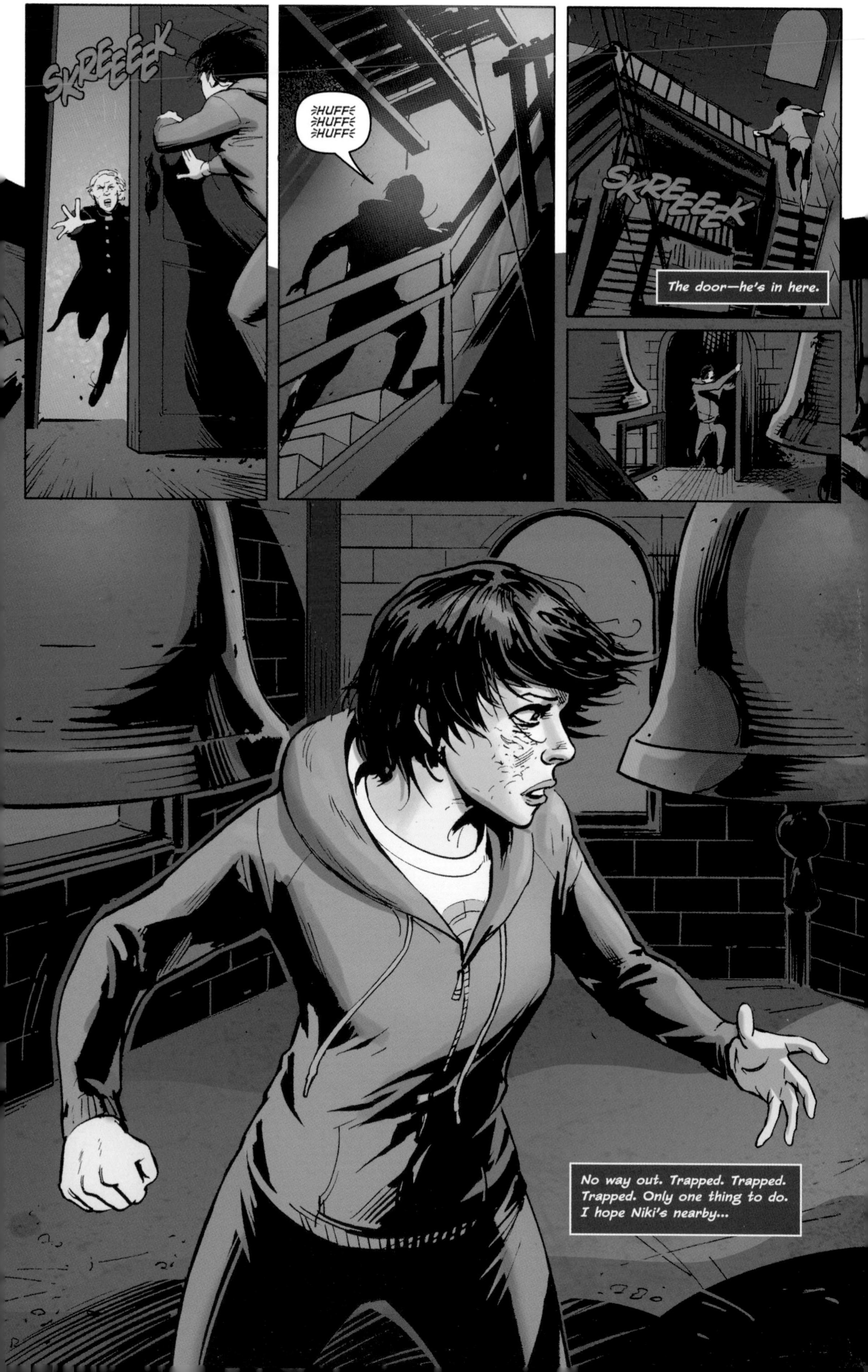
SKREEEEK
HUFF HUFF HUFF
SKREEEEK
The door—he's in here.
No way out. Trapped. Trapped. Trapped. Only one thing to do. I hope Niki's nearby...

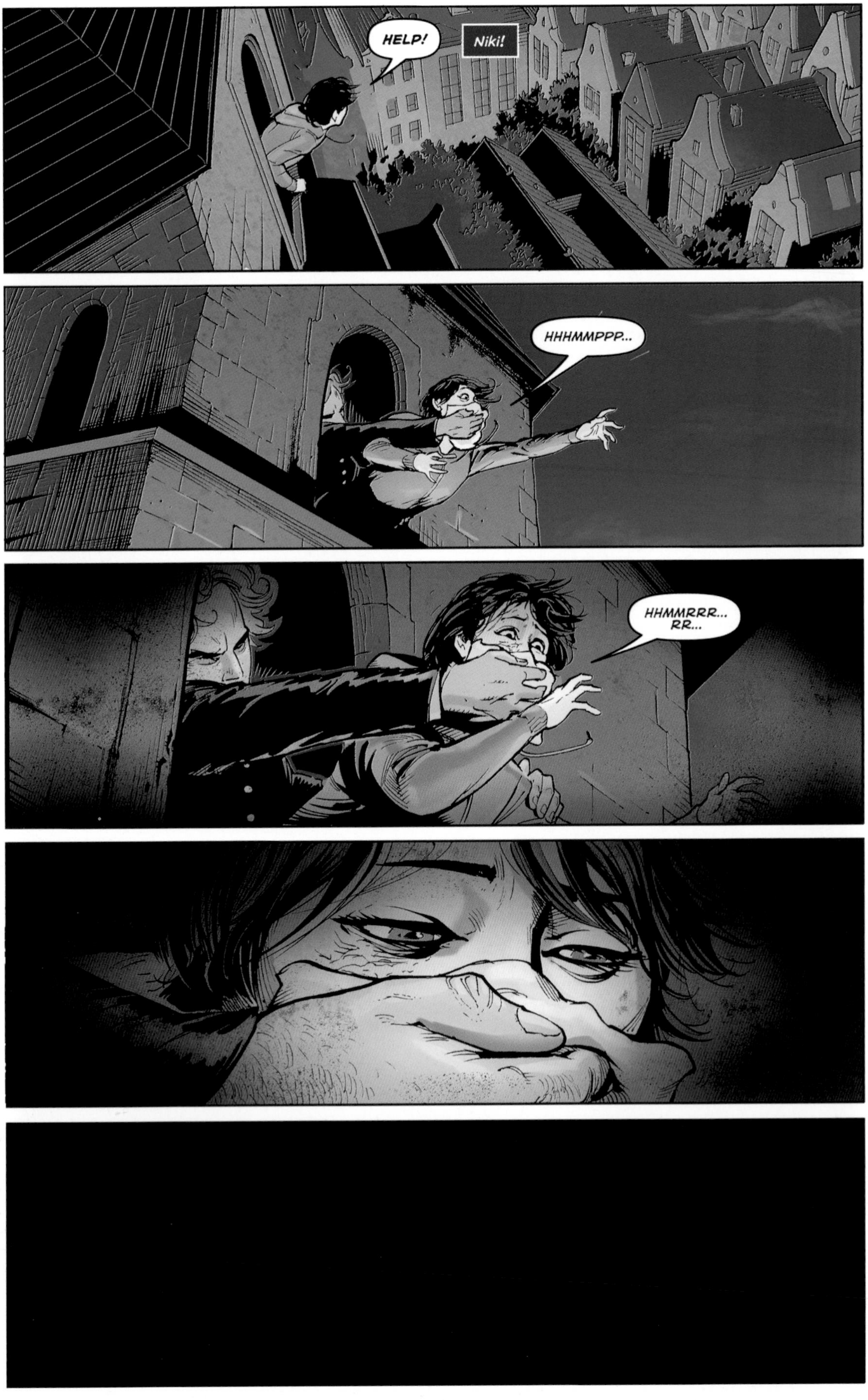
HELP!
Niki!
HHHMMPPP...
HHMMRRR... RR...

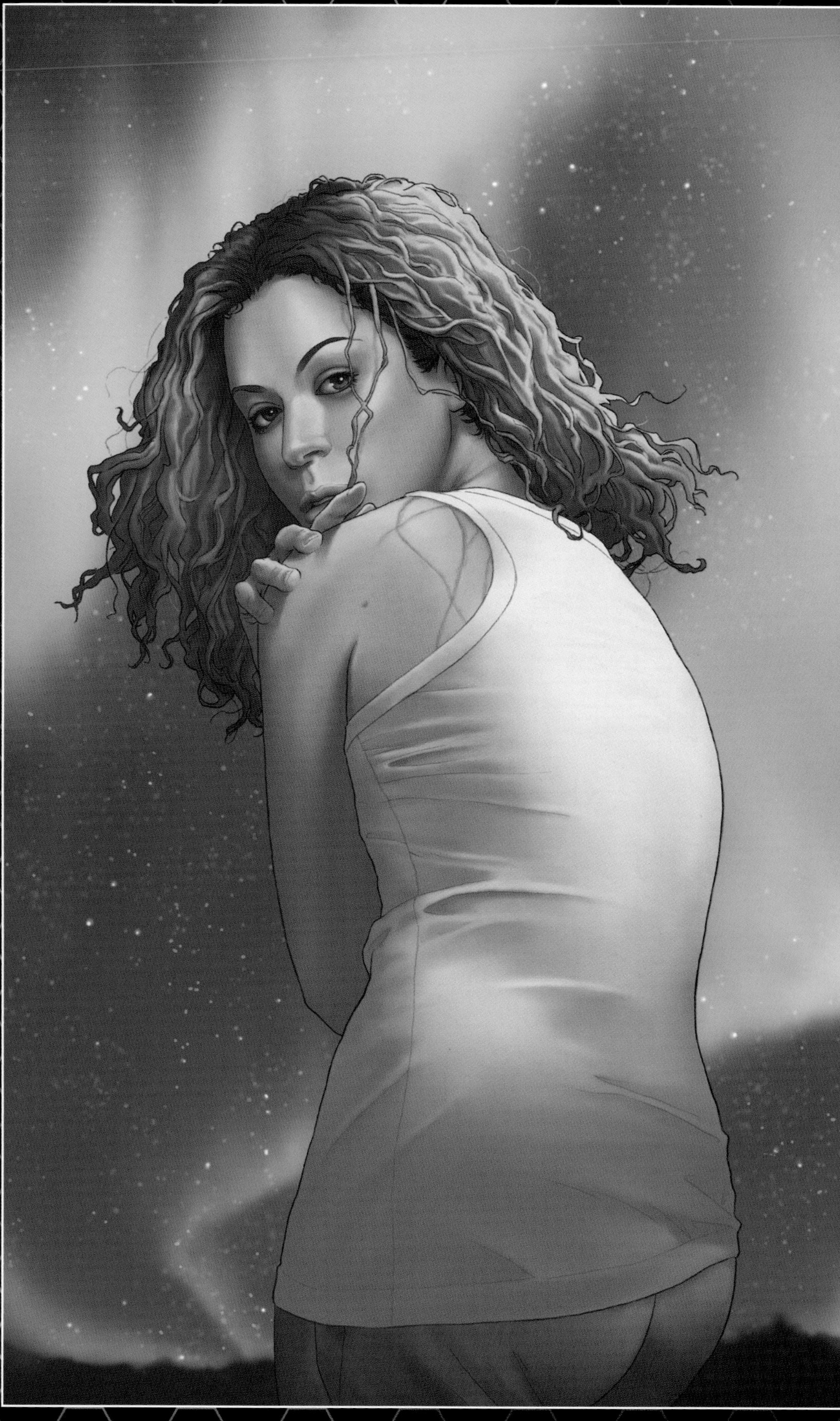

BY **RODIN ESQUEJO**

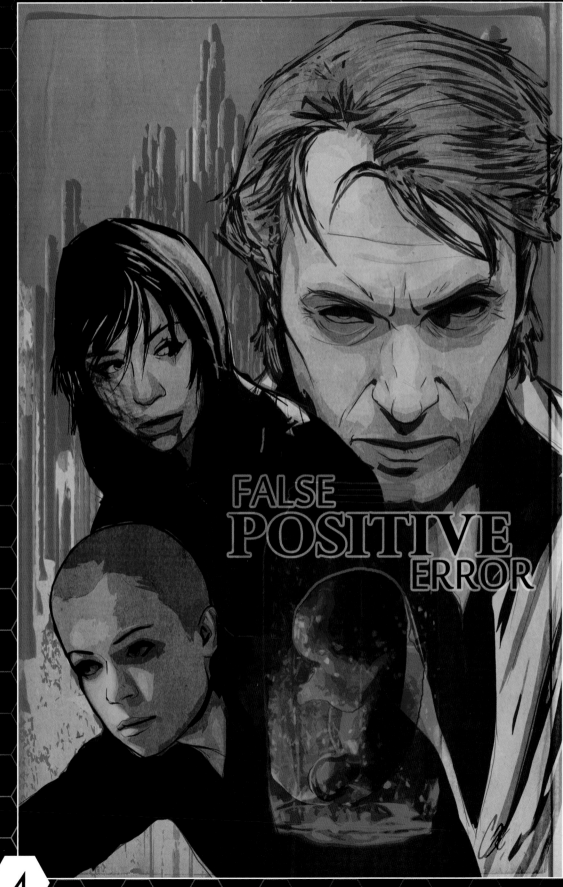

FALSE POSITIVE ERROR

4

BY CAT STAGGS

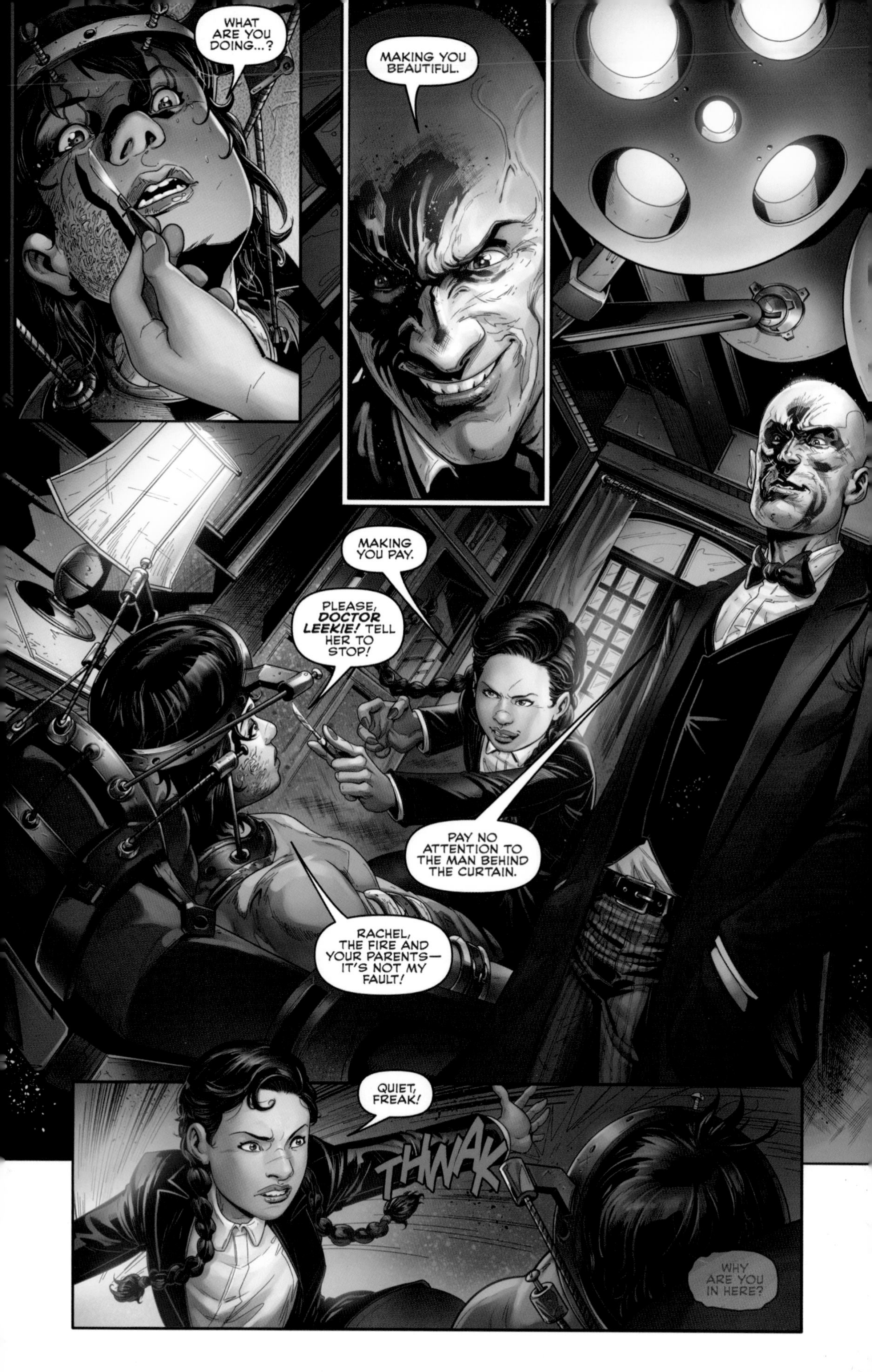
WHAT ARE YOU DOING...?
MAKING YOU BEAUTIFUL.
MAKING YOU PAY.
PLEASE, DOCTOR LEEKIE! TELL HER TO STOP!
PAY NO ATTENTION TO THE MAN BEHIND THE CURTAIN.
RACHEL, THE FIRE AND YOUR PARENTS— IT'S NOT MY FAULT!
QUIET, FREAK!
THWAK
WHY ARE YOU IN HERE?

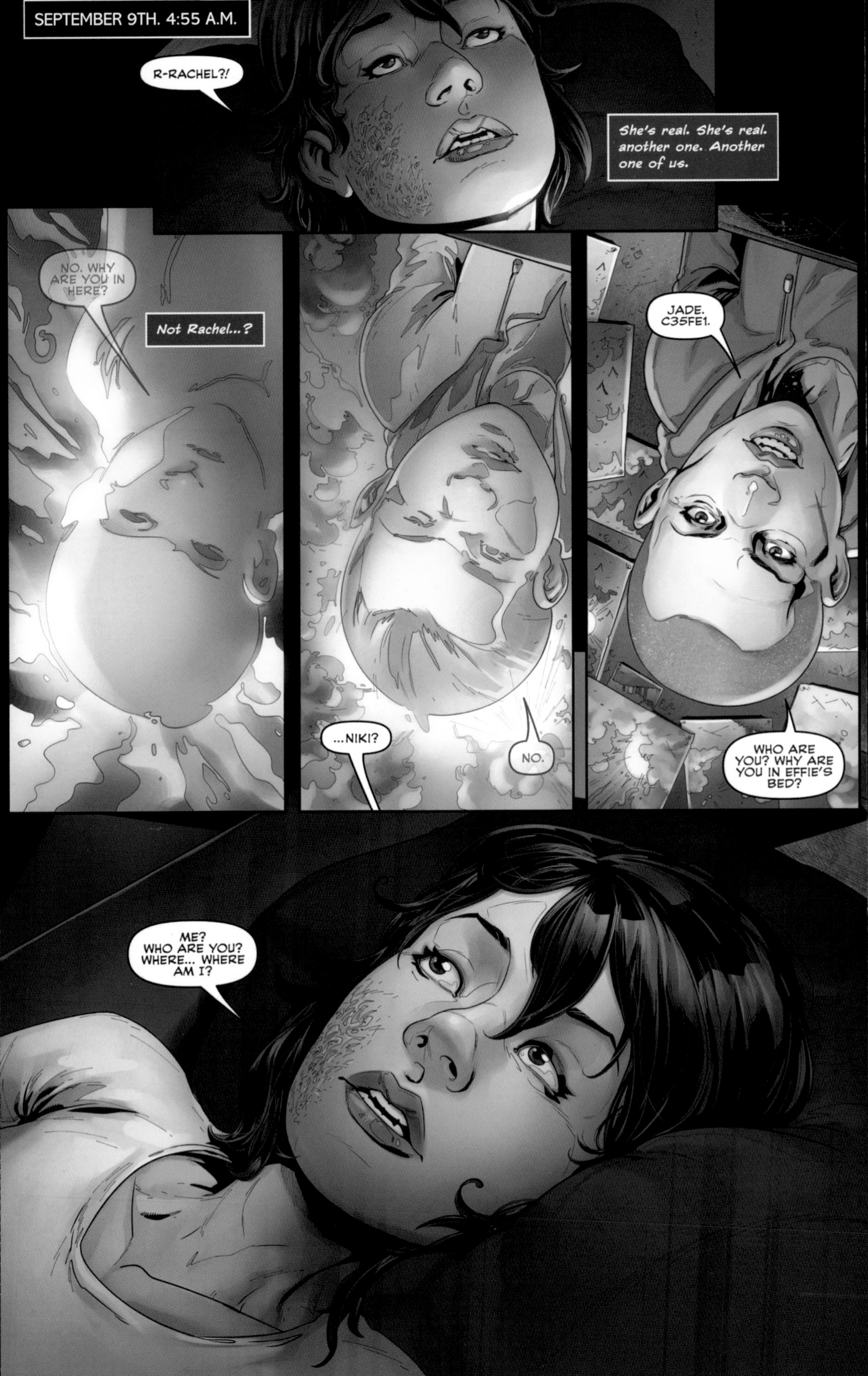
SEPTEMBER 9TH. 4:55 A.M.
R-RACHEL?!
She's real. She's real. another one. Another one of us.
NO. WHY ARE YOU IN HERE?
Not Rachel...?
...NIKI?
NO.
JADE. C35FE1.
WHO ARE YOU? WHY ARE YOU IN EFFIE'S BED?
ME? WHO ARE YOU? WHERE... WHERE AM I?

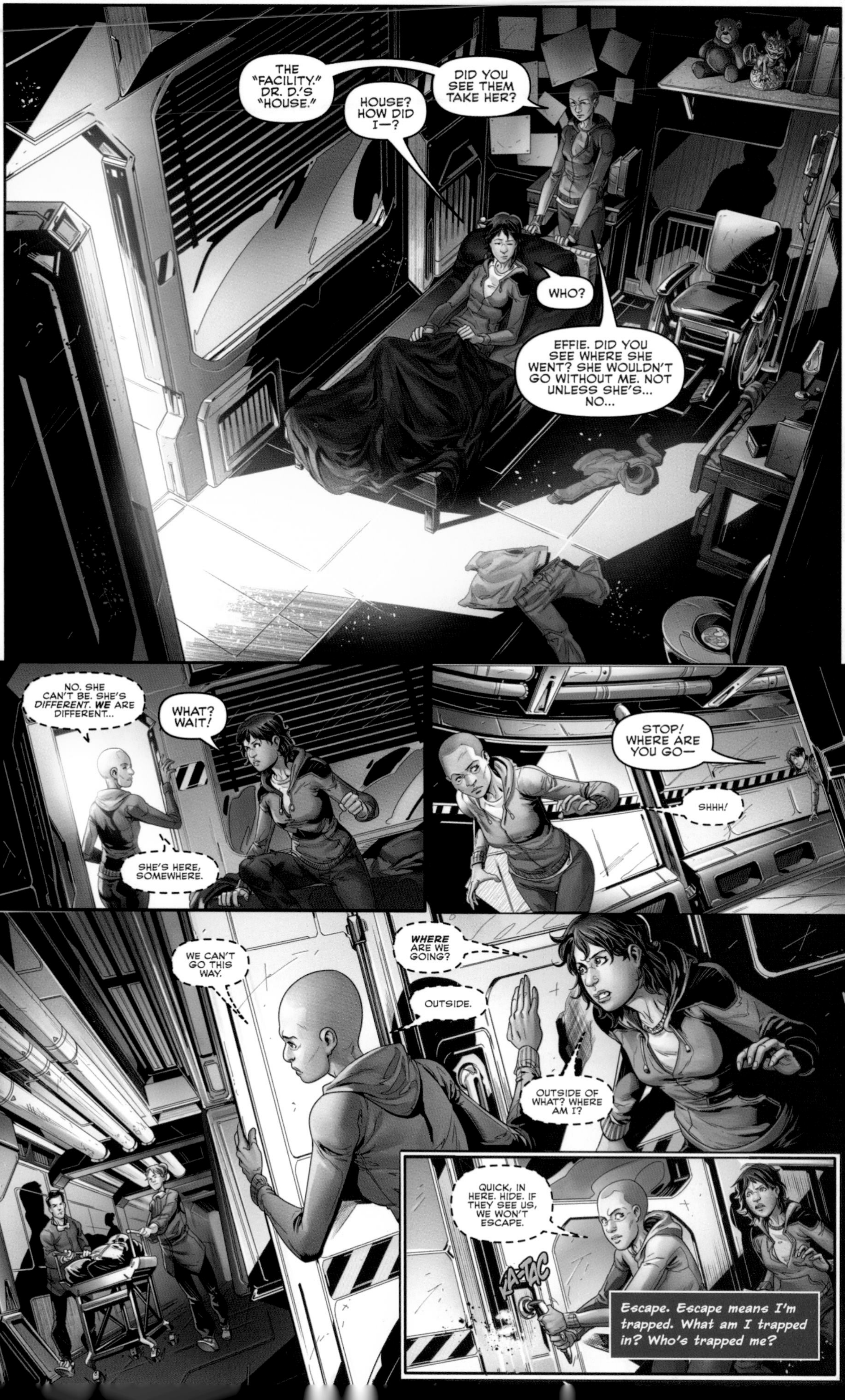
THE "FACILITY." DR. D.'S "HOUSE."
DID YOU SEE THEM TAKE HER?
HOUSE? HOW DID I—?
WHO?
EFFIE. DID YOU SEE WHERE SHE WENT? SHE WOULDN'T GO WITHOUT ME. NOT UNLESS SHE'S... NO...
NO. SHE CAN'T BE. SHE'S DIFFERENT. WE ARE DIFFERENT...
WHAT? WAIT!
SHE'S HERE, SOMEWHERE.
STOP! WHERE ARE YOU GO—
SHHH!
WE CAN'T GO THIS WAY.
WHERE ARE WE GOING?
OUTSIDE.
OUTSIDE OF WHAT? WHERE AM I?
QUICK, IN HERE. HIDE. IF THEY SEE US, WE WON'T ESCAPE.
KA-TAC
Escape. Escape means I'm trapped. What am I trapped in? Who's trapped me?

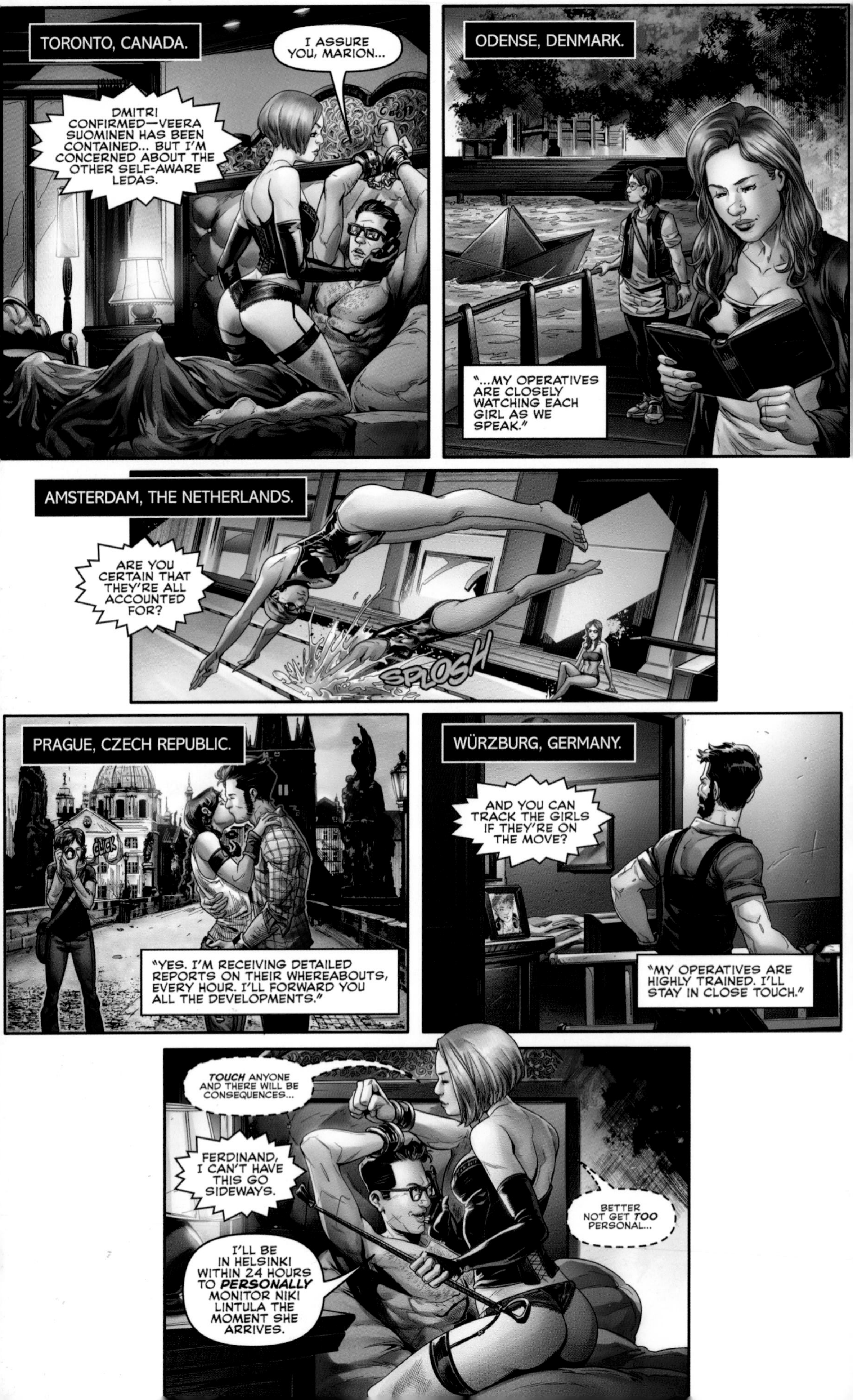
TORONTO, CANADA.
I ASSURE YOU, MARION...
DMITRI CONFIRMED—VEERA SUOMINEN HAS BEEN CONTAINED... BUT I'M CONCERNED ABOUT THE OTHER SELF-AWARE LEDAS.
ODENSE, DENMARK.
"...MY OPERATIVES ARE CLOSELY WATCHING EACH GIRL AS WE SPEAK."
AMSTERDAM, THE NETHERLANDS.
ARE YOU CERTAIN THAT THEY'RE ALL ACCOUNTED FOR?
SPLOSH
PRAGUE, CZECH REPUBLIC.
CLICK
"YES. I'M RECEIVING DETAILED REPORTS ON THEIR WHEREABOUTS, EVERY HOUR. I'LL FORWARD YOU ALL THE DEVELOPMENTS."
WÜRZBURG, GERMANY.
AND YOU CAN TRACK THE GIRLS IF THEY'RE ON THE MOVE?
"MY OPERATIVES ARE HIGHLY TRAINED. I'LL STAY IN CLOSE TOUCH."
TOUCH ANYONE AND THERE WILL BE CONSEQUENCES...
FERDINAND, I CAN'T HAVE THIS GO SIDEWAYS.
BETTER NOT GET TOO PERSONAL...
I'LL BE IN HELSINKI WITHIN 24 HOURS TO PERSONALLY MONITOR NIKI LINTULA THE MOMENT SHE ARRIVES.

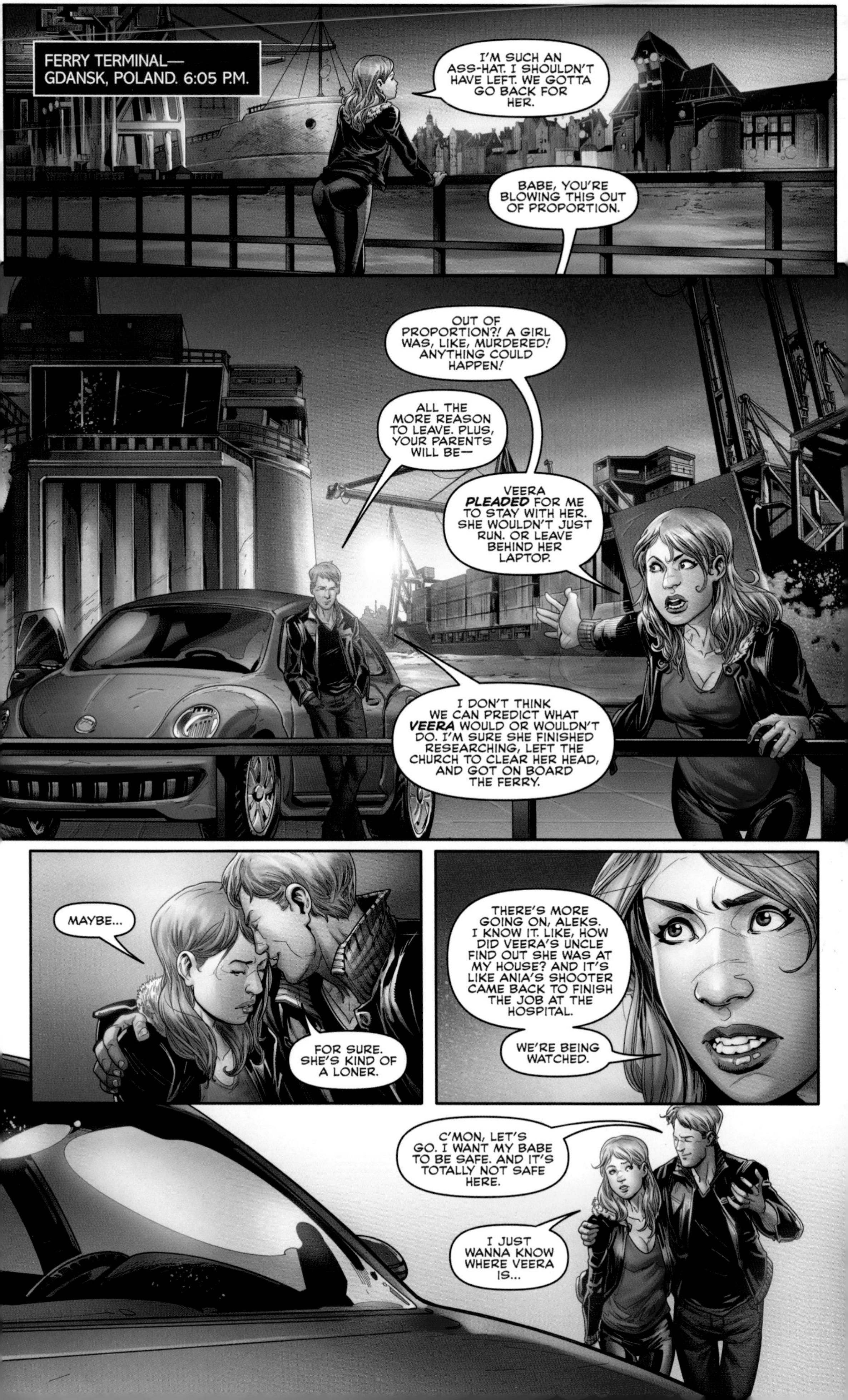
FERRY TERMINAL— GDANSK, POLAND. 6:05 P.M.
I'M SUCH AN ASS-HAT. I SHOULDN'T HAVE LEFT. WE GOTTA GO BACK FOR HER.
BABE, YOU'RE BLOWING THIS OUT OF PROPORTION.
OUT OF PROPORTION?! A GIRL WAS, LIKE, MURDERED! ANYTHING COULD HAPPEN!
ALL THE MORE REASON TO LEAVE. PLUS, YOUR PARENTS WILL BE—
VEERA PLEADED FOR ME TO STAY WITH HER. SHE WOULDN'T JUST RUN. OR LEAVE BEHIND HER LAPTOP.
I DON'T THINK WE CAN PREDICT WHAT VEERA WOULD OR WOULDN'T DO. I'M SURE SHE FINISHED RESEARCHING, LEFT THE CHURCH TO CLEAR HER HEAD, AND GOT ON BOARD THE FERRY.
MAYBE...
FOR SURE. SHE'S KIND OF A LONER.
THERE'S MORE GOING ON, ALEKS. I KNOW IT. LIKE, HOW DID VEERA'S UNCLE FIND OUT SHE WAS AT MY HOUSE? AND IT'S LIKE ANIA'S SHOOTER CAME BACK TO FINISH THE JOB AT THE HOSPITAL.
WE'RE BEING WATCHED.
C'MON, LET'S GO. I WANT MY BABE TO BE SAFE. AND IT'S TOTALLY NOT SAFE HERE.
I JUST WANNA KNOW WHERE VEERA IS...

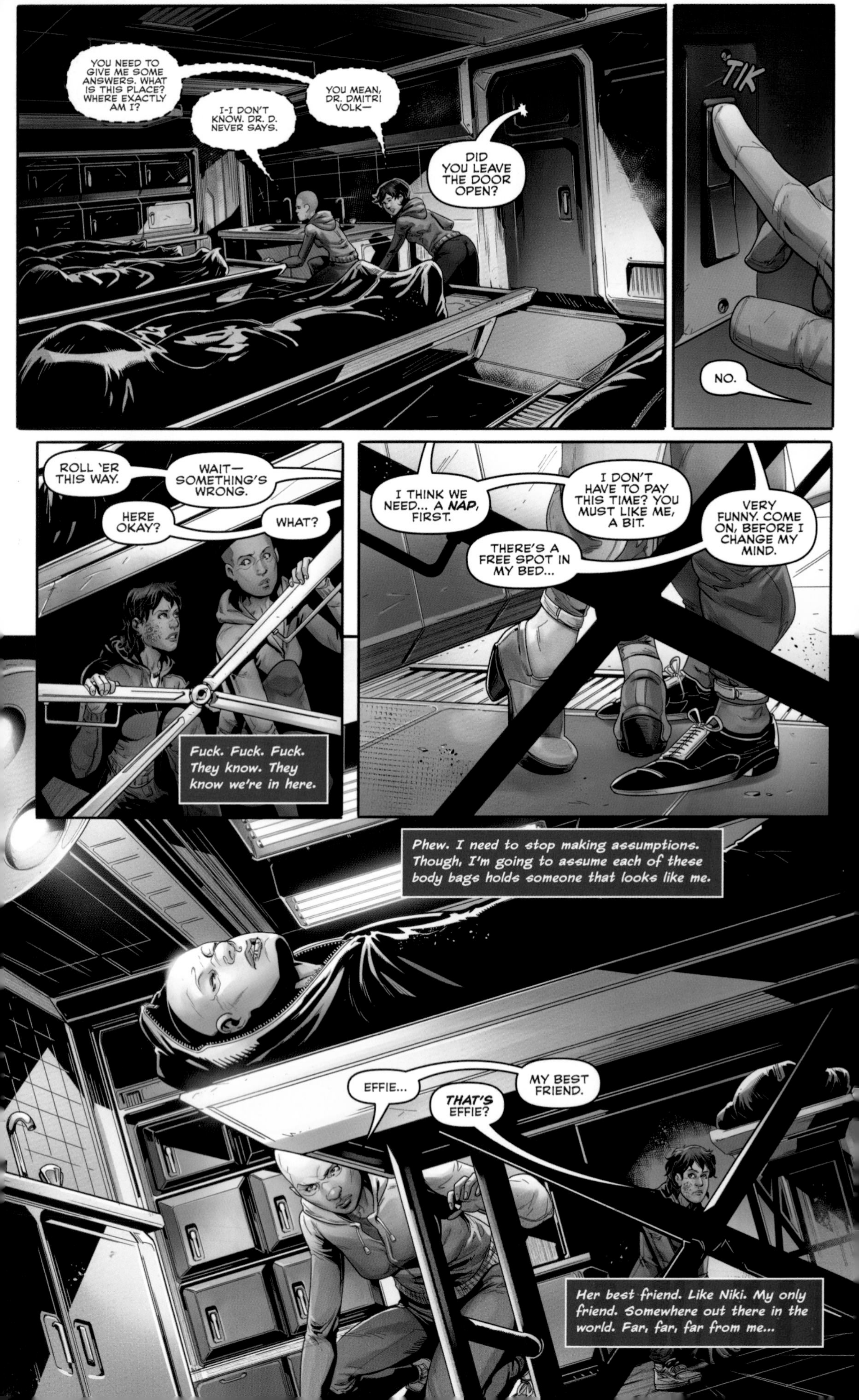
YOU NEED TO GIVE ME SOME ANSWERS. WHAT IS THIS PLACE? WHERE EXACTLY AM I?
I-I DON'T KNOW. DR. D. NEVER SAYS.
YOU MEAN, DR. DMITRI VOLK—
DID YOU LEAVE THE DOOR OPEN?
TIK
NO.
ROLL 'ER THIS WAY.
WAIT— SOMETHING'S WRONG.
HERE OKAY?
WHAT?
Fuck. Fuck. Fuck. They know. They know we're in here.
I THINK WE NEED... A NAP, FIRST.
I DON'T HAVE TO PAY THIS TIME? YOU MUST LIKE ME, A BIT.
THERE'S A FREE SPOT IN MY BED...
VERY FUNNY. COME ON, BEFORE I CHANGE MY MIND.
Phew. I need to stop making assumptions. Though, I'm going to assume each of these body bags holds someone that looks like me.
EFFIE...
MY BEST FRIEND.
THAT'S EFFIE?
Her best friend. Like Niki. My only friend. Somewhere out there in the world. Far, far, far from me...

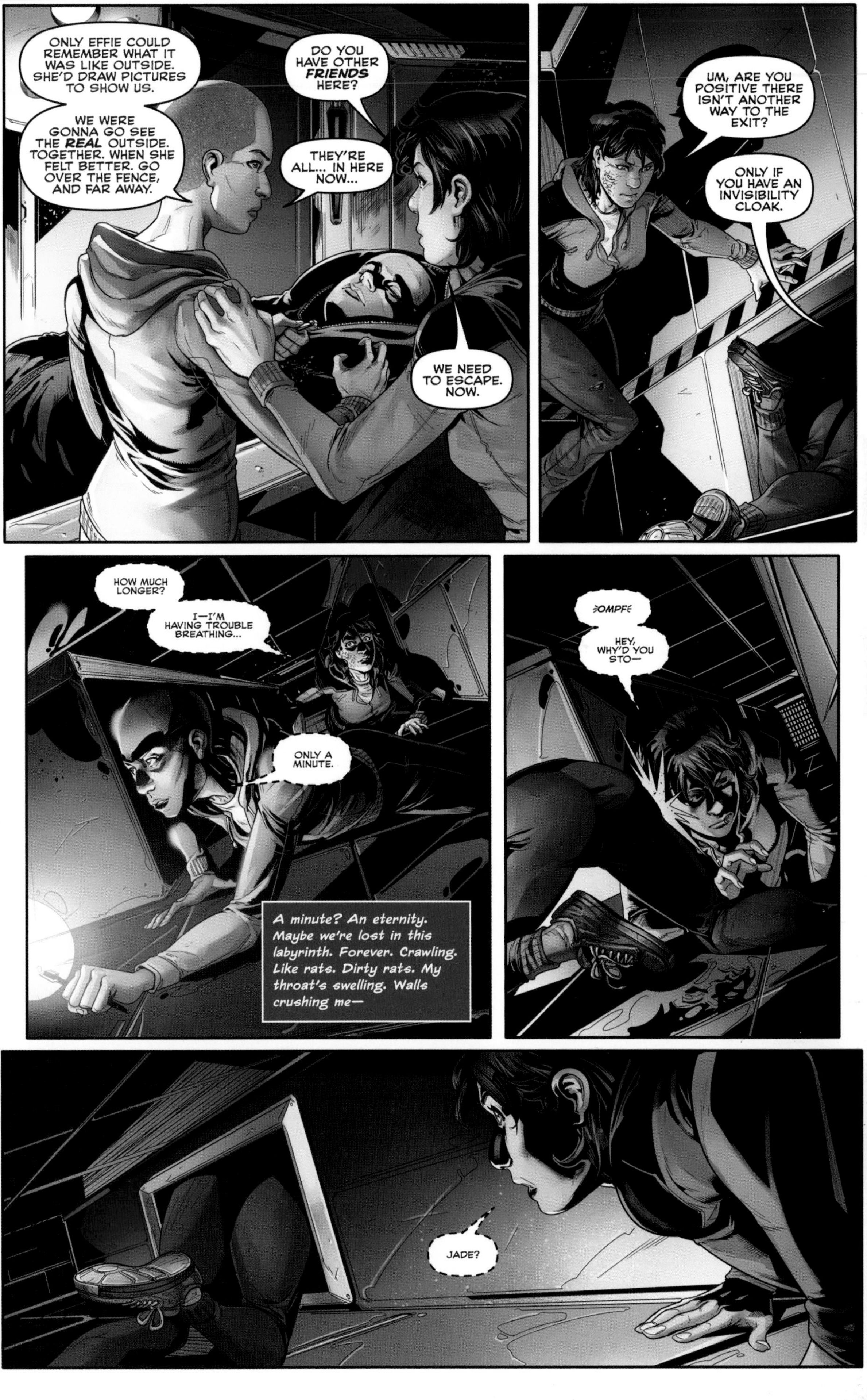
ONLY EFFIE COULD REMEMBER WHAT IT WAS LIKE OUTSIDE. SHE'D DRAW PICTURES TO SHOW US.
WE WERE GONNA GO SEE THE **REAL** OUTSIDE. TOGETHER. WHEN SHE FELT BETTER. GO OVER THE FENCE, AND FAR AWAY.
DO YOU HAVE OTHER **FRIENDS** HERE?
THEY'RE ALL... IN HERE NOW...
WE NEED TO ESCAPE. NOW.
UM, ARE YOU POSITIVE THERE ISN'T ANOTHER WAY TO THE EXIT?
ONLY IF YOU HAVE AN INVISIBILITY CLOAK.
HOW MUCH LONGER?
I—I'M HAVING TROUBLE BREATHING...
ONLY A MINUTE.
A minute? An eternity. Maybe we're lost in this labyrinth. Forever. Crawling. Like rats. Dirty rats. My throat's swelling. Walls crushing me—
OMPF
HEY, WHY'D YOU STO—
JADE?

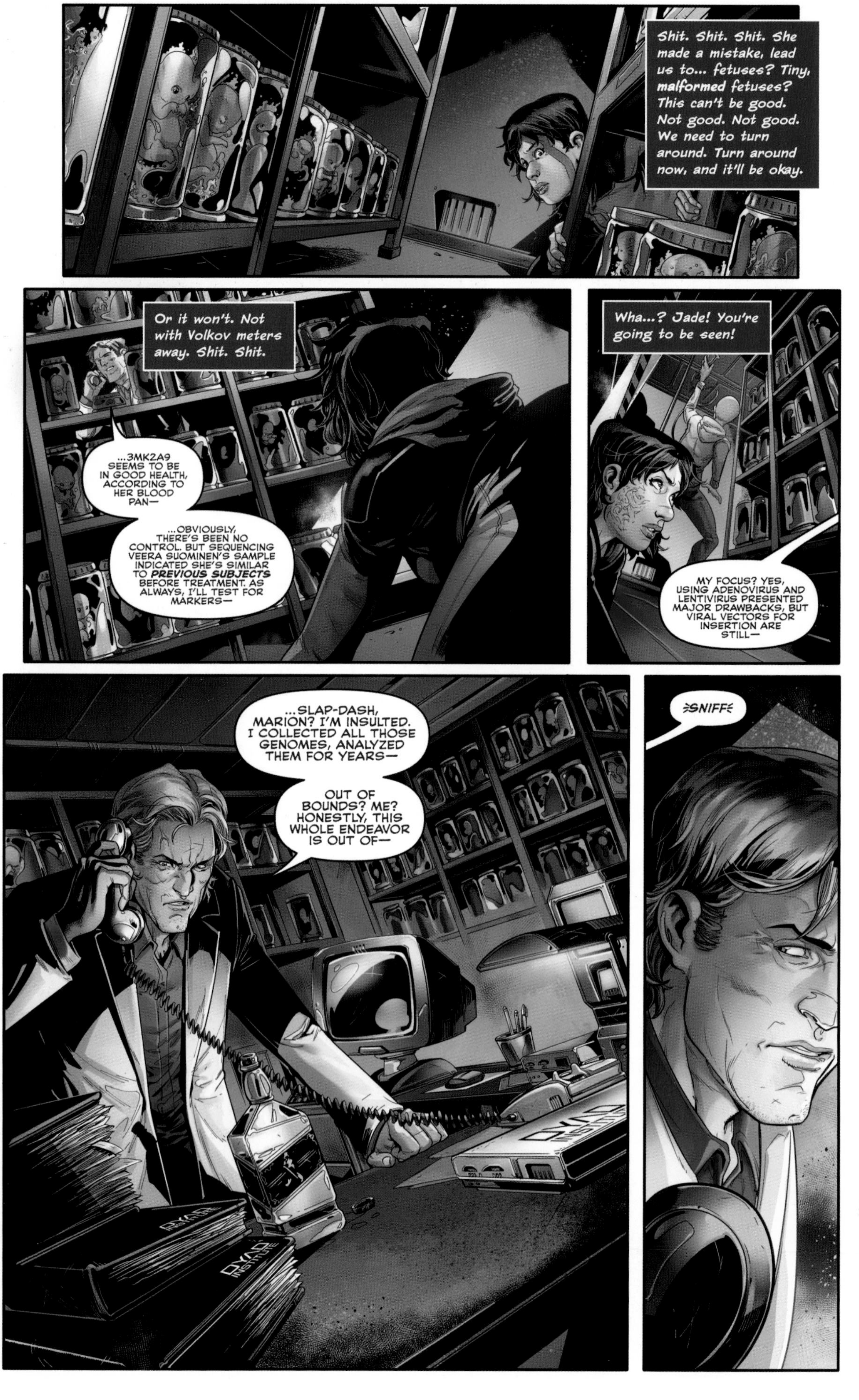
Shit. Shit. Shit. She made a mistake, lead us to... fetuses? Tiny, **malformed** fetuses? This can't be good. Not good. Not good. We need to turn around. Turn around now, and it'll be okay.
Or it won't. Not with Volkov meters away. Shit. Shit.
...3MK2A9 SEEMS TO BE IN GOOD HEALTH, ACCORDING TO HER BLOOD PAN—
...OBVIOUSLY, THERE'S BEEN NO CONTROL. BUT SEQUENCING VEERA SUOMINEN'S SAMPLE INDICATED SHE'S SIMILAR TO ***PREVIOUS SUBJECTS*** BEFORE TREATMENT. AS ALWAYS, I'LL TEST FOR MARKERS—
Wha...? Jade! You're going to be seen!
MY FOCUS? YES, USING ADENOVIRUS AND LENTIVIRUS PRESENTED MAJOR DRAWBACKS, BUT VIRAL VECTORS FOR INSERTION ARE STILL—
...SLAP-DASH, MARION? I'M INSULTED. I COLLECTED ALL THOSE GENOMES, ANALYZED THEM FOR YEARS—
OUT OF BOUNDS? ME? HONESTLY, THIS WHOLE ENDEAVOR IS OUT OF—
SNIFF

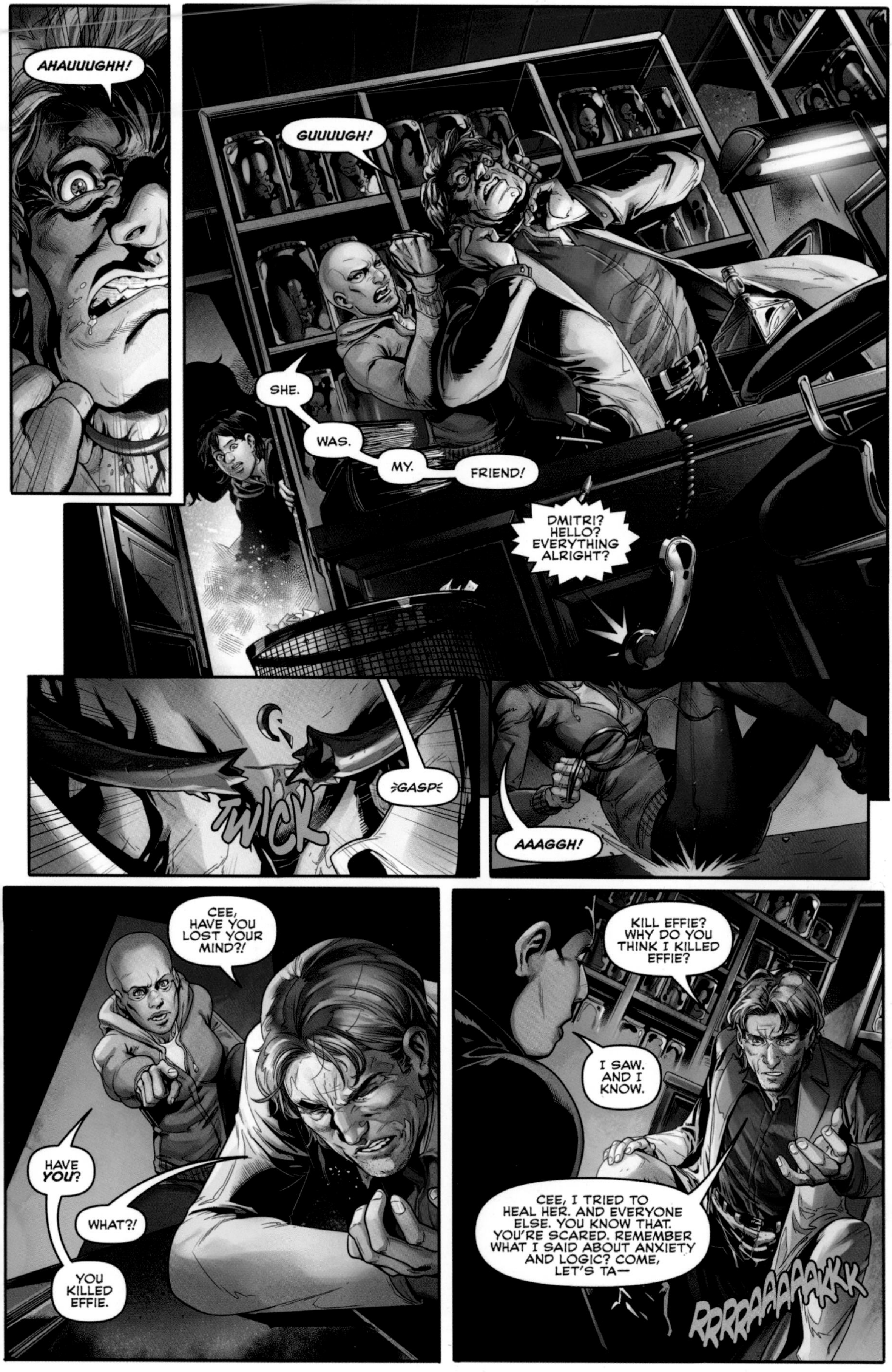
AHAUUUGHH!
GUUUUGH!
SHE.
WAS.
MY.
FRIEND!
DMITRI? HELLO? EVERYTHING ALRIGHT?
TWICK
GASP
AAAGGH!
CEE, HAVE YOU LOST YOUR MIND?!
HAVE YOU?
WHAT?!
YOU KILLED EFFIE.
KILL EFFIE? WHY DO YOU THINK I KILLED EFFIE?
I SAW. AND I KNOW.
CEE, I TRIED TO HEAL HER. AND EVERYONE ELSE. YOU KNOW THAT. YOU'RE SCARED. REMEMBER WHAT I SAID ABOUT ANXIETY AND LOGIC? COME, LET'S TA—
RRRRAAAAAKKK

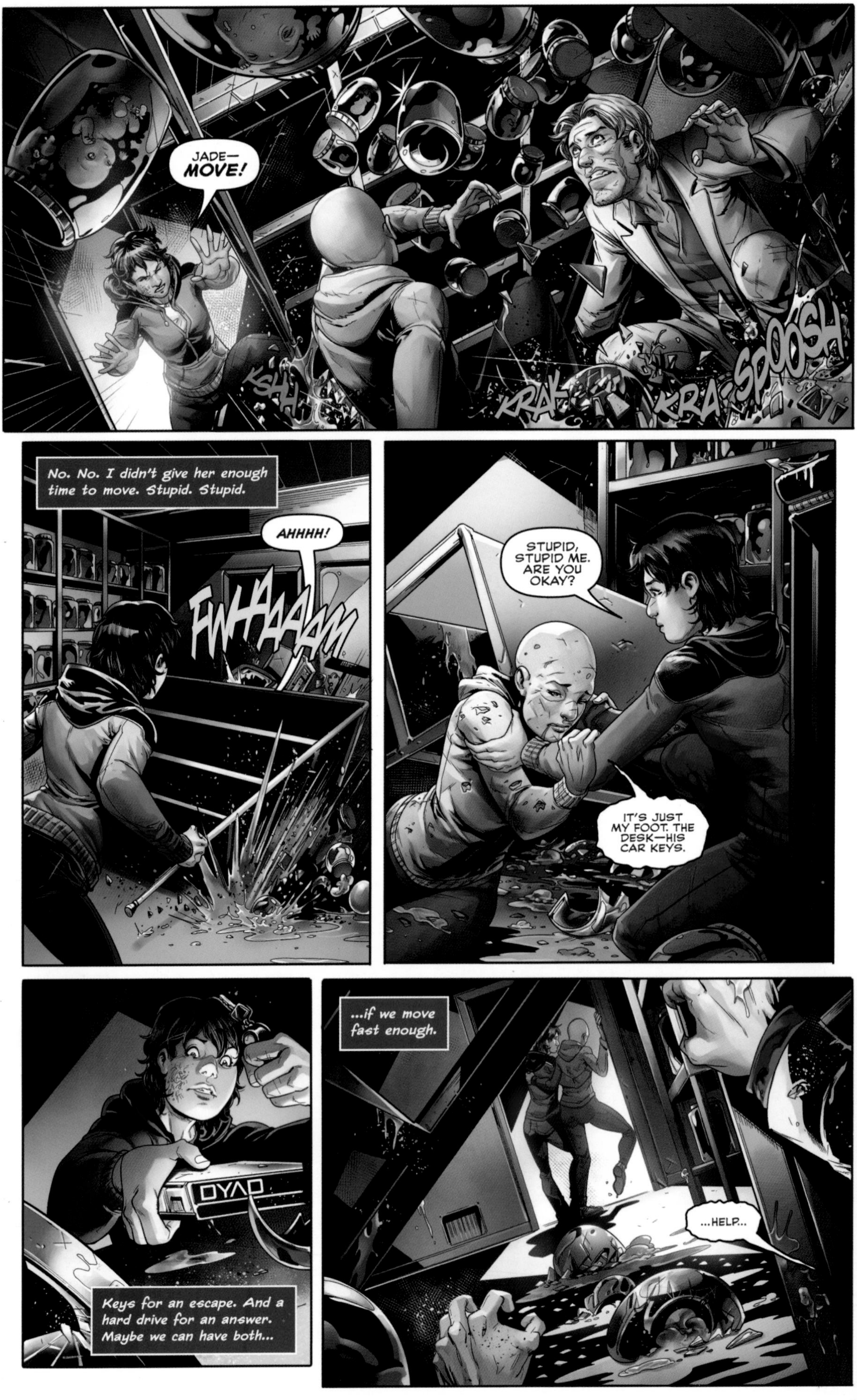

JADE—MOVE!
KSHH
KRAK
KRA-SPOOSH
No. No. I didn't give her enough time to move. Stupid. Stupid.
AHHHH!
FWHAAAAM
STUPID, STUPID ME. ARE YOU OKAY?
IT'S JUST MY FOOT. THE DESK—HIS CAR KEYS.
DYAD
Keys for an escape. And a hard drive for an answer. Maybe we can have both...
...if we move fast enough.
...HELP...

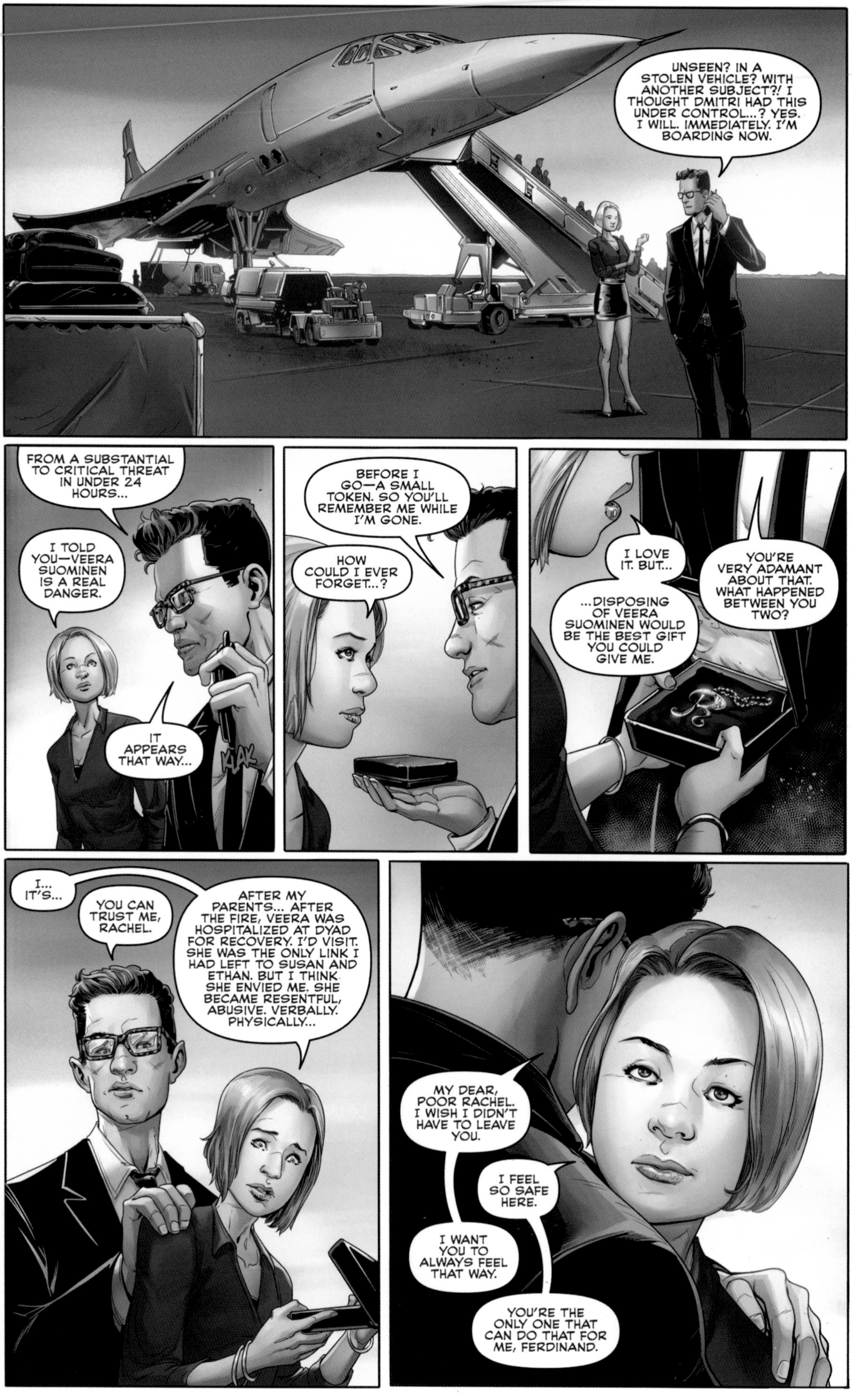
UNSEEN? IN A STOLEN VEHICLE? WITH ANOTHER SUBJECT?! I THOUGHT DMITRI HAD THIS UNDER CONTROL...? YES. I WILL. IMMEDIATELY. I'M BOARDING NOW.
FROM A SUBSTANTIAL TO CRITICAL THREAT IN UNDER 24 HOURS...
I TOLD YOU—VEERA SUOMINEN IS A REAL DANGER.
IT APPEARS THAT WAY...
KLAK
BEFORE I GO—A SMALL TOKEN. SO YOU'LL REMEMBER ME WHILE I'M GONE.
HOW COULD I EVER FORGET...?
I LOVE IT. BUT...
...DISPOSING OF VEERA SUOMINEN WOULD BE THE BEST GIFT YOU COULD GIVE ME.
YOU'RE VERY ADAMANT ABOUT THAT. WHAT HAPPENED BETWEEN YOU TWO?
I... IT'S...
YOU CAN TRUST ME, RACHEL.
AFTER MY PARENTS... AFTER THE FIRE, VEERA WAS HOSPITALIZED AT DYAD FOR RECOVERY. I'D VISIT. SHE WAS THE ONLY LINK I HAD LEFT TO SUSAN AND ETHAN. BUT I THINK SHE ENVIED ME. SHE BECAME RESENTFUL, ABUSIVE. VERBALLY. PHYSICALLY...
MY DEAR, POOR RACHEL. I WISH I DIDN'T HAVE TO LEAVE YOU.
I FEEL SO SAFE HERE.
I WANT YOU TO ALWAYS FEEL THAT WAY.
YOU'RE THE ONLY ONE THAT CAN DO THAT FOR ME, FERDINAND.

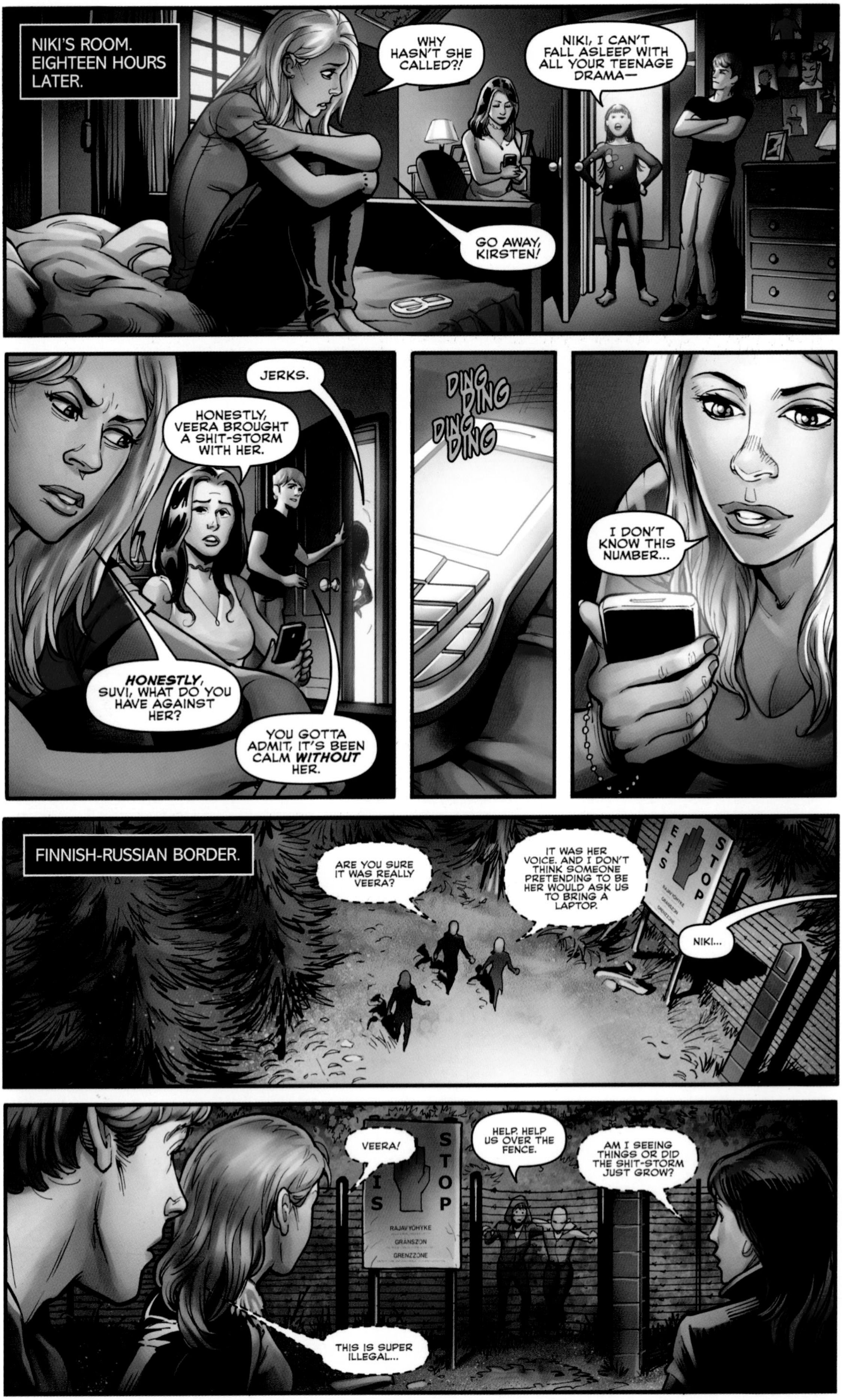
NIKI'S ROOM. EIGHTEEN HOURS LATER.
WHY HASN'T SHE CALLED?!
NIKI, I CAN'T FALL ASLEEP WITH ALL YOUR TEENAGE DRAMA—
GO AWAY, KIRSTEN!
JERKS.
HONESTLY, VEERA BROUGHT A SHIT-STORM WITH HER.
HONESTLY, SUVI, WHAT DO YOU HAVE AGAINST HER?
YOU GOTTA ADMIT, IT'S BEEN CALM WITHOUT HER.
DING DING DING DING
I DON'T KNOW THIS NUMBER...
FINNISH-RUSSIAN BORDER.
ARE YOU SURE IT WAS REALLY VEERA?
IT WAS HER VOICE. AND I DON'T THINK SOMEONE PRETENDING TO BE HER WOULD ASK US TO BRING A LAPTOP.
NIKI...
EIS STOP
VEERA!
HELP. HELP US OVER THE FENCE.
AM I SEEING THINGS OR DID THE SHIT-STORM JUST GROW?
THIS IS SUPER ILLEGAL...

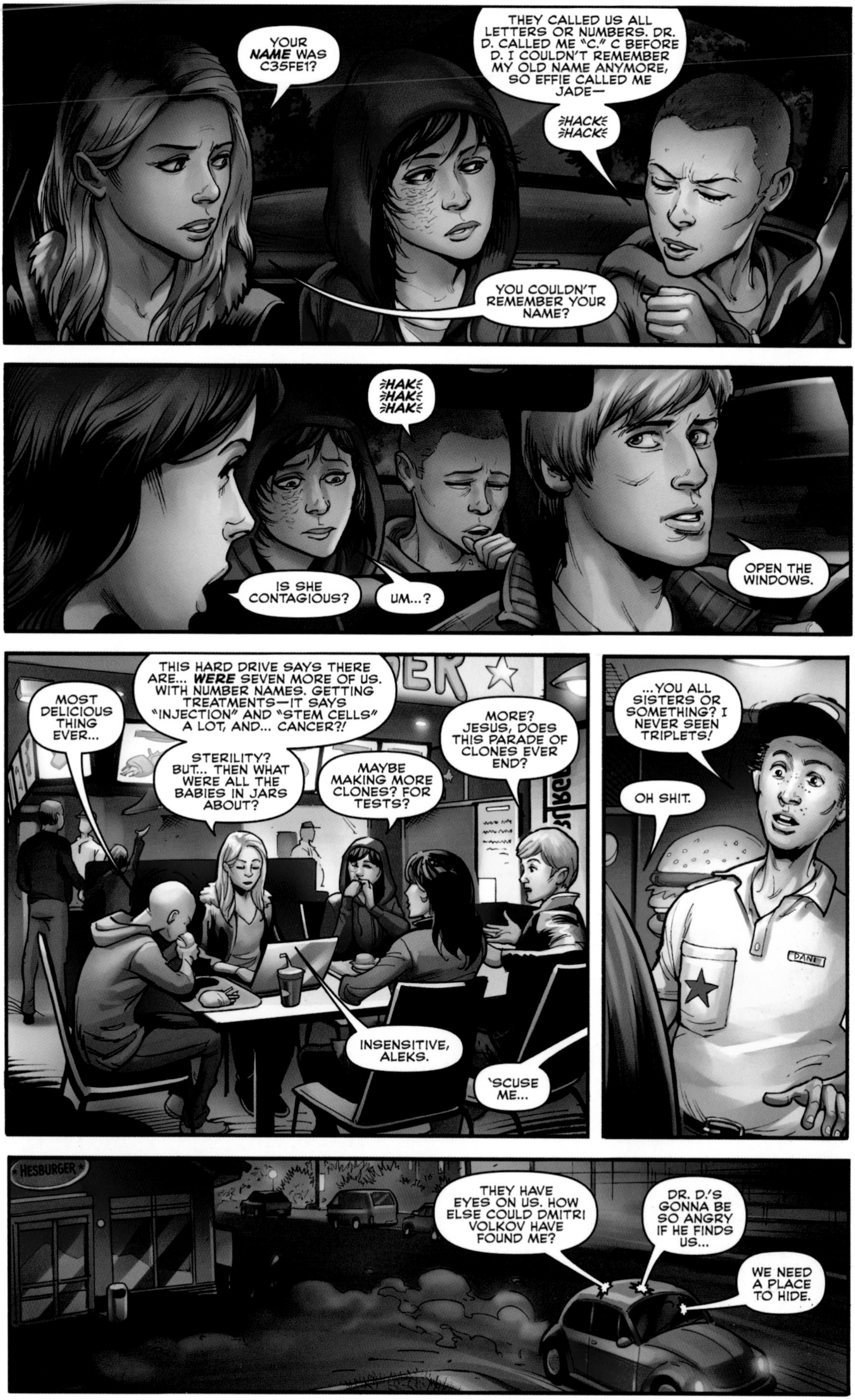
YOUR NAME WAS C35FE1?
THEY CALLED US ALL LETTERS OR NUMBERS. DR. D. CALLED ME "C." C BEFORE D. I COULDN'T REMEMBER MY OLD NAME ANYMORE, SO EFFIE CALLED ME JADE—
HACK HACK
YOU COULDN'T REMEMBER YOUR NAME?
HAK HAK HAK
IS SHE CONTAGIOUS?
UM...?
OPEN THE WINDOWS.
MOST DELICIOUS THING EVER...
THIS HARD DRIVE SAYS THERE ARE... WERE SEVEN MORE OF US. WITH NUMBER NAMES. GETTING TREATMENTS—IT SAYS "INJECTION" AND "STEM CELLS" A LOT, AND... CANCER?!
STERILITY? BUT... THEN WHAT WERE ALL THE BABIES IN JARS ABOUT?
MAYBE MAKING MORE CLONES? FOR TESTS?
MORE? JESUS, DOES THIS PARADE OF CLONES EVER END?
INSENSITIVE, ALEKS.
'SCUSE ME...
...YOU ALL SISTERS OR SOMETHING? I NEVER SEEN TRIPLETS!
OH SHIT.
HESBURGER
THEY HAVE EYES ON US. HOW ELSE COULD DMITRI VOLKOV HAVE FOUND ME?
DR. D.'S GONNA BE SO ANGRY IF HE FINDS US...
WE NEED A PLACE TO HIDE.

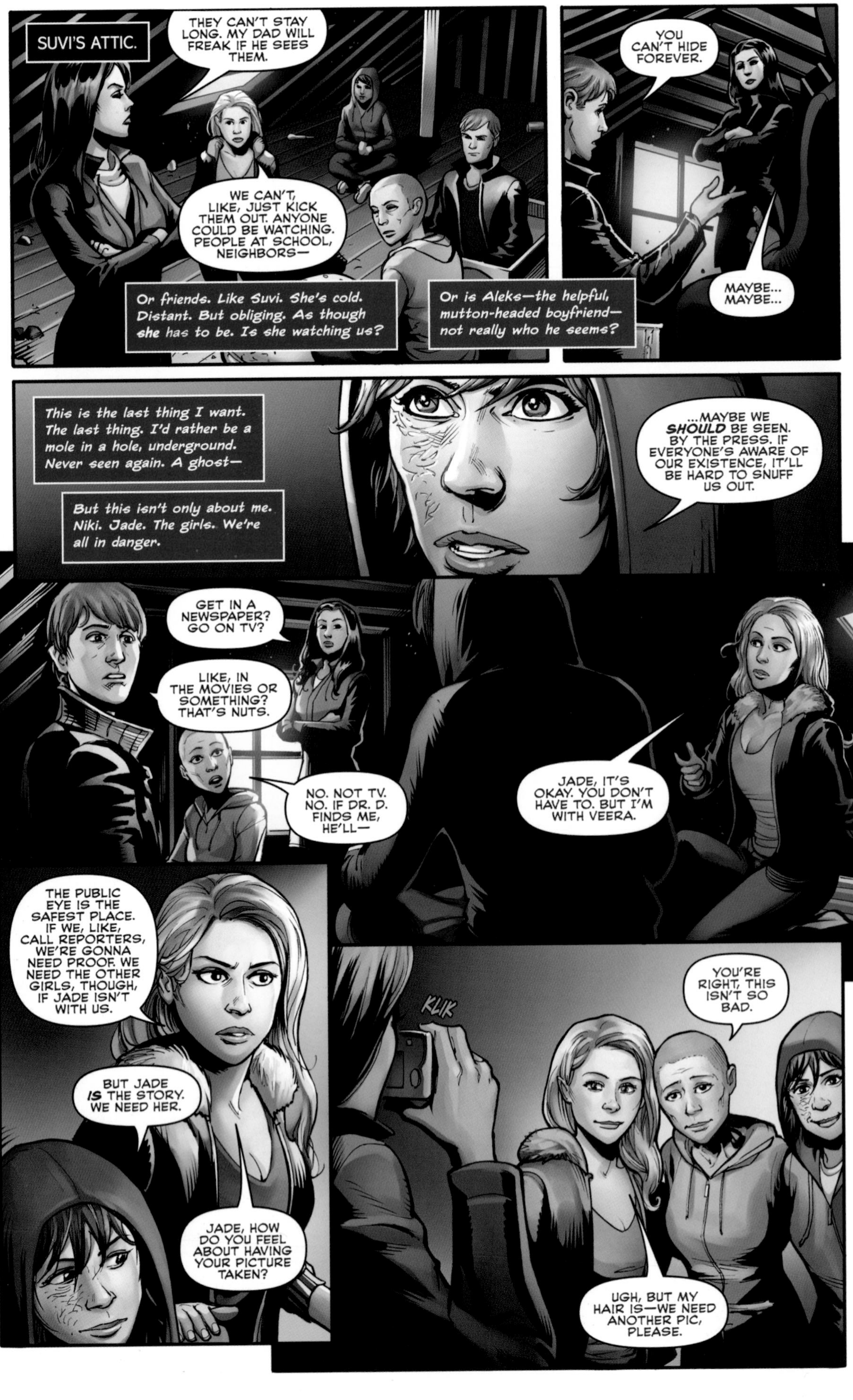

SUVI'S ATTIC.
THEY CAN'T STAY LONG. MY DAD WILL FREAK IF HE SEES THEM.
WE CAN'T, LIKE, JUST KICK THEM OUT. ANYONE COULD BE WATCHING. PEOPLE AT SCHOOL, NEIGHBORS—
Or friends. Like Suvi. She's cold. Distant. But obliging. As though she has to be. Is she watching us?
YOU CAN'T HIDE FOREVER.
Or is Aleks—the helpful, mutton-headed boyfriend—not really who he seems?
MAYBE... MAYBE...
This is the last thing I want. The last thing. I'd rather be a mole in a hole, underground. Never seen again. A ghost—
But this isn't only about me. Niki. Jade. The girls. We're all in danger.
...MAYBE WE SHOULD BE SEEN. BY THE PRESS. IF EVERYONE'S AWARE OF OUR EXISTENCE, IT'LL BE HARD TO SNUFF US OUT.
GET IN A NEWSPAPER? GO ON TV?
LIKE, IN THE MOVIES OR SOMETHING? THAT'S NUTS.
NO. NOT TV. NO. IF DR. D. FINDS ME, HE'LL—
JADE, IT'S OKAY. YOU DON'T HAVE TO. BUT I'M WITH VEERA.
THE PUBLIC EYE IS THE SAFEST PLACE. IF WE, LIKE, CALL REPORTERS, WE'RE GONNA NEED PROOF. WE NEED THE OTHER GIRLS, THOUGH, IF JADE ISN'T WITH US.
BUT JADE IS THE STORY. WE NEED HER.
JADE, HOW DO YOU FEEL ABOUT HAVING YOUR PICTURE TAKEN?
KLIK
YOU'RE RIGHT, THIS ISN'T SO BAD.
UGH, BUT MY HAIR IS—WE NEED ANOTHER PIC, PLEASE.

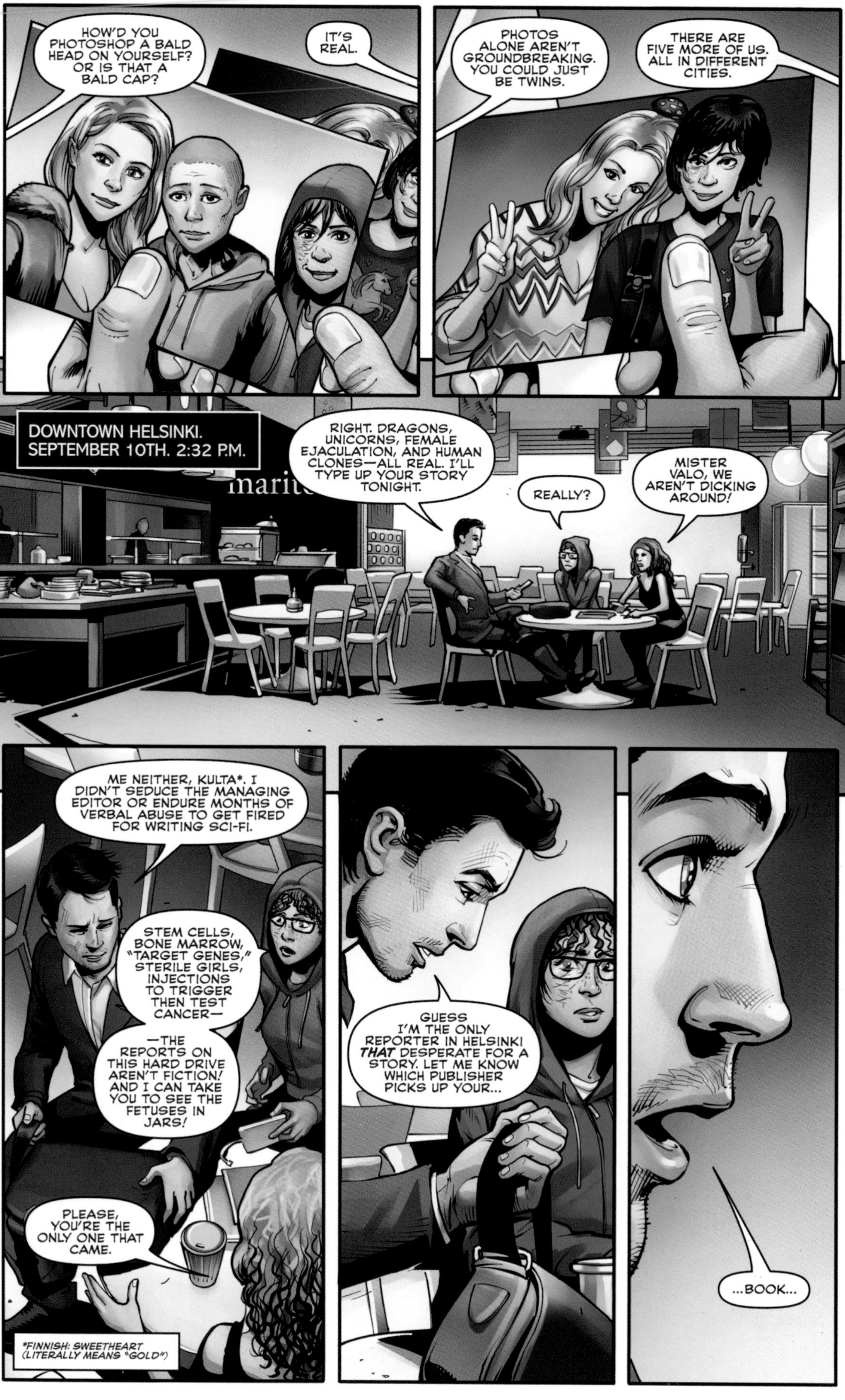
HOW'D YOU PHOTOSHOP A BALD HEAD ON YOURSELF? OR IS THAT A BALD CAP?
IT'S REAL.
PHOTOS ALONE AREN'T GROUNDBREAKING. YOU COULD JUST BE TWINS.
THERE ARE FIVE MORE OF US. ALL IN DIFFERENT CITIES.
DOWNTOWN HELSINKI. SEPTEMBER 10TH. 2:32 P.M.
RIGHT. DRAGONS, UNICORNS, FEMALE EJACULATION, AND HUMAN CLONES—ALL REAL. I'LL TYPE UP YOUR STORY TONIGHT.
REALLY?
MISTER VALO, WE AREN'T DICKING AROUND!
ME NEITHER, KULTA*. I DIDN'T SEDUCE THE MANAGING EDITOR OR ENDURE MONTHS OF VERBAL ABUSE TO GET FIRED FOR WRITING SCI-FI.
STEM CELLS, BONE MARROW, "TARGET GENES," STERILE GIRLS, INJECTIONS TO TRIGGER THEN TEST CANCER—
—THE REPORTS ON THIS HARD DRIVE AREN'T FICTION! AND I CAN TAKE YOU TO SEE THE FETUSES IN JARS!
PLEASE, YOU'RE THE ONLY ONE THAT CAME.
*FINNISH: SWEETHEART (LITERALLY MEANS "GOLD")
GUESS I'M THE ONLY REPORTER IN HELSINKI *THAT* DESPERATE FOR A STORY. LET ME KNOW WHICH PUBLISHER PICKS UP YOUR...
...BOOK...

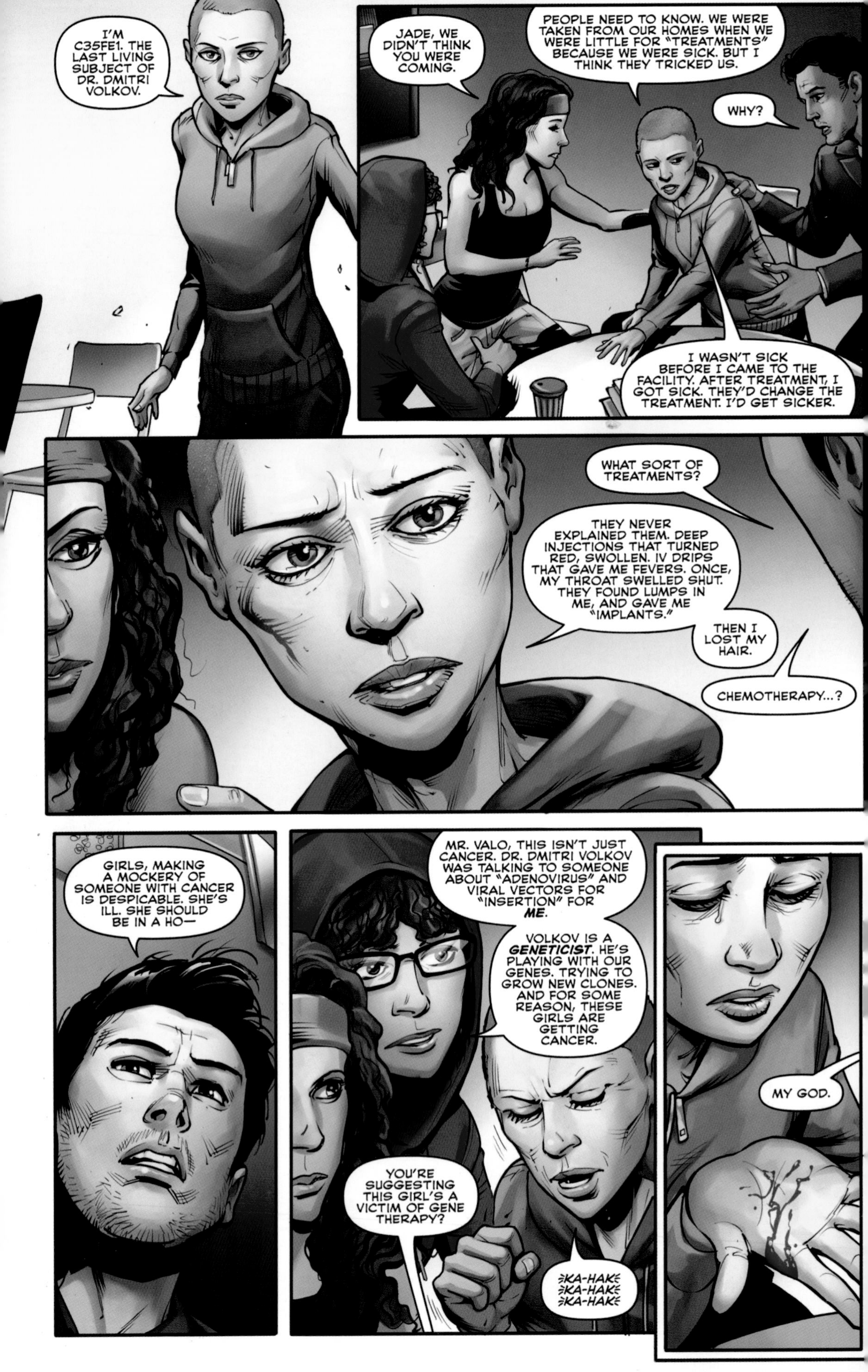
I'M C35FE1. THE LAST LIVING SUBJECT OF DR. DMITRI VOLKOV.
JADE, WE DIDN'T THINK YOU WERE COMING.
PEOPLE NEED TO KNOW. WE WERE TAKEN FROM OUR HOMES WHEN WE WERE LITTLE FOR "TREATMENTS" BECAUSE WE WERE SICK. BUT I THINK THEY TRICKED US.
WHY?
I WASN'T SICK BEFORE I CAME TO THE FACILITY. AFTER TREATMENT, I GOT SICK. THEY'D CHANGE THE TREATMENT. I'D GET SICKER.
WHAT SORT OF TREATMENTS?
THEY NEVER EXPLAINED THEM. DEEP INJECTIONS THAT TURNED RED, SWOLLEN. IV DRIPS THAT GAVE ME FEVERS. ONCE, MY THROAT SWELLED SHUT. THEY FOUND LUMPS IN ME, AND GAVE ME "IMPLANTS."
THEN I LOST MY HAIR.
CHEMOTHERAPY...?
GIRLS, MAKING A MOCKERY OF SOMEONE WITH CANCER IS DESPICABLE. SHE'S ILL. SHE SHOULD BE IN A HO—
MR. VALO, THIS ISN'T JUST CANCER. DR. DMITRI VOLKOV WAS TALKING TO SOMEONE ABOUT "ADENOVIRUS" AND VIRAL VECTORS FOR "INSERTION" FOR ***ME***.
VOLKOV IS A ***GENETICIST***. HE'S PLAYING WITH OUR GENES. TRYING TO GROW NEW CLONES. AND FOR SOME REASON, THESE GIRLS ARE GETTING CANCER.
YOU'RE SUGGESTING THIS GIRL'S A VICTIM OF GENE THERAPY?
KA-HAK
KA-HAK
KA-HAK
MY GOD.

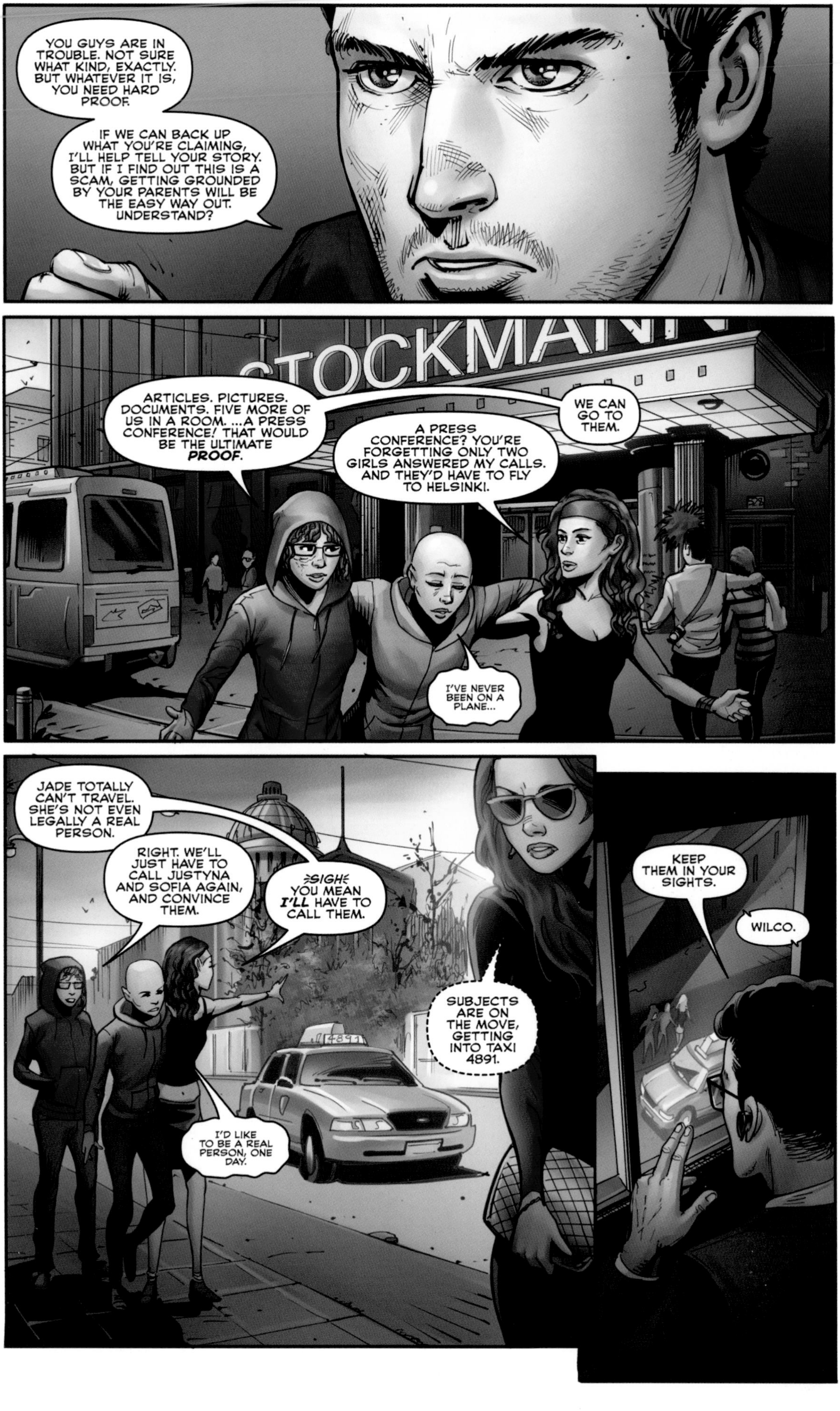
YOU GUYS ARE IN TROUBLE. NOT SURE WHAT KIND, EXACTLY. BUT WHATEVER IT IS, YOU NEED HARD PROOF.
IF WE CAN BACK UP WHAT YOU'RE CLAIMING, I'LL HELP TELL YOUR STORY. BUT IF I FIND OUT THIS IS A SCAM, GETTING GROUNDED BY YOUR PARENTS WILL BE THE EASY WAY OUT. UNDERSTAND?
STOCKMANN
ARTICLES. PICTURES. DOCUMENTS. FIVE MORE OF US IN A ROOM. ...A PRESS CONFERENCE! THAT WOULD BE THE ULTIMATE **PROOF**.
WE CAN GO TO THEM.
A PRESS CONFERENCE? YOU'RE FORGETTING ONLY TWO GIRLS ANSWERED MY CALLS. AND THEY'D HAVE TO FLY TO HELSINKI.
I'VE NEVER BEEN ON A PLANE...
JADE TOTALLY CAN'T TRAVEL. SHE'S NOT EVEN LEGALLY A REAL PERSON.
RIGHT. WE'LL JUST HAVE TO CALL JUSTYNA AND SOFIA AGAIN, AND CONVINCE THEM.
≈SIGH≈ YOU MEAN ***I'LL*** HAVE TO CALL THEM.
I'D LIKE TO BE A REAL PERSON, ONE DAY.
4891
SUBJECTS ARE ON THE MOVE, GETTING INTO TAXI 4891.
KEEP THEM IN YOUR SIGHTS.
WILCO.

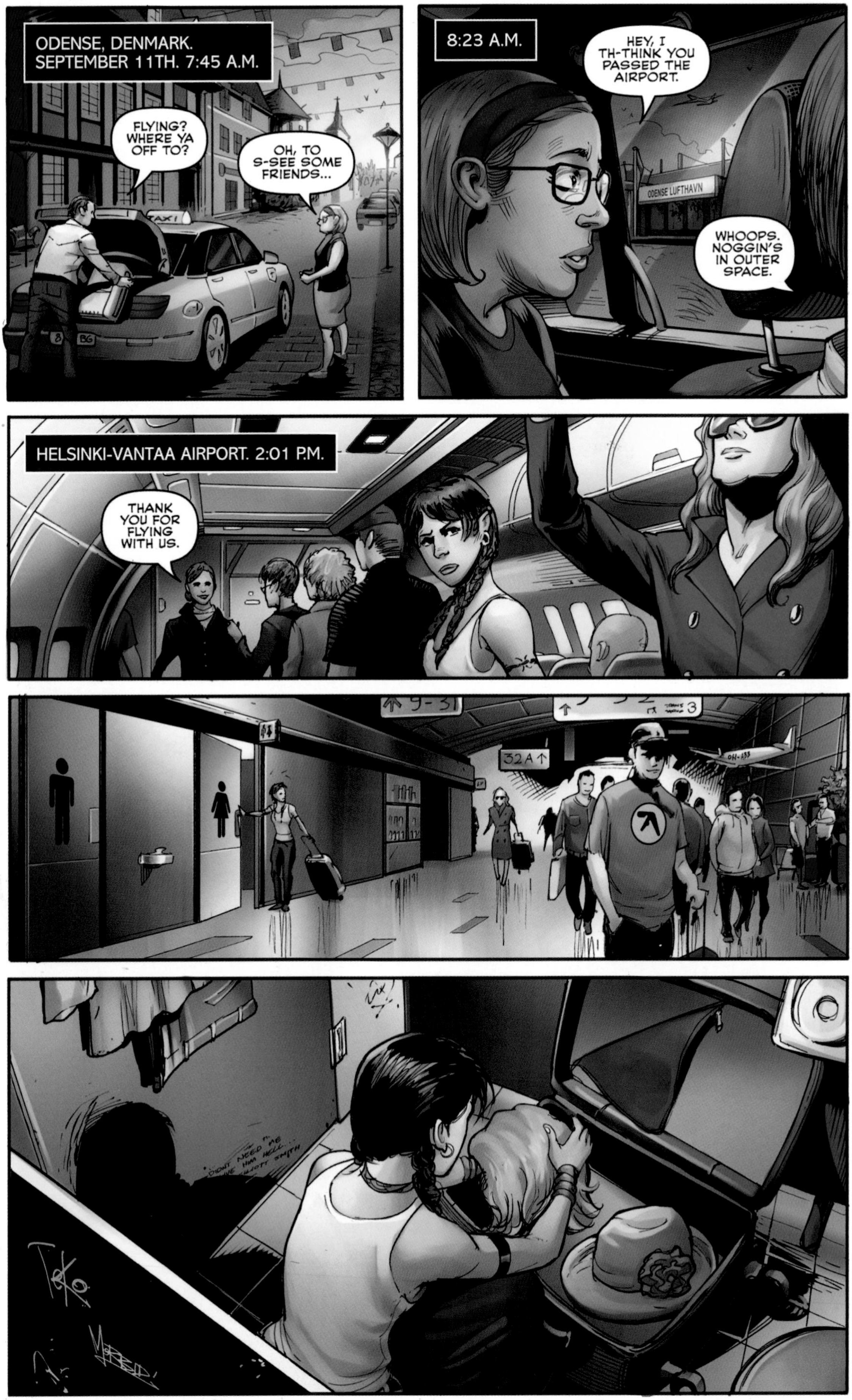
ODENSE, DENMARK.
SEPTEMBER 11TH. 7:45 A.M.
FLYING? WHERE YA OFF TO?
OH, TO S-SEE SOME FRIENDS...
8:23 A.M.
HEY, I TH-THINK YOU PASSED THE AIRPORT.
ODENSE LUFTHAVN
WHOOPS. NOGGIN'S IN OUTER SPACE.
HELSINKI-VANTAA AIRPORT. 2:01 P.M.
THANK YOU FOR FLYING WITH US.
32A

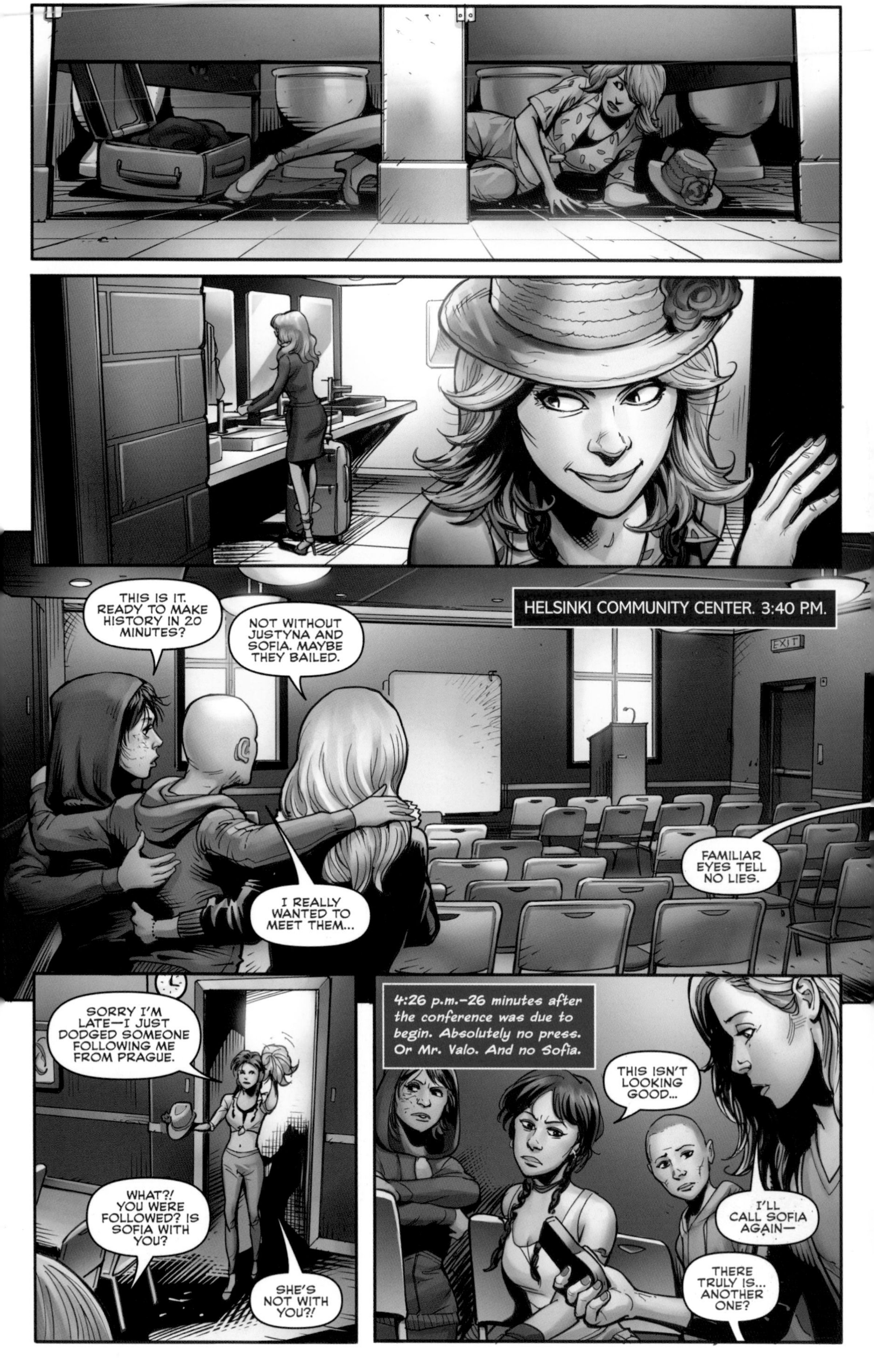
HELSINKI COMMUNITY CENTER. 3:40 P.M.
THIS IS IT. READY TO MAKE HISTORY IN 20 MINUTES?
NOT WITHOUT JUSTYNA AND SOFIA. MAYBE THEY BAILED.
I REALLY WANTED TO MEET THEM...
FAMILIAR EYES TELL NO LIES.
EXIT
SORRY I'M LATE—I JUST DODGED SOMEONE FOLLOWING ME FROM PRAGUE.
WHAT?! YOU WERE FOLLOWED? IS SOFIA WITH YOU?
SHE'S NOT WITH YOU?!
4:26 p.m.—26 minutes after the conference was due to begin. Absolutely no press. Or Mr. Valo. And no Sofia.
THIS ISN'T LOOKING GOOD...
I'LL CALL SOFIA AGAIN—
THERE TRULY IS... ANOTHER ONE?

RIGHT HERE. IN THE FLESH. I CAN'T BELIEVE THIS DAY JUST GOT STRANGER...

WHERE HAVE YOU BEEN?

YOU DON'T KNOW?!

KNOW WHAT?

OH MY GOD. THIS CAN'T BE REAL...

IT STARTED ABOUT 40 MINUTES AGO.

NO WONDER NO ONE SHOWED.

SO WHY DID YOU, MR. VALO?

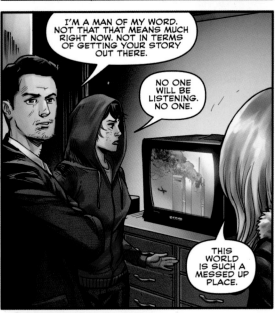

I'M A MAN OF MY WORD. NOT THAT THAT MEANS MUCH RIGHT NOW. NOT IN TERMS OF GETTING YOUR STORY OUT THERE.

NO ONE WILL BE LISTENING. NO ONE.

THIS WORLD IS SUCH A MESSED UP PLACE.

WHAT DO WE DO?

I DON'T KNOW. KEEP GOING? UNTIL SOMEONE LISTENS?

MAYBE WE'RE BLOWING EVERYTHING OUT OF PROPORTION. MAYBE WE'RE OKAY...

MARION, THEY'VE GATHERED A SECOND TIME FOR A PRESS CONFERENCE, WHICH WOULD EXPOSE EVERYTHING. THEY HAVE A REPORTER, ERIK VALO.

GOOD LORD.

THIS COULD QUICKLY SPIRAL INTO CHAOS. I PROPOSE MOVING FORWARD WITH OUR LAST RESORT: THE HELSINKI PROTOCOL. NO MORE MOLLYCODDLING.

YOU HAVE THE GO-AHEAD. BUT IF WE FUMBLE AND *SHE* FINDS OUT, IT'LL BE COMPLETE SLAUGHTER. FOR EVERYONE.

WE WON'T FUMBLE. I'LL INITIATE PHASE TWO IMMEDIATELY.

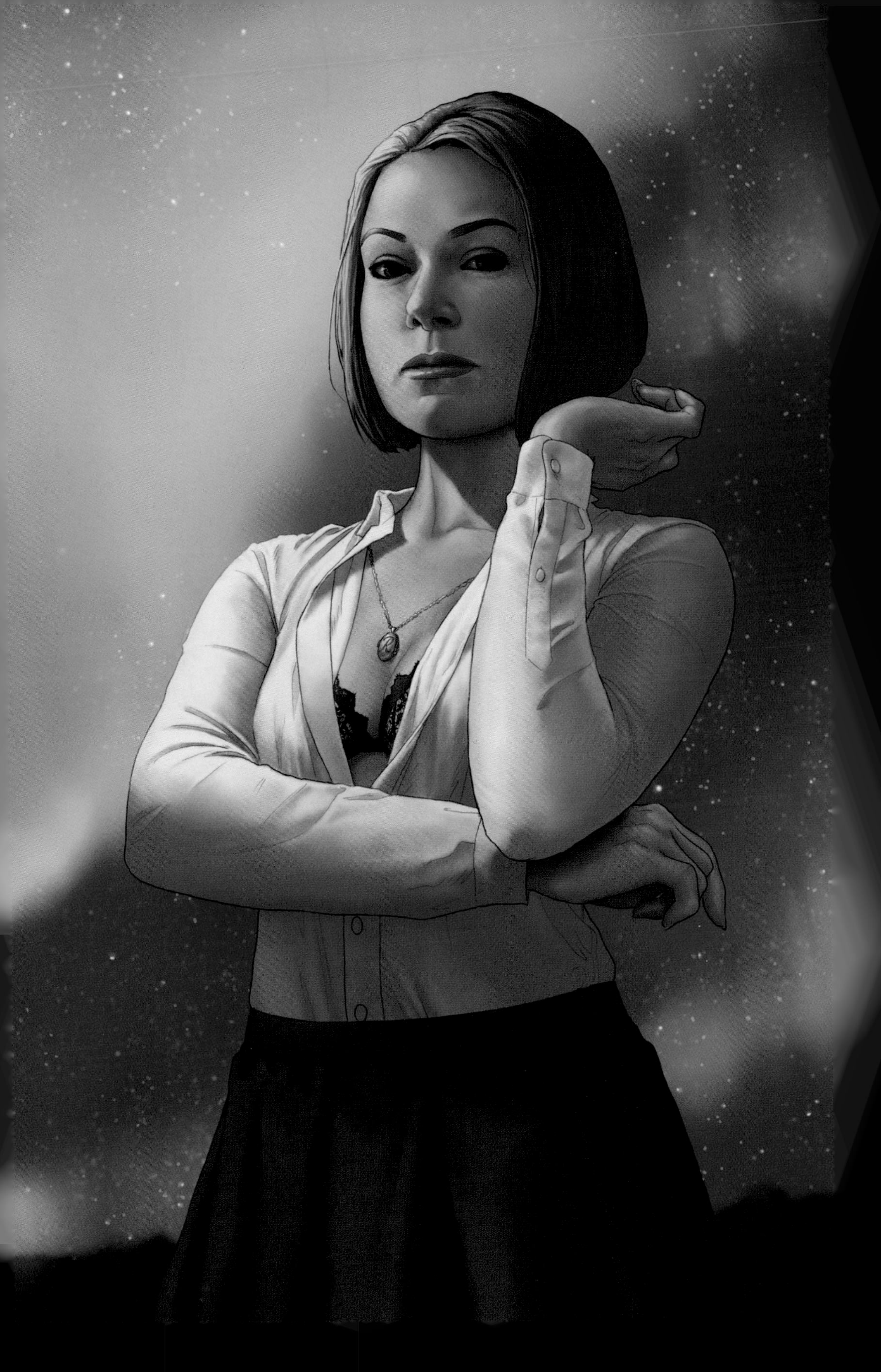

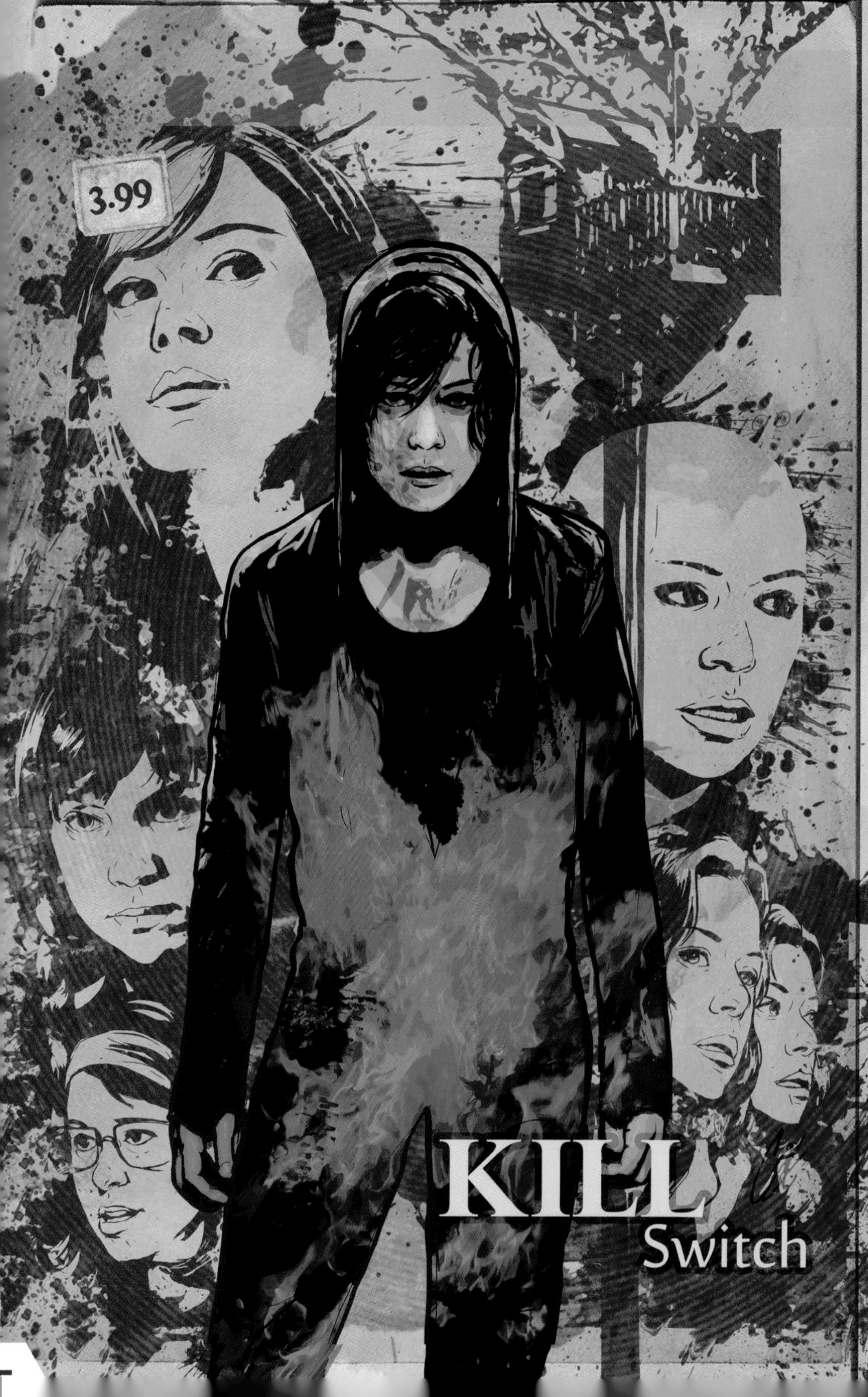
3.99
KILL
Switch

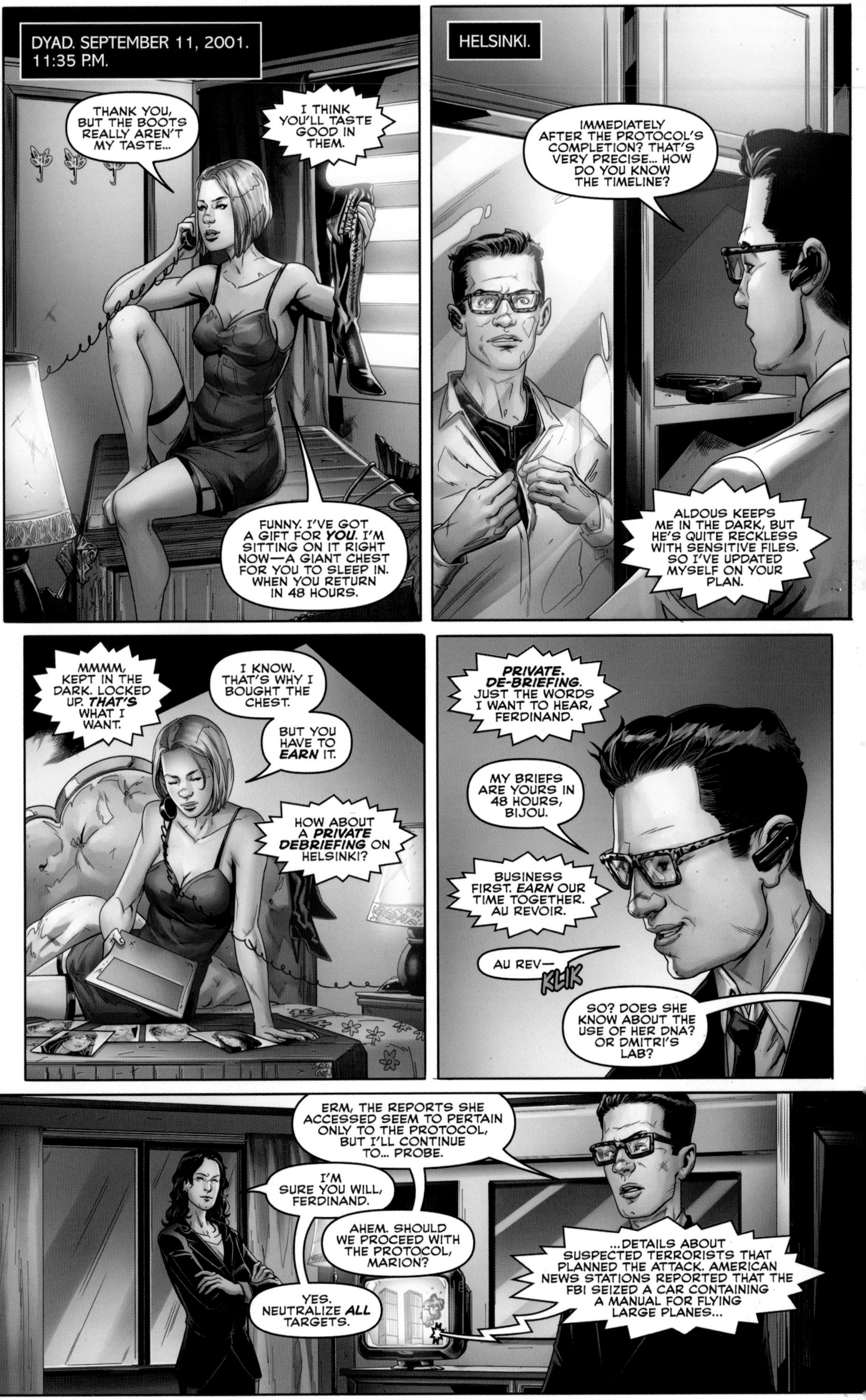
DYAD. SEPTEMBER 11, 2001. 11:35 P.M.
THANK YOU, BUT THE BOOTS REALLY AREN'T MY TASTE...
I THINK YOU'LL TASTE GOOD IN THEM.
FUNNY. I'VE GOT A GIFT FOR YOU. I'M SITTING ON IT RIGHT NOW—A GIANT CHEST FOR YOU TO SLEEP IN. WHEN YOU RETURN IN 48 HOURS.
HELSINKI.
IMMEDIATELY AFTER THE PROTOCOL'S COMPLETION? THAT'S VERY PRECISE... HOW DO YOU KNOW THE TIMELINE?
ALDOUS KEEPS ME IN THE DARK, BUT HE'S QUITE RECKLESS WITH SENSITIVE FILES. SO I'VE UPDATED MYSELF ON YOUR PLAN.
MMMM, KEPT IN THE DARK. LOCKED UP. THAT'S WHAT I WANT.
I KNOW. THAT'S WHY I BOUGHT THE CHEST.
BUT YOU HAVE TO EARN IT.
HOW ABOUT A PRIVATE DEBRIEFING ON HELSINKI?
PRIVATE. DE-BRIEFING. JUST THE WORDS I WANT TO HEAR, FERDINAND.
MY BRIEFS ARE YOURS IN 48 HOURS, BIJOU.
BUSINESS FIRST. EARN OUR TIME TOGETHER. AU REVOIR.
AU REV—
KLIK
SO? DOES SHE KNOW ABOUT THE USE OF HER DNA? OR DMITRI'S LAB?
ERM, THE REPORTS SHE ACCESSED SEEM TO PERTAIN ONLY TO THE PROTOCOL, BUT I'LL CONTINUE TO... PROBE.
I'M SURE YOU WILL, FERDINAND.
AHEM. SHOULD WE PROCEED WITH THE PROTOCOL, MARION?
YES. NEUTRALIZE ALL TARGETS.
...DETAILS ABOUT SUSPECTED TERRORISTS THAT PLANNED THE ATTACK. AMERICAN NEWS STATIONS REPORTED THAT THE FBI SEIZED A CAR CONTAINING A MANUAL FOR FLYING LARGE PLANES...

HELSINKI-VANTAA AIRPORT.
SEPTEMBER 12. 7:59 A.M.

Sixteen hours since our
failed press conference.
Sixteen hours of silence.
From them. From us.
The world around us is
in chaos...

IT'S
CRAZY HERE.
ALL FLIGHTS ARE
GROUNDED.

EARLIEST
I CAN FLY IS
TOMORROW
MORNING.

BUT
MY LONDON
MEETING!

I'M SURE IT'LL
BE RESCHEDULED,
JUST LIKE ALL
OUR FLIGHTS,
SIR.

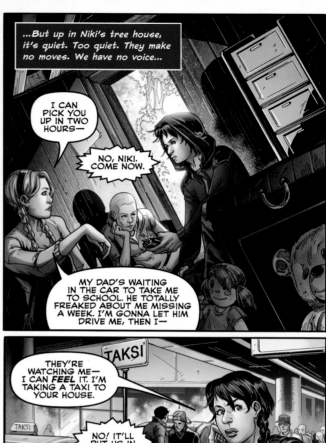

...But up in Niki's tree house,
it's quiet. Too quiet. They make
no moves. We have no voice...

I CAN
PICK YOU
UP IN TWO
HOURS—

NO, NIKI.
COME NOW.

MY DAD'S WAITING
IN THE CAR TO TAKE ME
TO SCHOOL. HE TOTALLY
FREAKED ABOUT ME MISSING
A WEEK. I'M GONNA LET HIM
DRIVE ME, THEN I—

THEY'RE
WATCHING ME—
I CAN FEEL IT. I'M
TAKING A TAXI TO
YOUR HOUSE.

TAKSI

NO! IT'LL
PUT US IN
DANGER.

I HAVE
NOWHERE
TO GO!

DANGER...?

NIKI, SHE'S
VULNERABLE, ALL
ALONE. IF JUSTYNA
SNEAKS THROUGH
THE WOODS TO THE
TREEHOUSE, SHE
WON'T BE SEEN.
SHE CAN HELP US
FIGURE OUT
A PLAN.

FINE.

JUSTYNA,
MAKE SURE NO
ONE FOLLOWS
YOU. SWITCH
CABS.

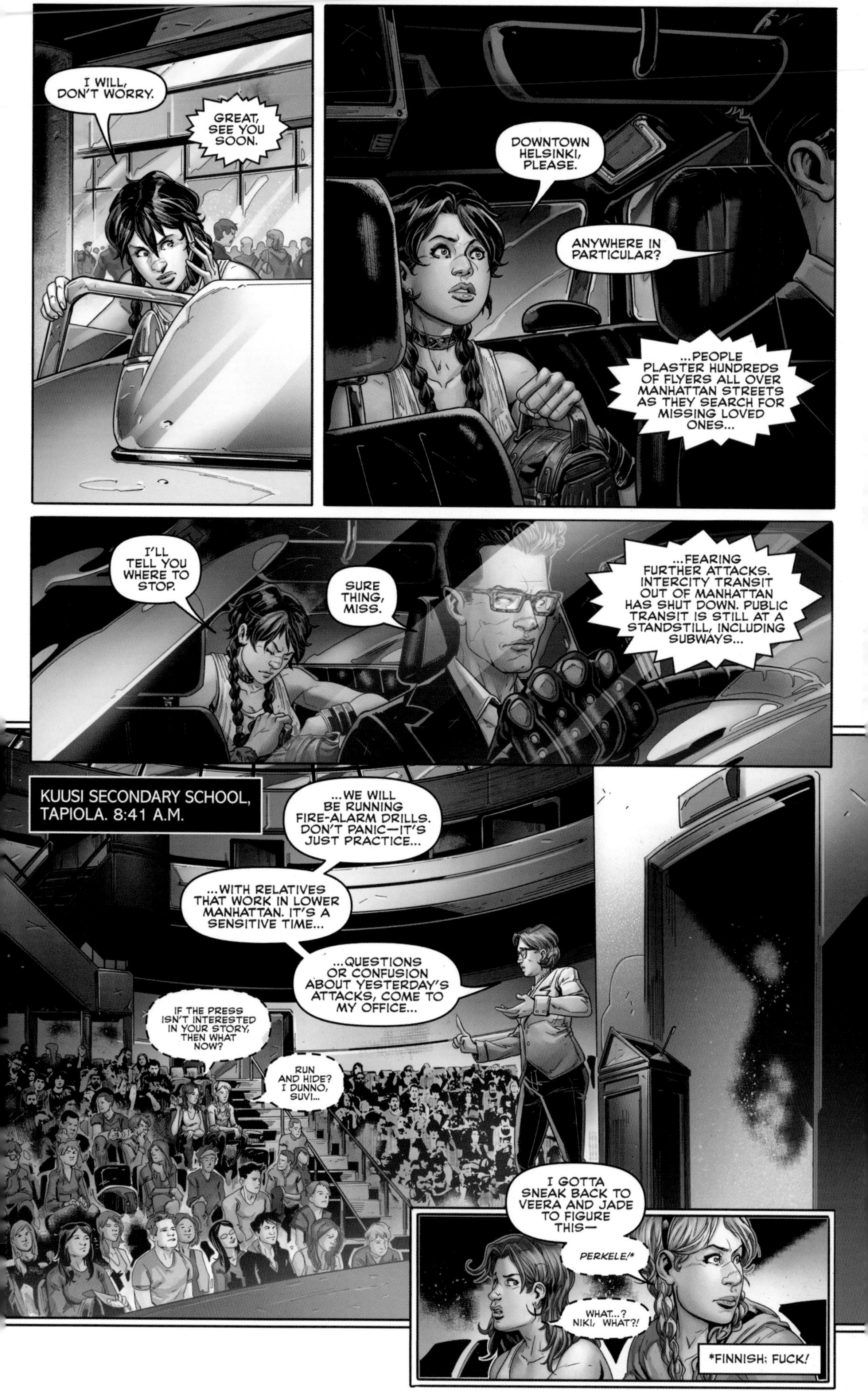

I WILL, DON'T WORRY.
GREAT, SEE YOU SOON.
DOWNTOWN HELSINKI, PLEASE.
ANYWHERE IN PARTICULAR?
...PEOPLE PLASTER HUNDREDS OF FLYERS ALL OVER MANHATTAN STREETS AS THEY SEARCH FOR MISSING LOVED ONES...
I'LL TELL YOU WHERE TO STOP.
SURE THING, MISS.
...FEARING FURTHER ATTACKS. INTERCITY TRANSIT OUT OF MANHATTAN HAS SHUT DOWN. PUBLIC TRANSIT IS STILL AT A STANDSTILL, INCLUDING SUBWAYS...
KUUSI SECONDARY SCHOOL, TAPIOLA. 8:41 A.M.
...WE WILL BE RUNNING FIRE-ALARM DRILLS. DON'T PANIC—IT'S JUST PRACTICE...
...WITH RELATIVES THAT WORK IN LOWER MANHATTAN. IT'S A SENSITIVE TIME...
...QUESTIONS OR CONFUSION ABOUT YESTERDAY'S ATTACKS, COME TO MY OFFICE...
IF THE PRESS ISN'T INTERESTED IN YOUR STORY, THEN WHAT NOW?
RUN AND HIDE? I DUNNO, SUVI...
I GOTTA SNEAK BACK TO VEERA AND JADE TO FIGURE THIS—
PERKELE!*
WHAT...? NIKI, WHAT?!
*FINNISH: FUCK!

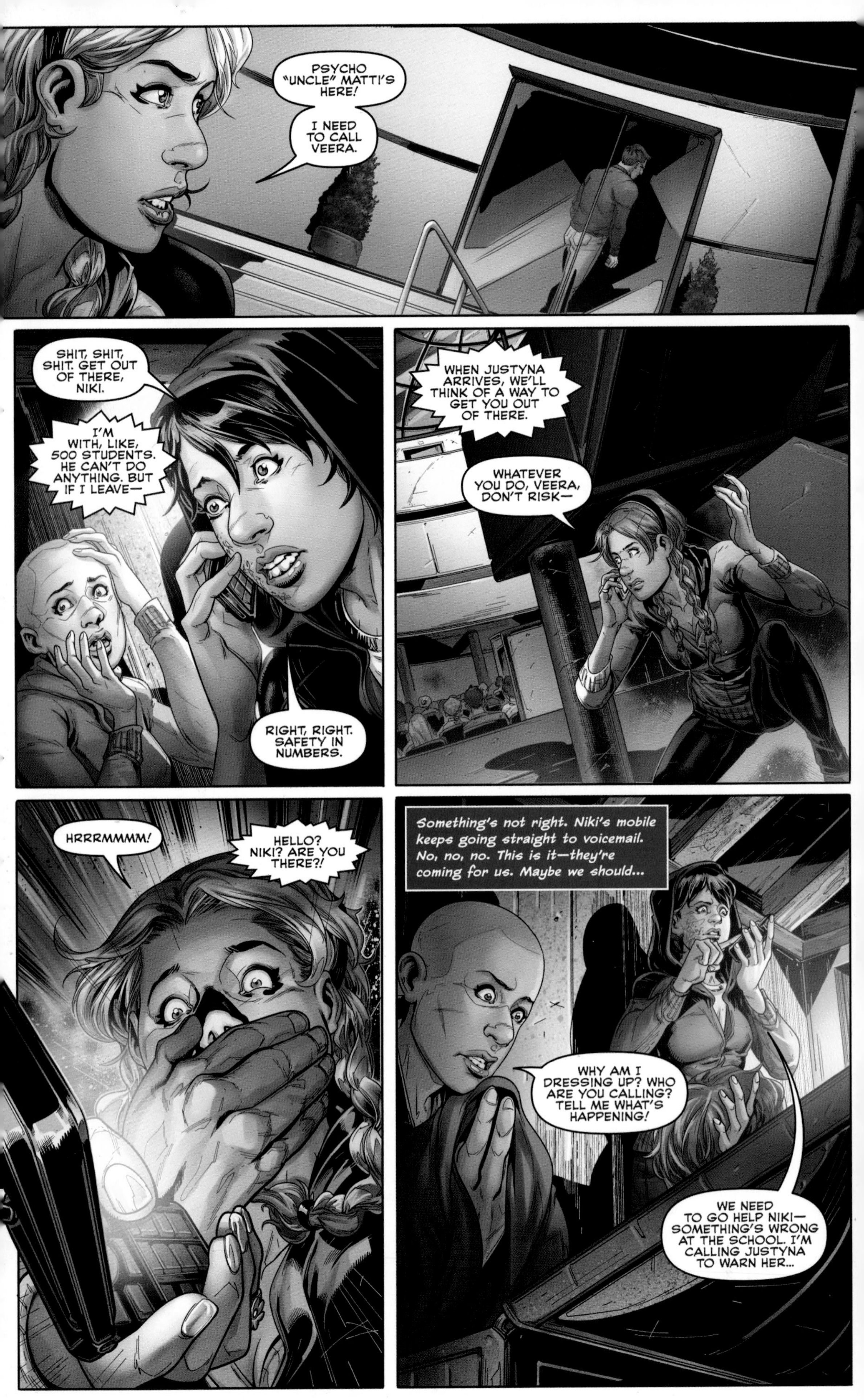
PSYCHO "UNCLE" MATTI'S HERE!
I NEED TO CALL VEERA.
SHIT, SHIT, SHIT. GET OUT OF THERE, NIKI.
I'M WITH, LIKE, 500 STUDENTS. HE CAN'T DO ANYTHING. BUT IF I LEAVE—
RIGHT, RIGHT. SAFETY IN NUMBERS.
WHEN JUSTYNA ARRIVES, WE'LL THINK OF A WAY TO GET YOU OUT OF THERE.
WHATEVER YOU DO, VEERA, DON'T RISK—
HRRRMMMM!
HELLO? NIKI? ARE YOU THERE?!
Something's not right. Niki's mobile keeps going straight to voicemail. No, no, no. This is it—they're coming for us. Maybe we should...
WHY AM I DRESSING UP? WHO ARE YOU CALLING? TELL ME WHAT'S HAPPENING!
WE NEED TO GO HELP NIKI—SOMETHING'S WRONG AT THE SCHOOL. I'M CALLING JUSTYNA TO WARN HER...

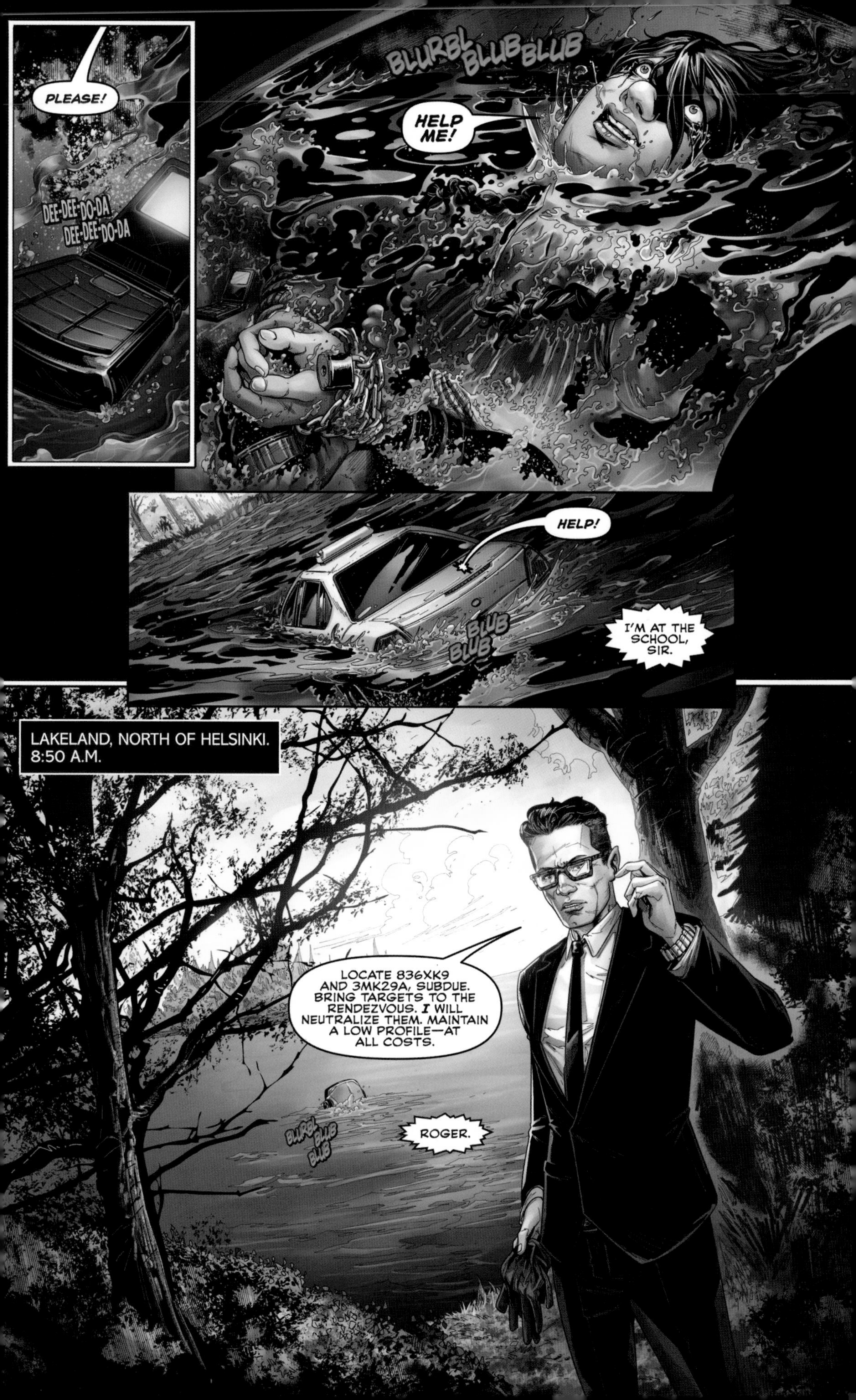
PLEASE!
DEE-DEE-DO-DA DEE-DEE-DO-DA
BLURBL BLUB BLUB
HELP ME!
HELP!
BLUB BLUB
I'M AT THE SCHOOL, SIR.
LAKELAND, NORTH OF HELSINKI.
8:50 A.M.
LOCATE 836XK9 AND 3MK29A, SUBDUE. BRING TARGETS TO THE RENDEZVOUS. I WILL NEUTRALIZE THEM. MAINTAIN A LOW PROFILE—AT ALL COSTS.
BLURBL BLUB BLUB
ROGER.

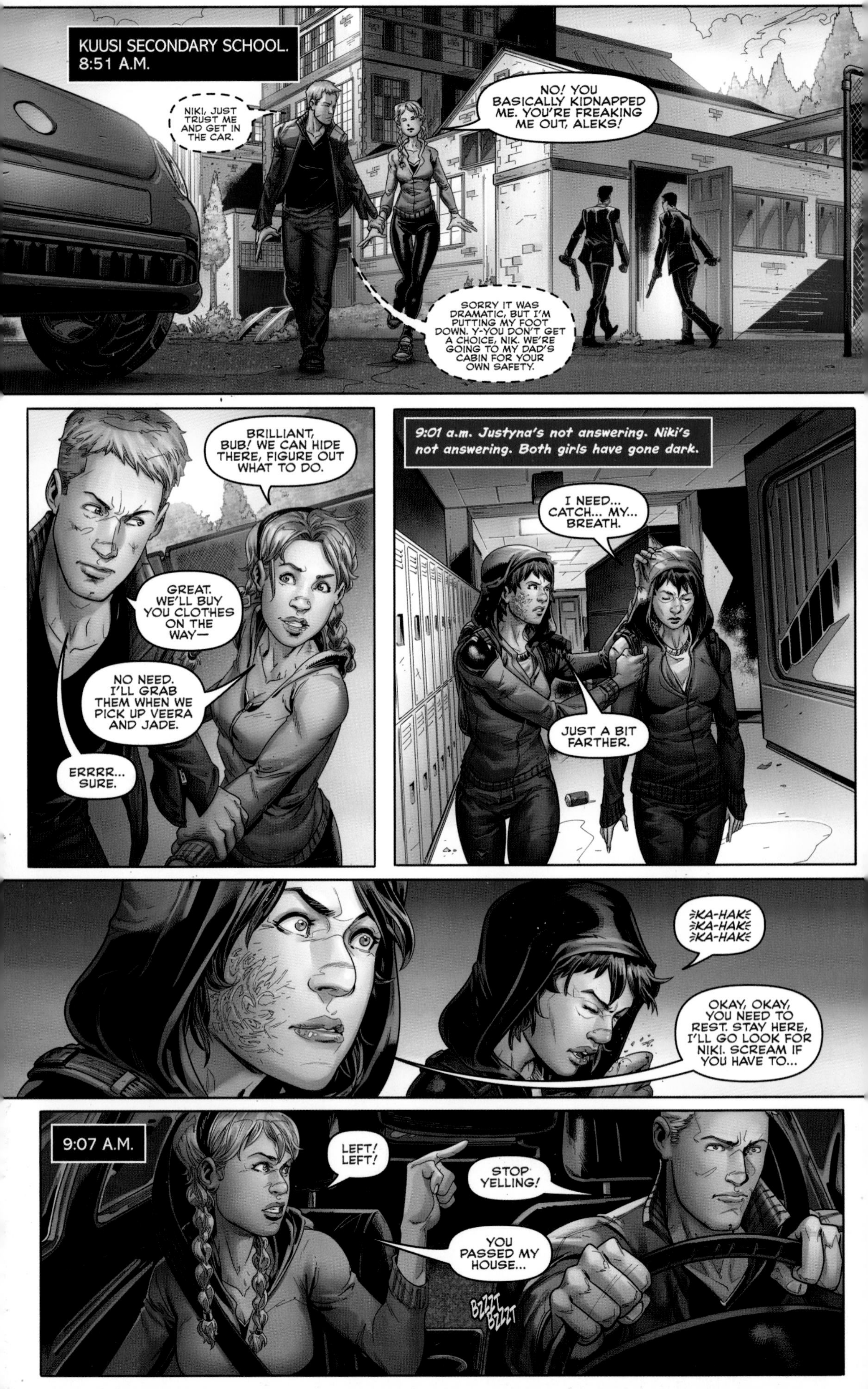
KUUSI SECONDARY SCHOOL.
8:51 A.M.
NIKI, JUST TRUST ME AND GET IN THE CAR.
NO! YOU BASICALLY KIDNAPPED ME. YOU'RE FREAKING ME OUT, ALEKS!
SORRY IT WAS DRAMATIC, BUT I'M PUTTING MY FOOT DOWN. Y-YOU DON'T GET A CHOICE, NIK. WE'RE GOING TO MY DAD'S CABIN FOR YOUR OWN SAFETY.
BRILLIANT, BUB! WE CAN HIDE THERE, FIGURE OUT WHAT TO DO.
GREAT. WE'LL BUY YOU CLOTHES ON THE WAY—
NO NEED. I'LL GRAB THEM WHEN WE PICK UP VEERA AND JADE.
ERRRR... SURE.
9:01 a.m. Justyna's not answering. Niki's not answering. Both girls have gone dark.
I NEED... CATCH... MY... BREATH.
JUST A BIT FARTHER.
KA-HAK
KA-HAK
KA-HAK
OKAY, OKAY, YOU NEED TO REST. STAY HERE, I'LL GO LOOK FOR NIKI. SCREAM IF YOU HAVE TO...
9:07 A.M.
LEFT! LEFT!
STOP YELLING!
YOU PASSED MY HOUSE...
BZZZT BZZZT

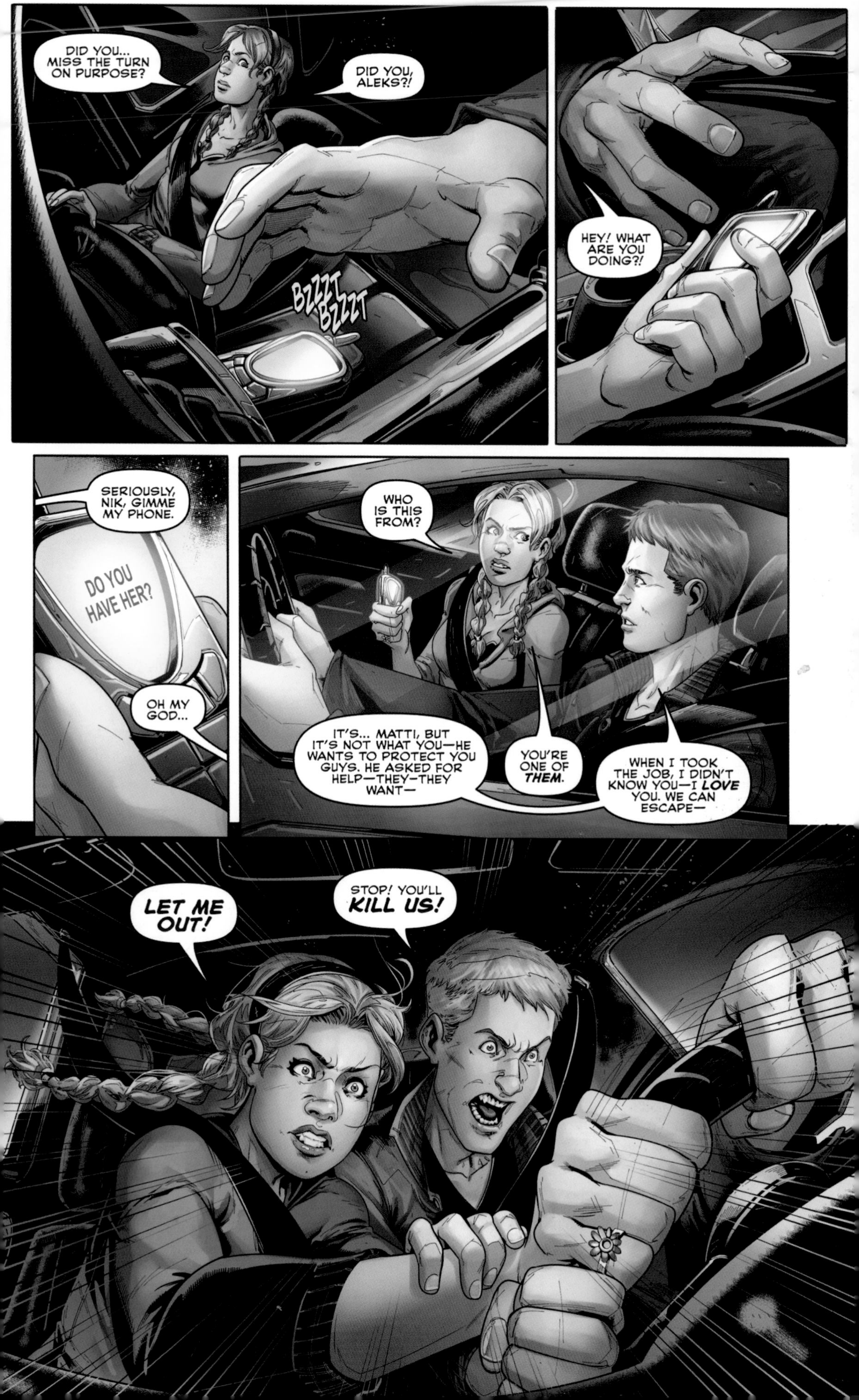
DID YOU... MISS THE TURN ON PURPOSE?
DID YOU, ALEKS?!
BZZZT BZZZT
HEY! WHAT ARE YOU DOING?!
SERIOUSLY, NIK, GIMME MY PHONE.
DO YOU HAVE HER?
OH MY GOD...
WHO IS THIS FROM?
IT'S... MATTI, BUT IT'S NOT WHAT YOU—HE WANTS TO PROTECT YOU GUYS. HE ASKED FOR HELP—THEY—THEY WANT—
YOU'RE ONE OF *THEM*.
WHEN I TOOK THE JOB, I DIDN'T KNOW YOU—I *LOVE* YOU. WE CAN ESCAPE—
LET ME OUT!
STOP! YOU'LL *KILL US!*

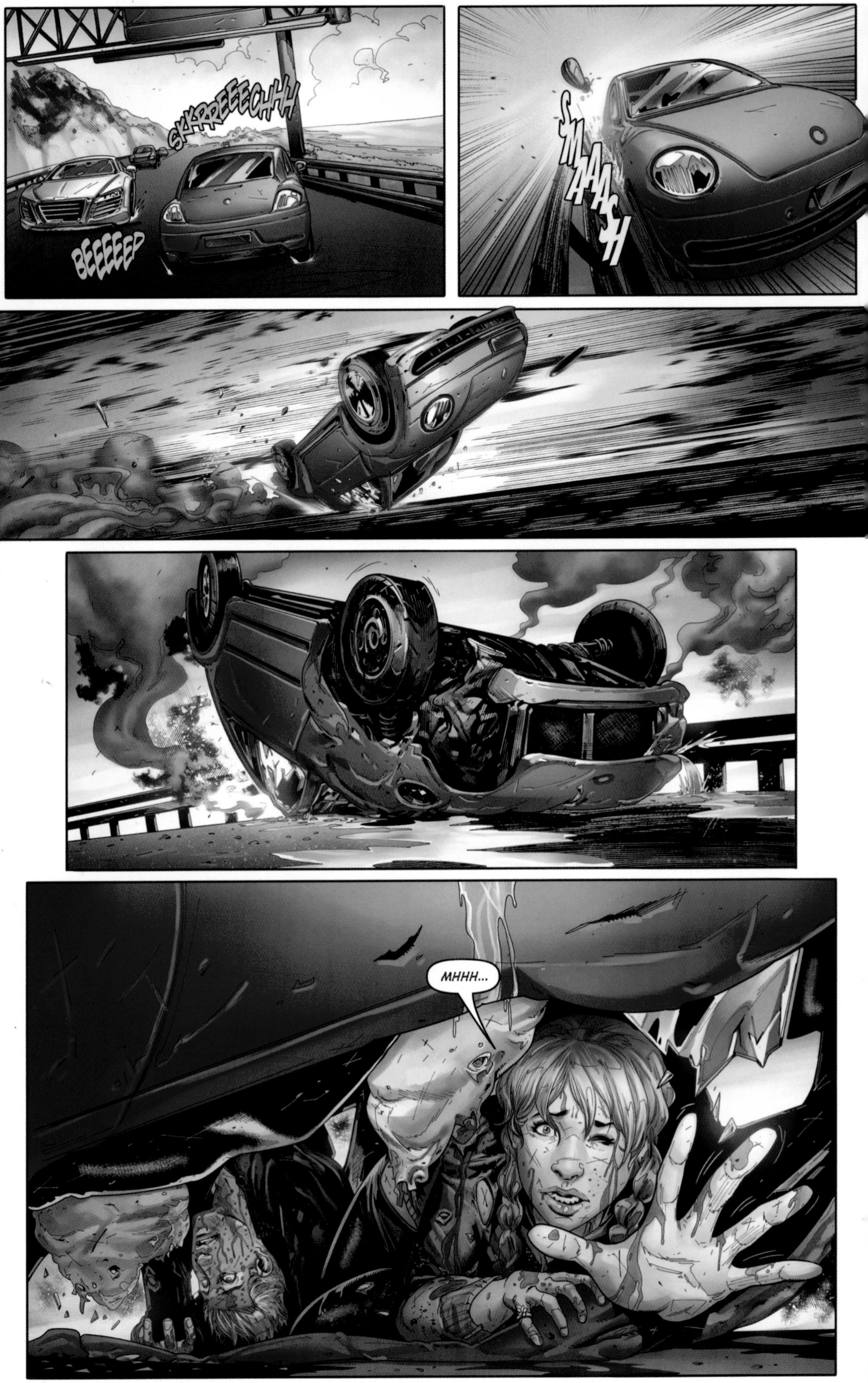
SKRREEECHHH
BEEEEEP
SMAAASH
MHHH...

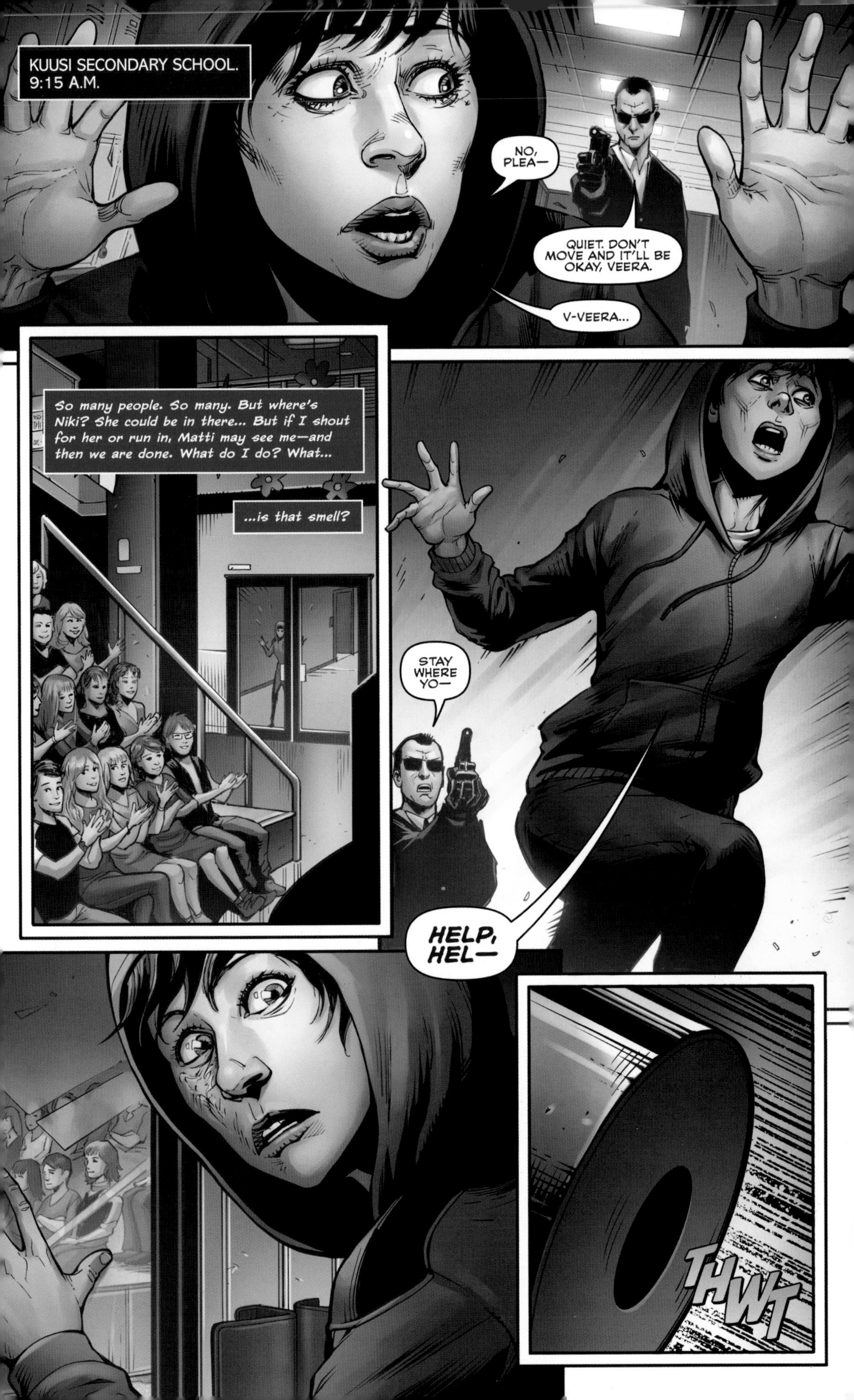
KUUSI SECONDARY SCHOOL.
9:15 A.M.
NO, PLEA—
QUIET. DON'T MOVE AND IT'LL BE OKAY, VEERA.
V-VEERA...
So many people. So many. But where's Niki? She could be in there... But if I shout for her or run in, Matti may see me—and then we are done. What do I do? What...
...is that smell?
STAY WHERE YO—
HELP, HEL—
THWT

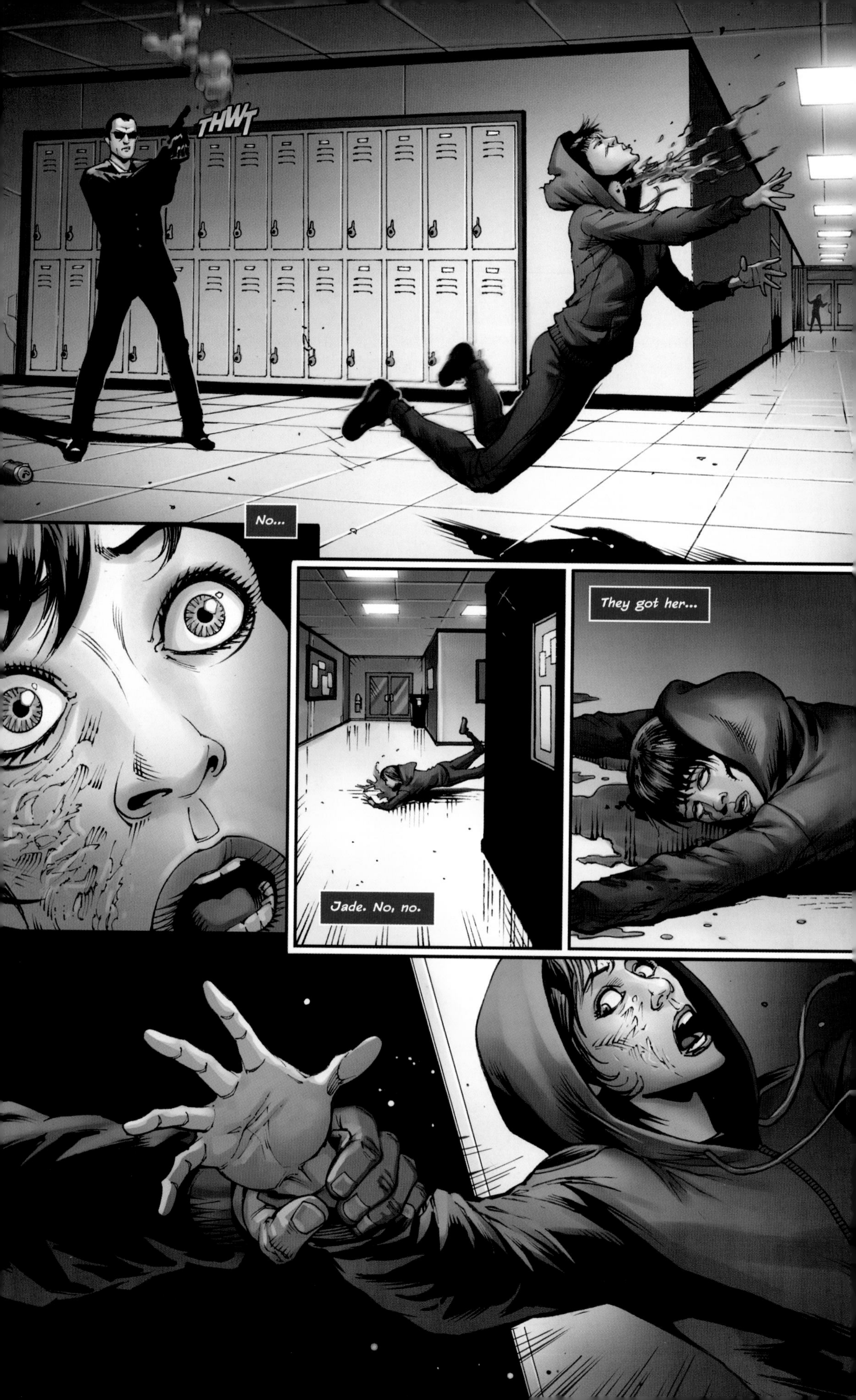
THWT
No...
They got her...
Jade. No, no.

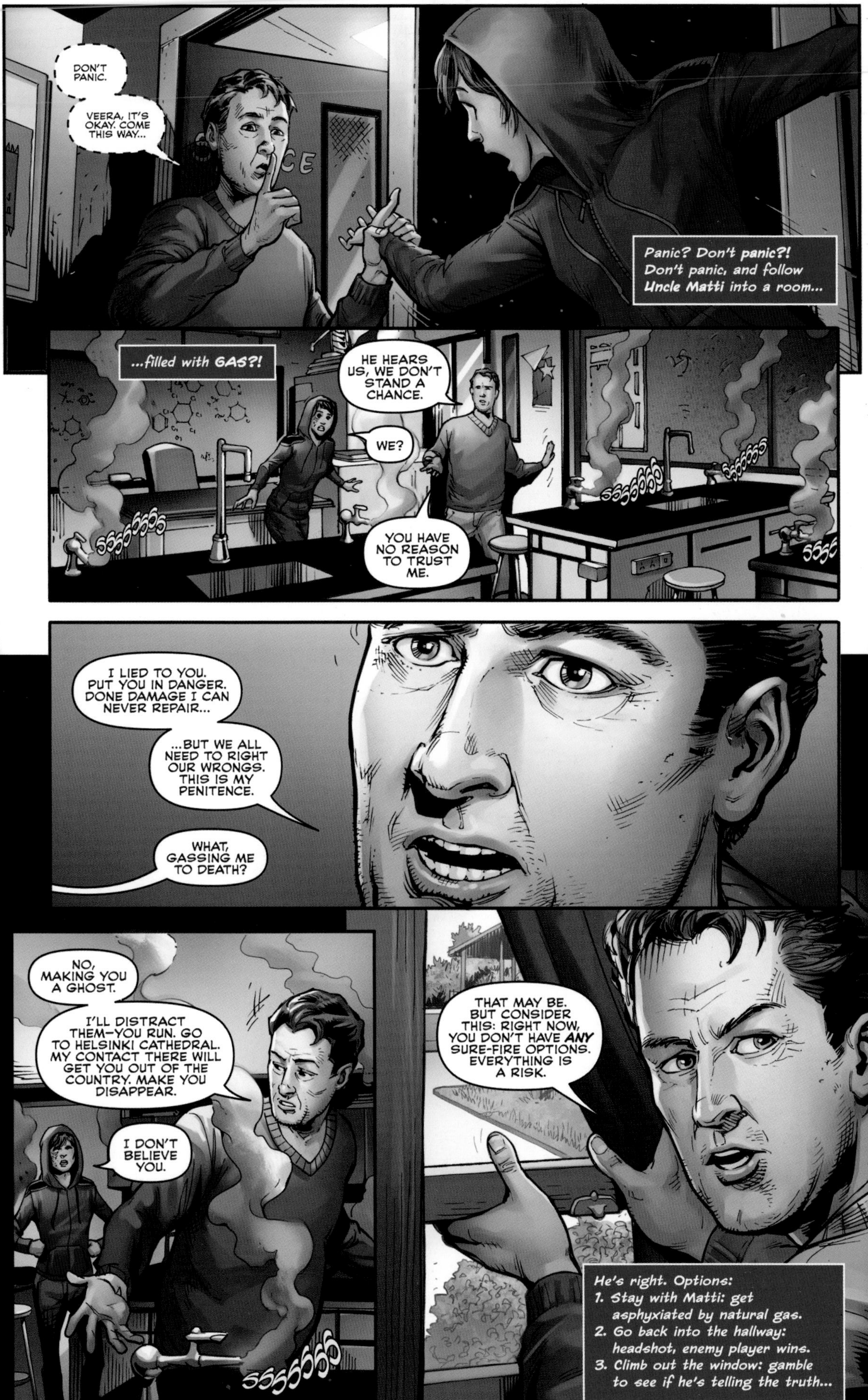
DON'T PANIC.
VEERA, IT'S OKAY. COME THIS WAY...
Panic? Don't panic?! Don't panic, and follow Uncle Matti into a room...
...filled with GAS?!
HE HEARS US, WE DON'T STAND A CHANCE.
WE?
YOU HAVE NO REASON TO TRUST ME.
SSSSSSS
I LIED TO YOU. PUT YOU IN DANGER. DONE DAMAGE I CAN NEVER REPAIR...
...BUT WE ALL NEED TO RIGHT OUR WRONGS. THIS IS MY PENITENCE.
WHAT, GASSING ME TO DEATH?
NO, MAKING YOU A GHOST.
I'LL DISTRACT THEM—YOU RUN. GO TO HELSINKI CATHEDRAL. MY CONTACT THERE WILL GET YOU OUT OF THE COUNTRY. MAKE YOU DISAPPEAR.
I DON'T BELIEVE YOU.
SSSSSSS
THAT MAY BE. BUT CONSIDER THIS: RIGHT NOW, YOU DON'T HAVE ANY SURE-FIRE OPTIONS. EVERYTHING IS A RISK.
He's right. Options:
1. Stay with Matti: get asphyxiated by natural gas.
2. Go back into the hallway: headshot, enemy player wins.
3. Climb out the window: gamble to see if he's telling the truth...

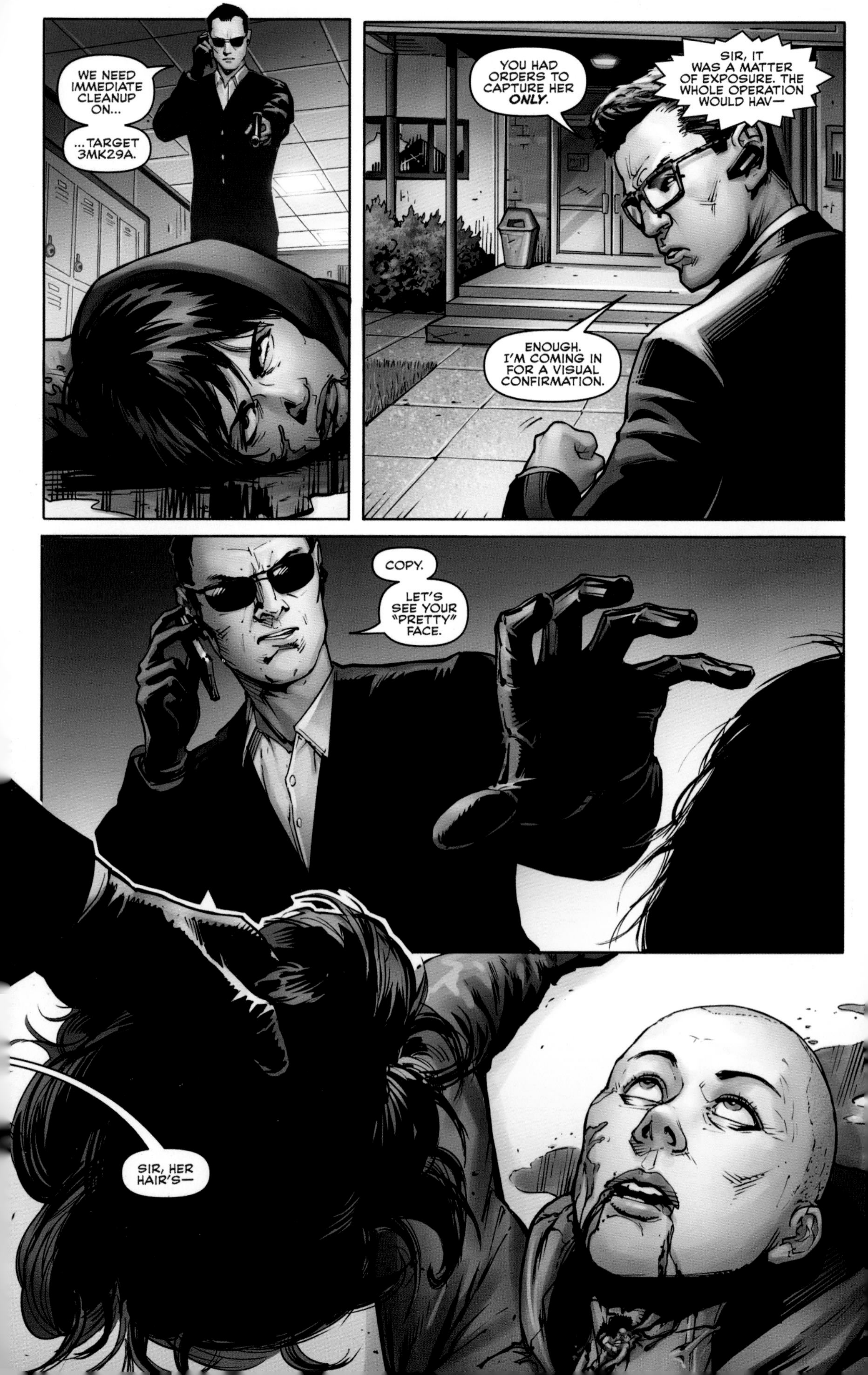
WE NEED IMMEDIATE CLEANUP ON...
...TARGET 3MK29A.
YOU HAD ORDERS TO CAPTURE HER *ONLY*.
SIR, IT WAS A MATTER OF EXPOSURE. THE WHOLE OPERATION WOULD HAV—
ENOUGH. I'M COMING IN FOR A VISUAL CONFIRMATION.
COPY.
LET'S SEE YOUR "PRETTY" FACE.
SIR, HER HAIR'S—

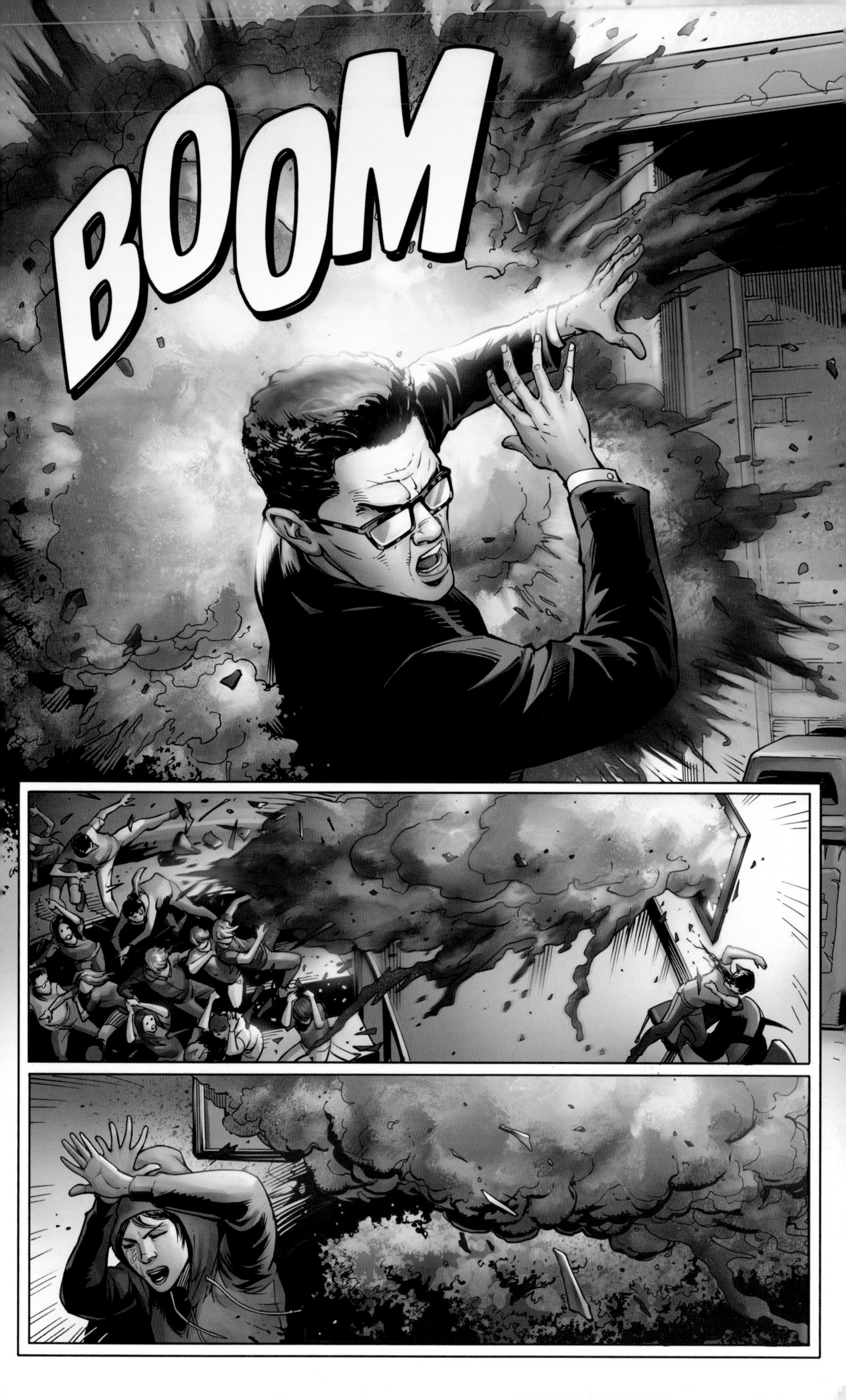
BOOM

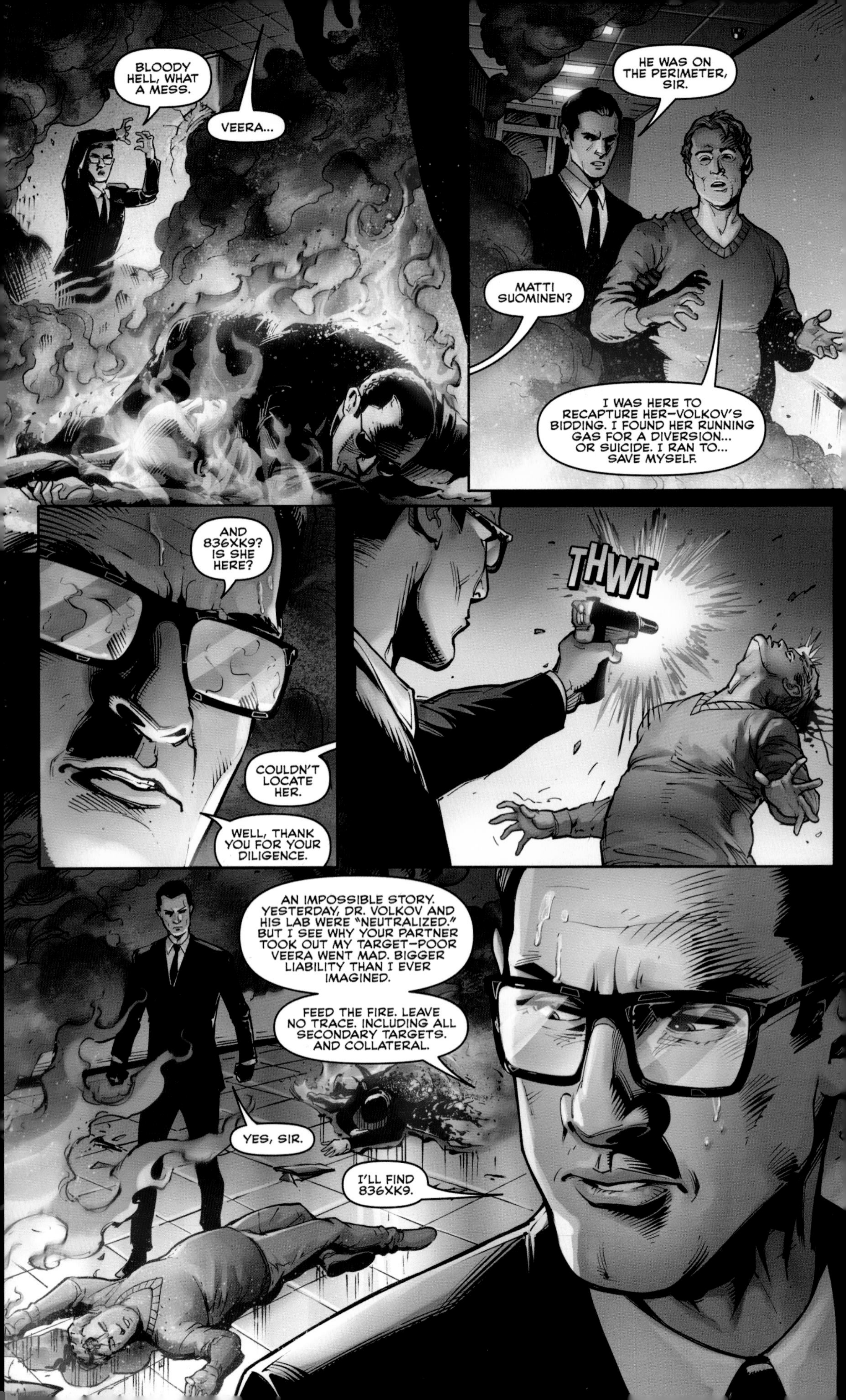
BLOODY HELL, WHAT A MESS.
VEERA...
HE WAS ON THE PERIMETER, SIR.
MATTI SUOMINEN?
I WAS HERE TO RECAPTURE HER—VOLKOV'S BIDDING. I FOUND HER RUNNING GAS FOR A DIVERSION... OR SUICIDE. I RAN TO... SAVE MYSELF.
AND 836XK9? IS SHE HERE?
COULDN'T LOCATE HER.
WELL, THANK YOU FOR YOUR DILIGENCE.
THWT
AN IMPOSSIBLE STORY. YESTERDAY, DR. VOLKOV AND HIS LAB WERE "NEUTRALIZED." BUT I SEE WHY YOUR PARTNER TOOK OUT MY TARGET—POOR VEERA WENT MAD. BIGGER LIABILITY THAN I EVER IMAGINED.
FEED THE FIRE. LEAVE NO TRACE. INCLUDING ALL SECONDARY TARGETS. AND COLLATERAL.
YES, SIR.
I'LL FIND 836XK9.

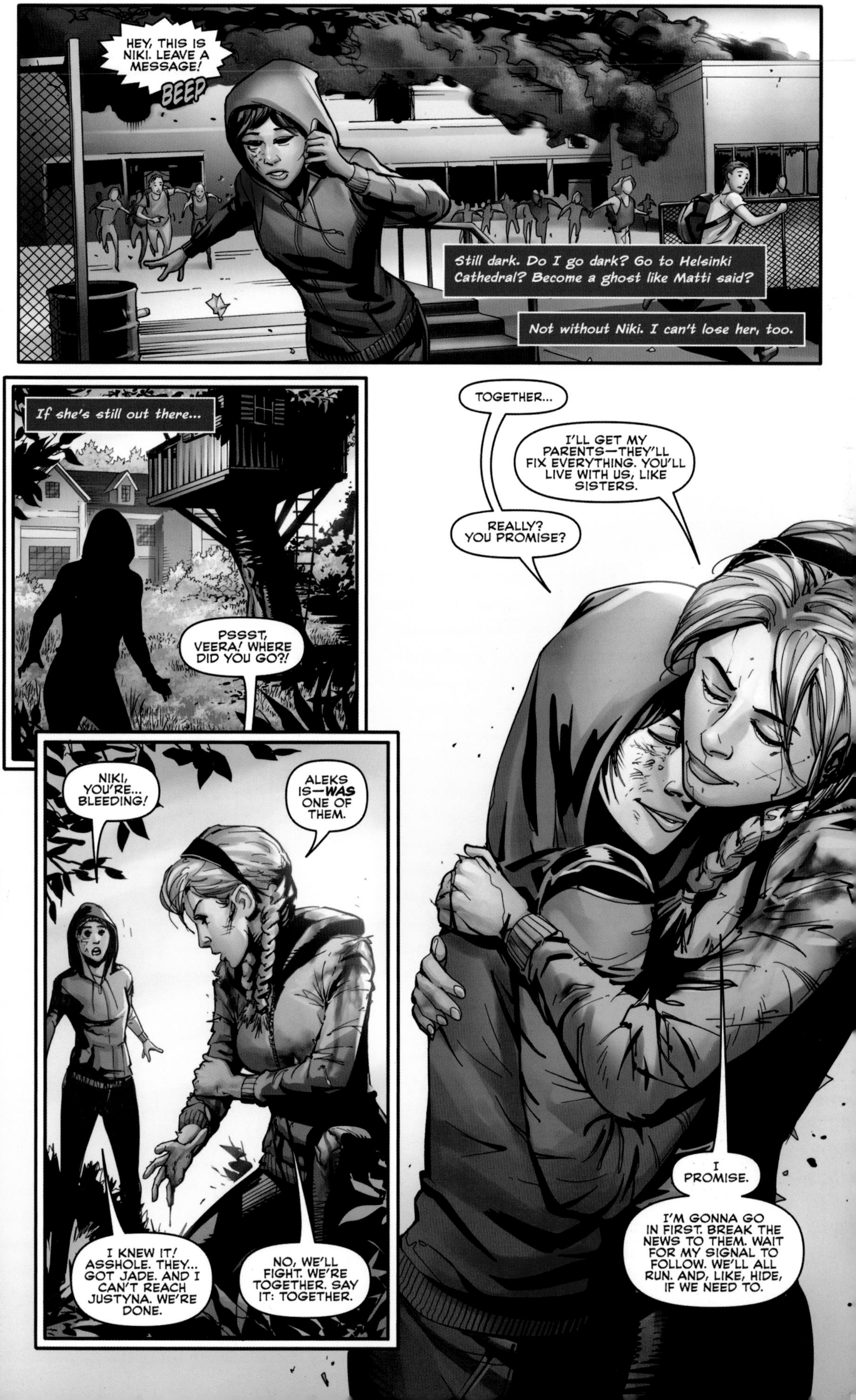
HEY, THIS IS NIKI. LEAVE A MESSAGE!
BEEP
Still dark. Do I go dark? Go to Helsinki Cathedral? Become a ghost like Matti said?
Not without Niki. I can't lose her, too.
If she's still out there...
PSSST, VEERA! WHERE DID YOU GO?!
NIKI, YOU'RE... BLEEDING!
ALEKS IS—WAS ONE OF THEM.
I KNEW IT! ASSHOLE. THEY... GOT JADE. AND I CAN'T REACH JUSTYNA. WE'RE DONE.
NO, WE'LL FIGHT. WE'RE TOGETHER. SAY IT: TOGETHER.
TOGETHER...
I'LL GET MY PARENTS—THEY'LL FIX EVERYTHING. YOU'LL LIVE WITH US, LIKE SISTERS.
REALLY? YOU PROMISE?
I PROMISE.
I'M GONNA GO IN FIRST. BREAK THE NEWS TO THEM. WAIT FOR MY SIGNAL TO FOLLOW. WE'LL ALL RUN. AND, LIKE, HIDE, IF WE NEED TO.

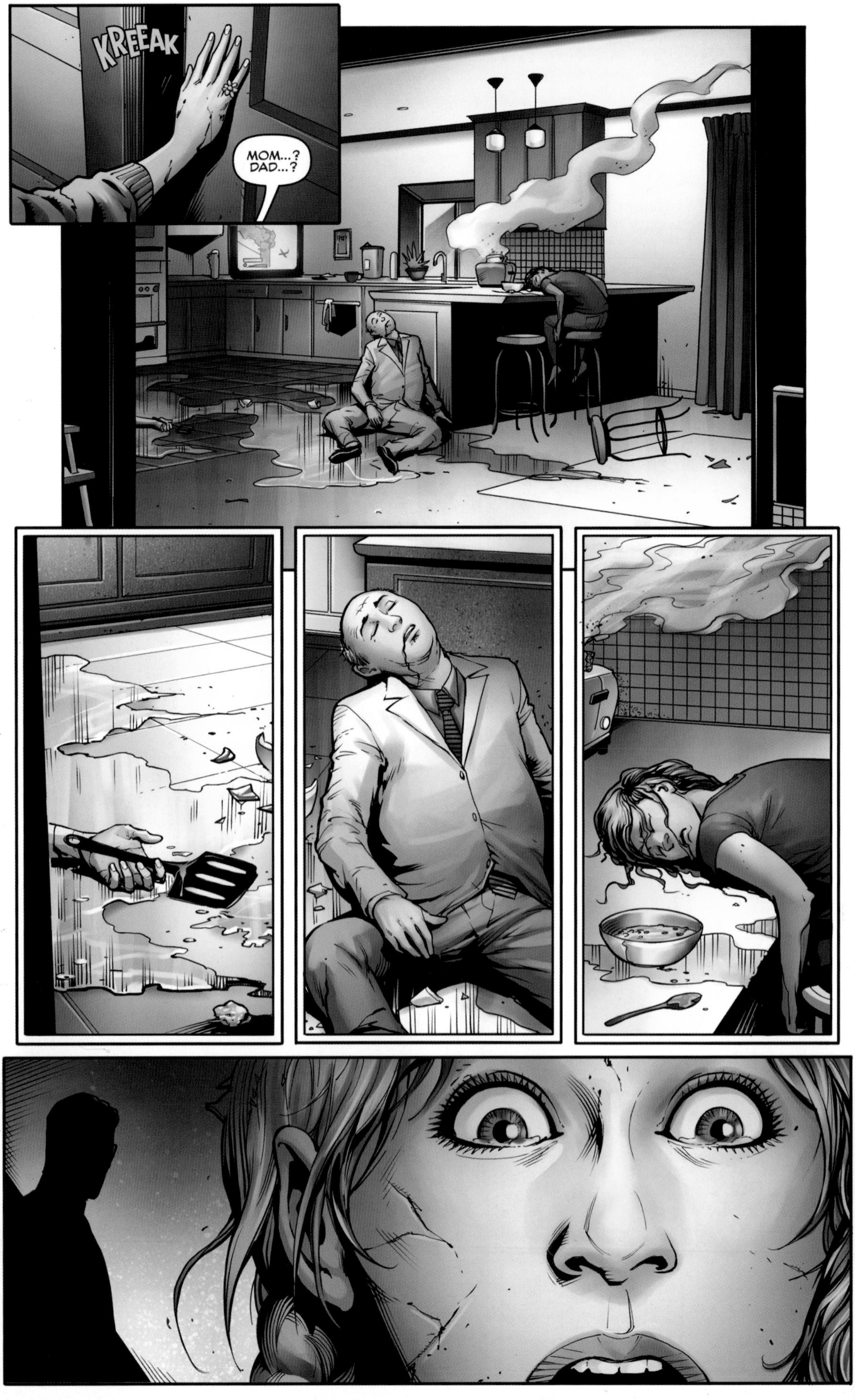
KREEAK
MOM...? DAD...?

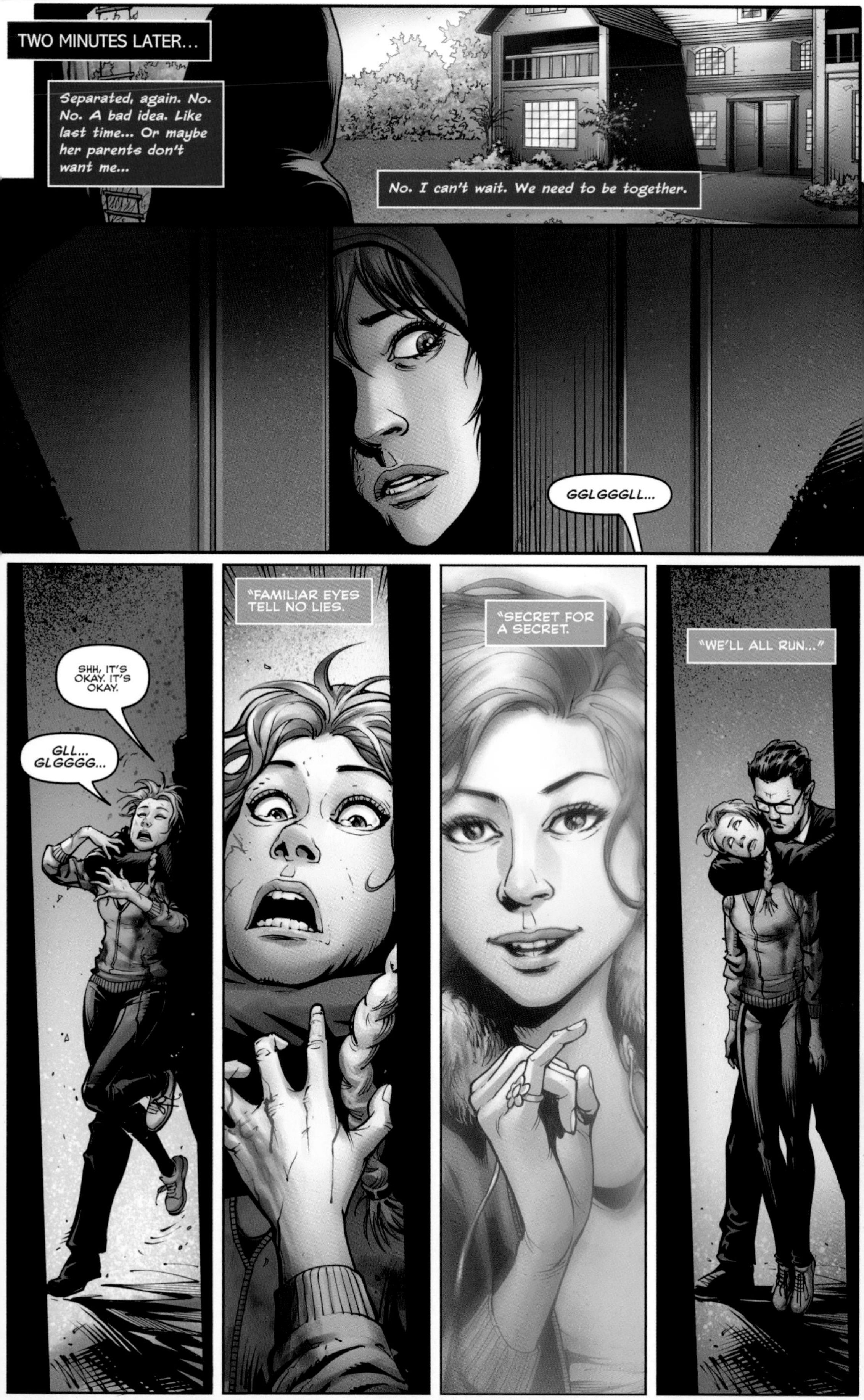
TWO MINUTES LATER...
Separated, again. No. No. A bad idea. Like last time... Or maybe her parents don't want me...
No. I can't wait. We need to be together.
GGLGGGLL...
SHH, IT'S OKAY. IT'S OKAY.
GLL... GLGGGG...
"FAMILIAR EYES TELL NO LIES.
"SECRET FOR A SECRET.
"WE'LL ALL RUN..."

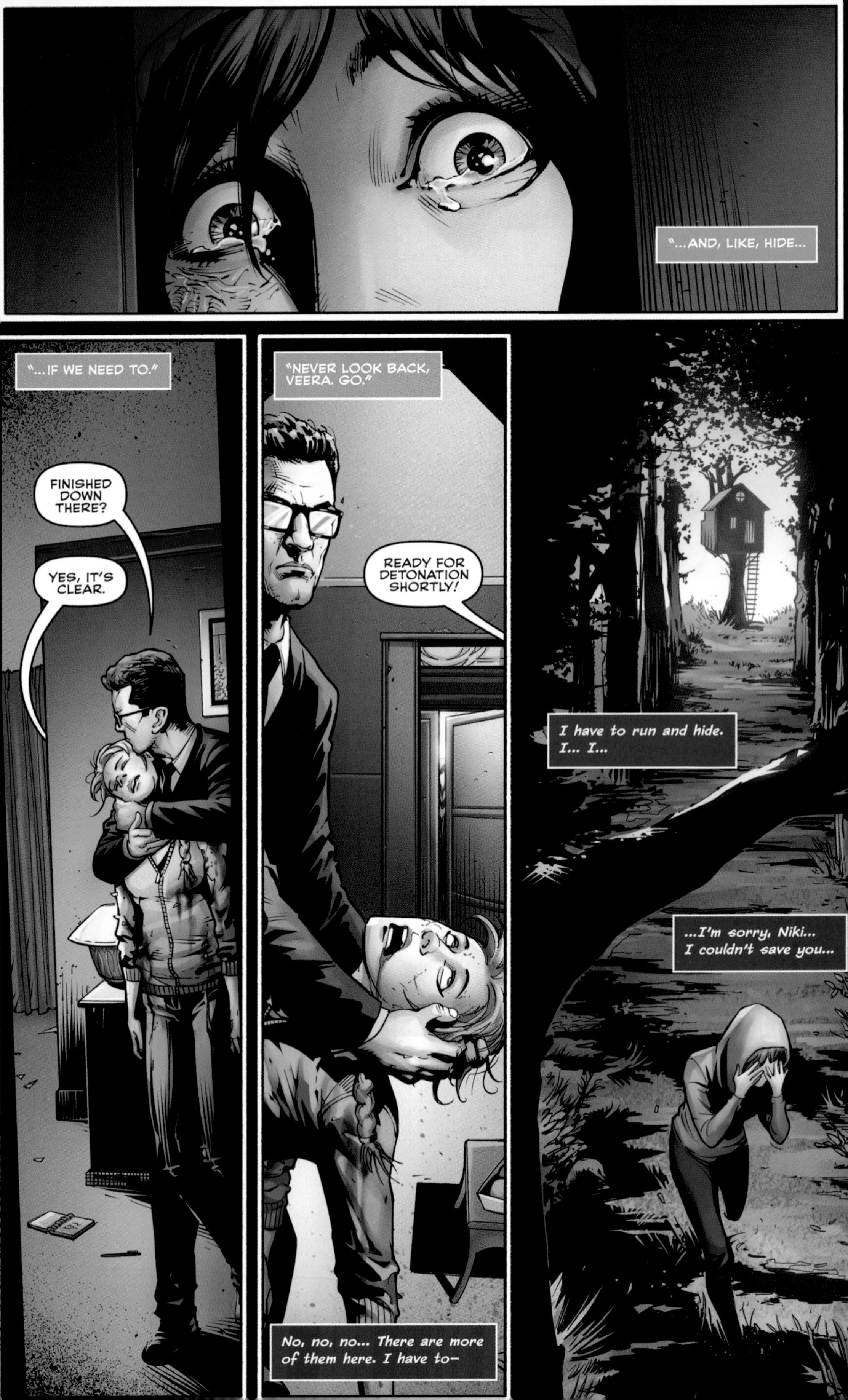
"...AND, LIKE, HIDE...
"...IF WE NEED TO."
FINISHED DOWN THERE?
YES, IT'S CLEAR.
"NEVER LOOK BACK, VEERA. GO."
READY FOR DETONATION SHORTLY!
No, no, no... There are more of them here. I have to—
I have to run and hide. I... I...
...I'm sorry, Niki... I couldn't save you...

AND YOU'RE CERTAIN VEERA SUOMINEN IS DEAD?

YES, RACHEL. AND NIKI LINTULA. I... *PERSONALLY* CONFIRMED IT.

SIX GIRLS, 32 CIVILIANS. IN 24 HOURS. ONE OF MY MOST COMPLEX JOBS.

SIX LEDAS... AND 32 *CIVILIANS*...?

"AN UNFORTUNATE CAR 'ACCIDENT' IN AMSTERDAM KILLED 'TWIN' TEENS AND THEIR MOTHER. DRIVERS ARE SO RECKLESS THESE DAYS.

"THE 'SUICIDE' OF A SAD RUNAWAY IN DENMARK. I ADMIT, IT'S ALMOST THE STEREOTYPICAL OPENING OF A SCANDINAVIAN MYSTERY.

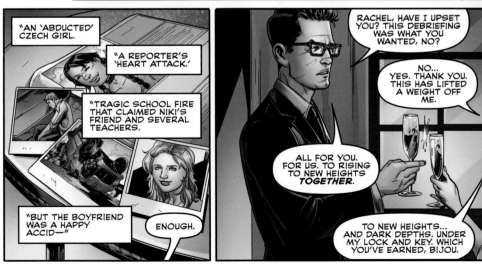

"AN 'ABDUCTED' CZECH GIRL.

"A REPORTER'S 'HEART ATTACK.'

"TRAGIC SCHOOL FIRE THAT CLAIMED NIKI'S FRIEND AND SEVERAL TEACHERS.

"BUT THE BOYFRIEND WAS A HAPPY ACCID—"

ENOUGH.

RACHEL, HAVE I UPSET YOU? THIS DEBRIEFING WAS WHAT YOU WANTED, NO?

NO... YES. THANK YOU. THIS HAS LIFTED A WEIGHT OFF ME.

ALL FOR YOU. FOR US. TO RISING TO NEW HEIGHTS *TOGETHER.*

TO NEW HEIGHTS... AND DARK DEPTHS. UNDER MY LOCK AND KEY. WHICH YOU'VE EARNED, BIJOU.

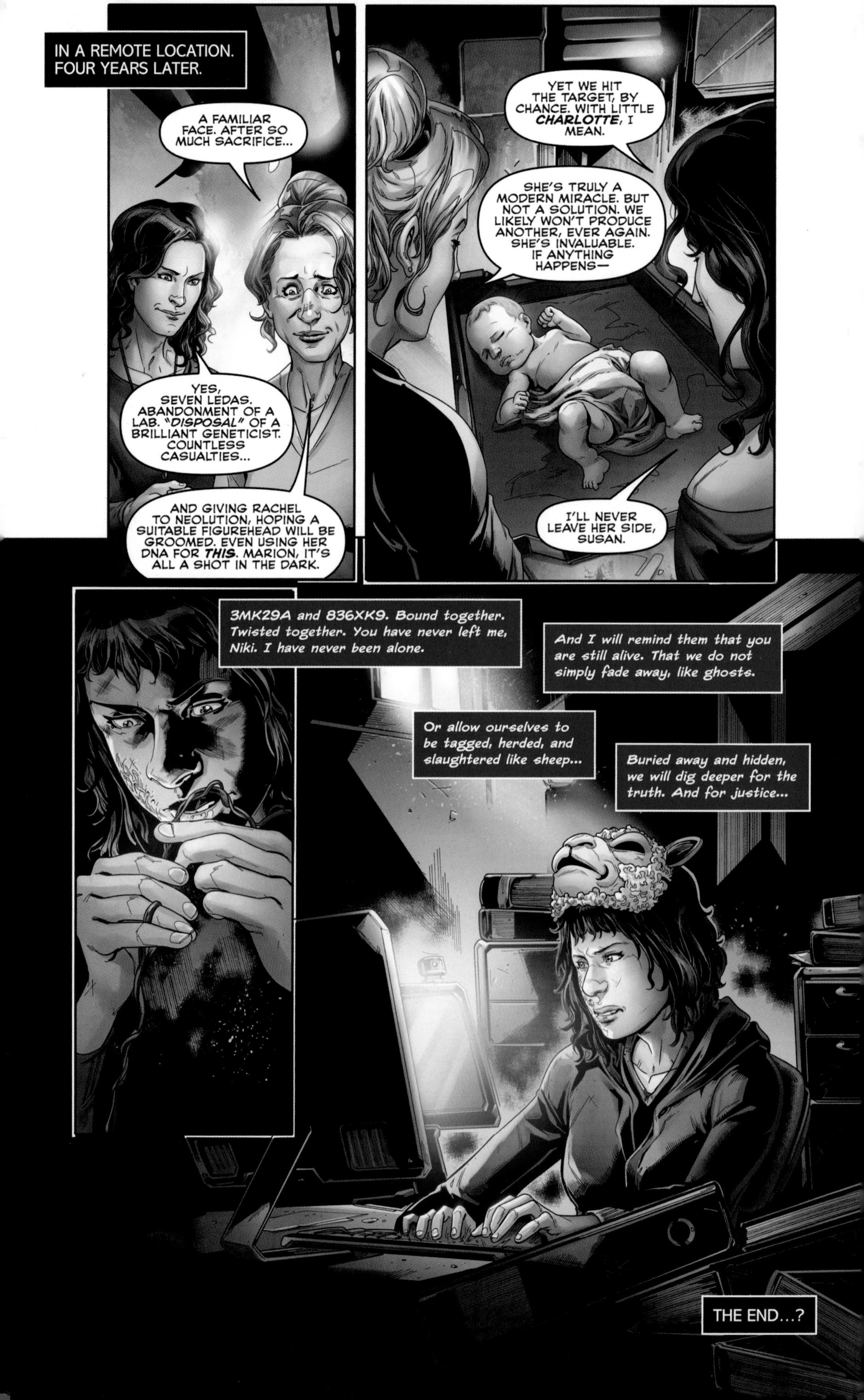
IN A REMOTE LOCATION. FOUR YEARS LATER.
A FAMILIAR FACE. AFTER SO MUCH SACRIFICE...
YES, SEVEN LEDAS. ABANDONMENT OF A LAB. "DISPOSAL" OF A BRILLIANT GENETICIST. COUNTLESS CASUALTIES...
AND GIVING RACHEL TO NEOLUTION, HOPING A SUITABLE FIGUREHEAD WILL BE GROOMED. EVEN USING HER DNA FOR THIS. MARION, IT'S ALL A SHOT IN THE DARK.
YET WE HIT THE TARGET, BY CHANCE. WITH LITTLE CHARLOTTE, I MEAN.
SHE'S TRULY A MODERN MIRACLE. BUT NOT A SOLUTION. WE LIKELY WON'T PRODUCE ANOTHER, EVER AGAIN. SHE'S INVALUABLE. IF ANYTHING HAPPENS—
I'LL NEVER LEAVE HER SIDE, SUSAN.
3MK29A and 836XK9. Bound together. Twisted together. You have never left me, Niki. I have never been alone.
And I will remind them that you are still alive. That we do not simply fade away, like ghosts.
Or allow ourselves to be tagged, herded, and slaughtered like sheep...
Buried away and hidden, we will dig deeper for the truth. And for justice...
THE END...?

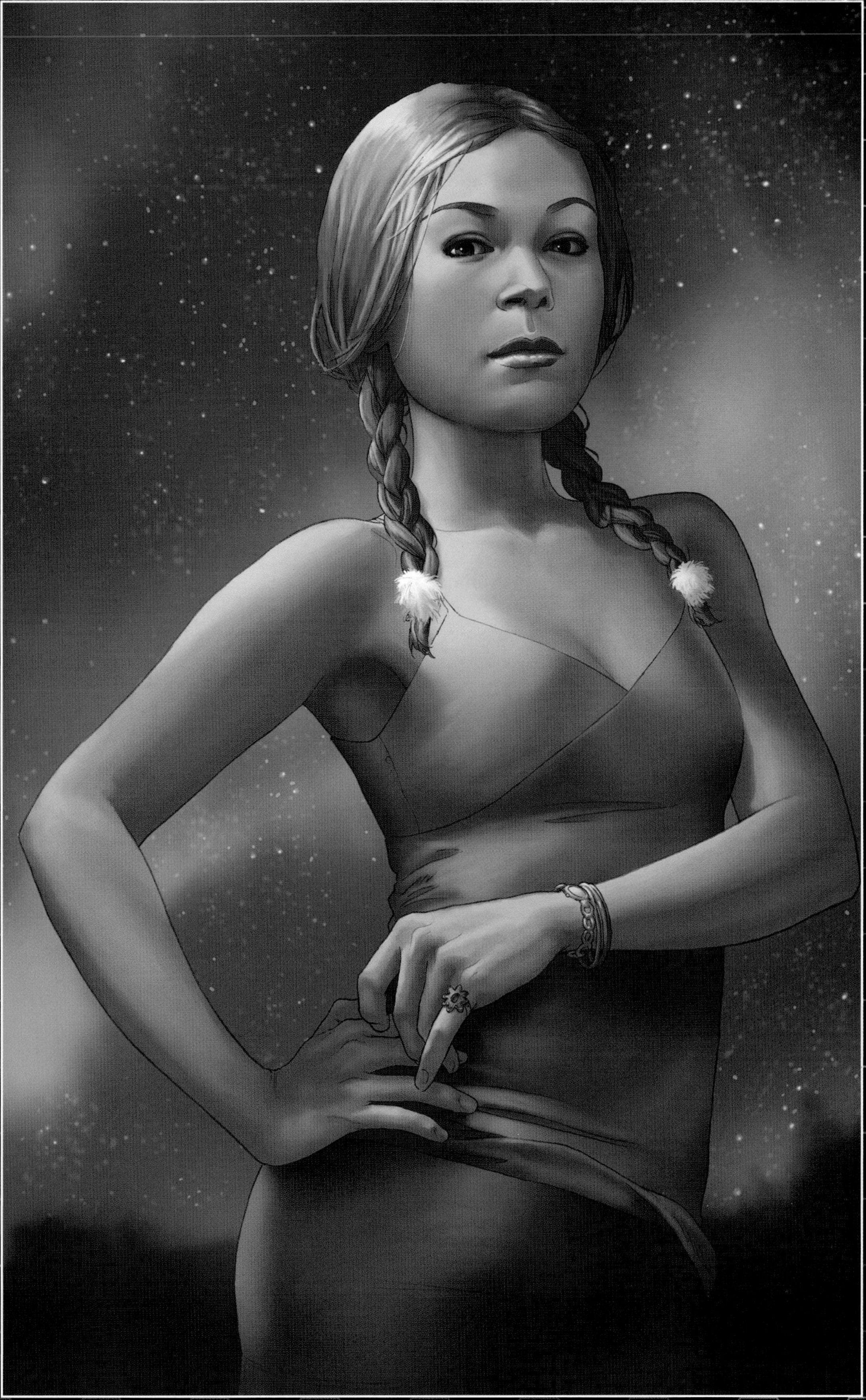

BY **RODIN ESQUEJO**

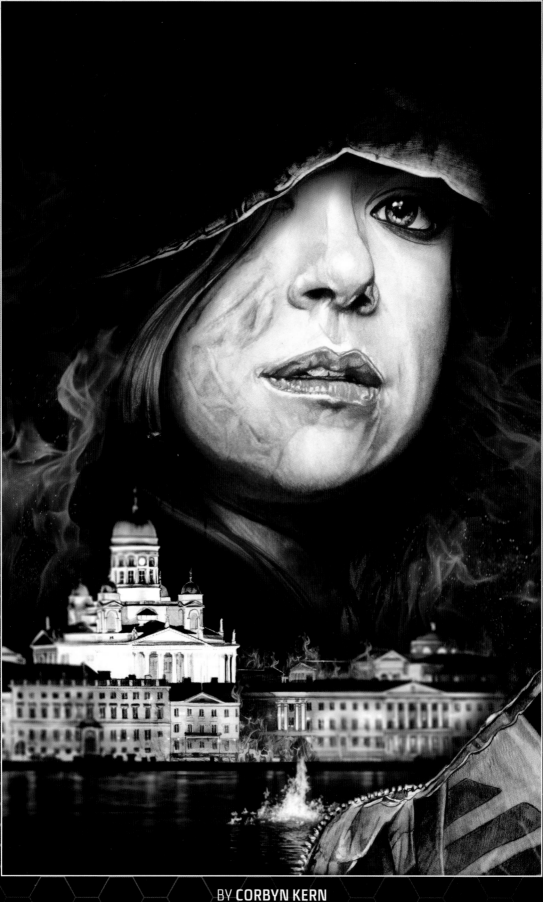

BY CORBYN KERN

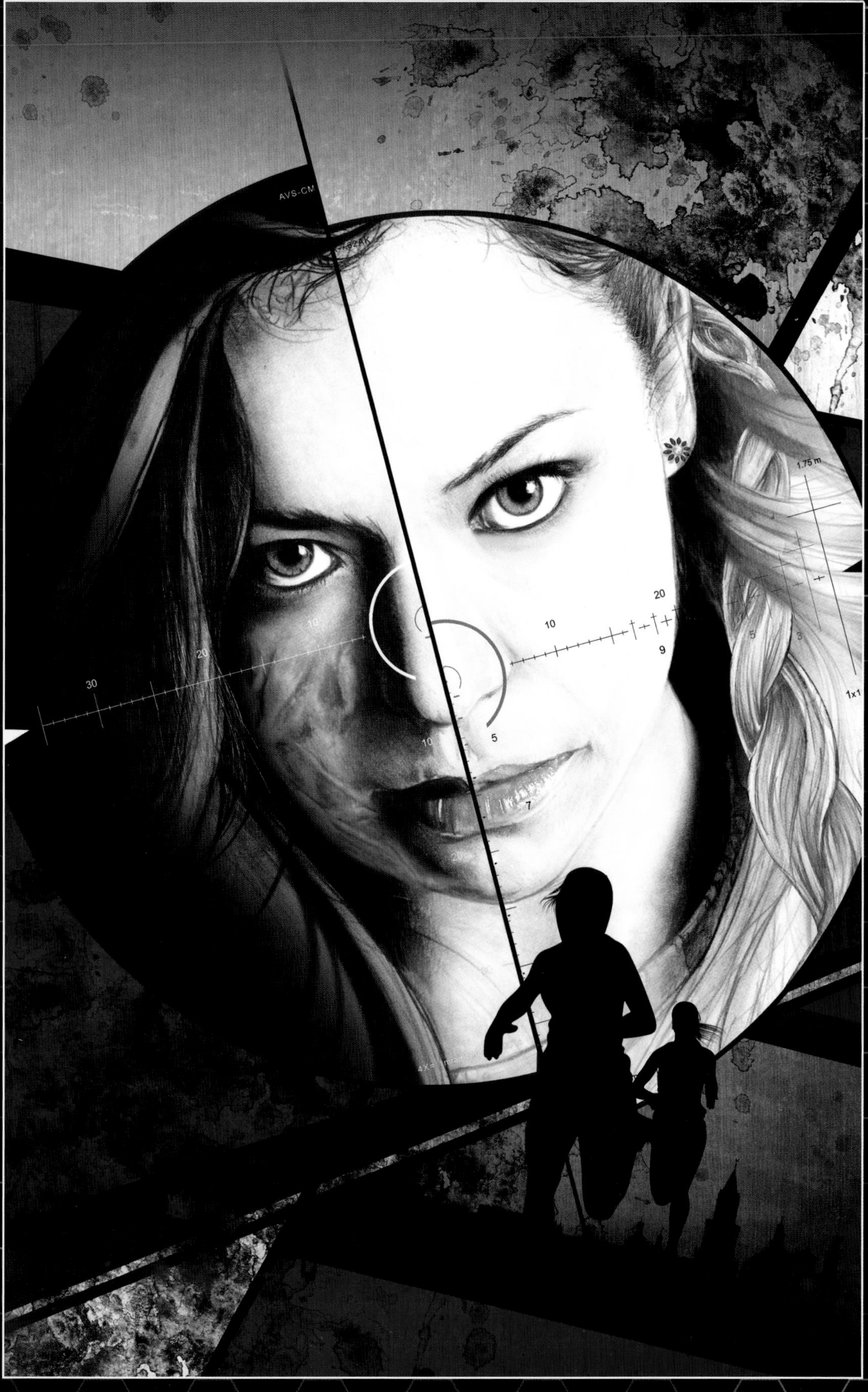
AVS-CM
1.75 m
1x1

BY **CORBYN KERN**

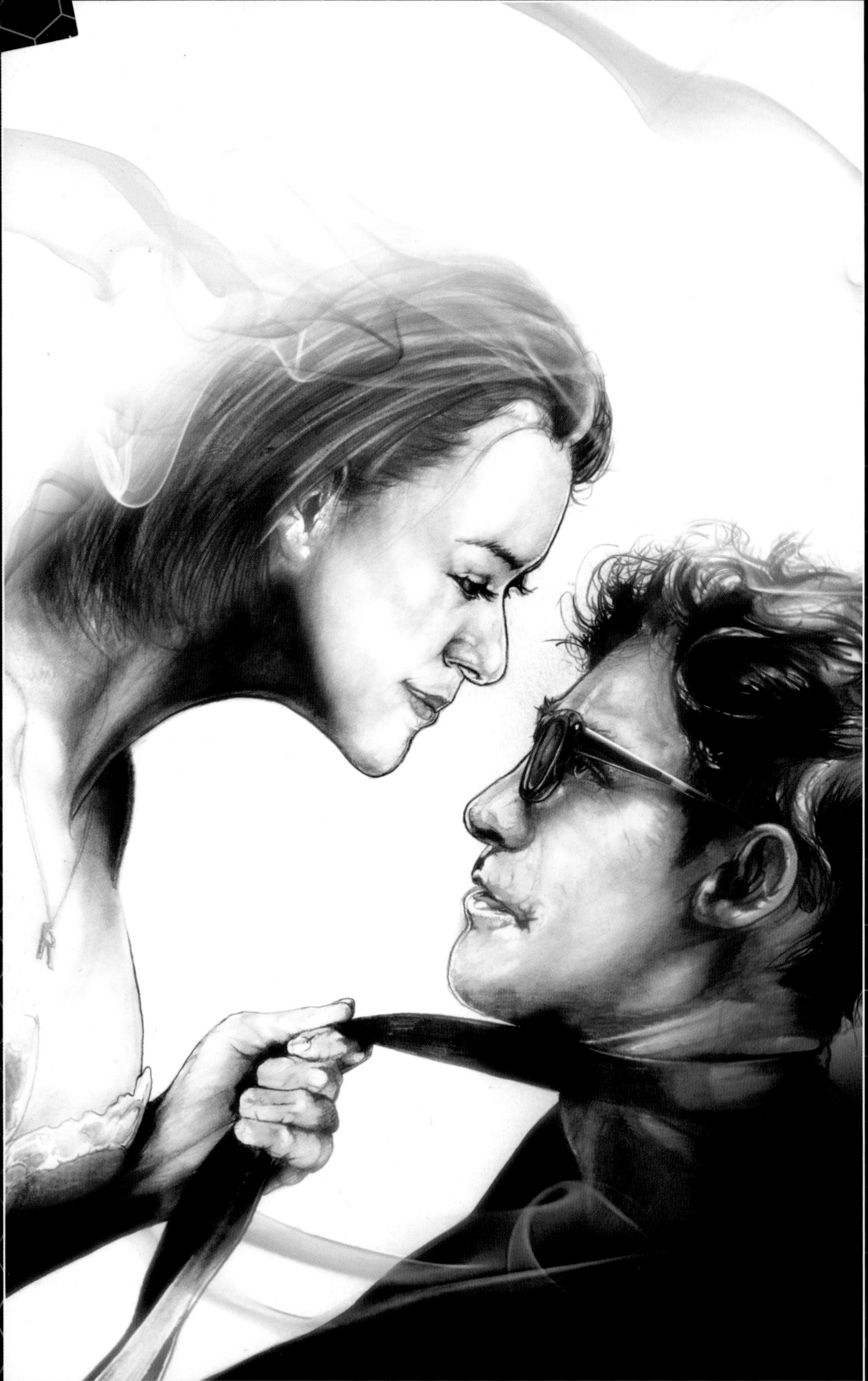

BY **CORBYN KERN**

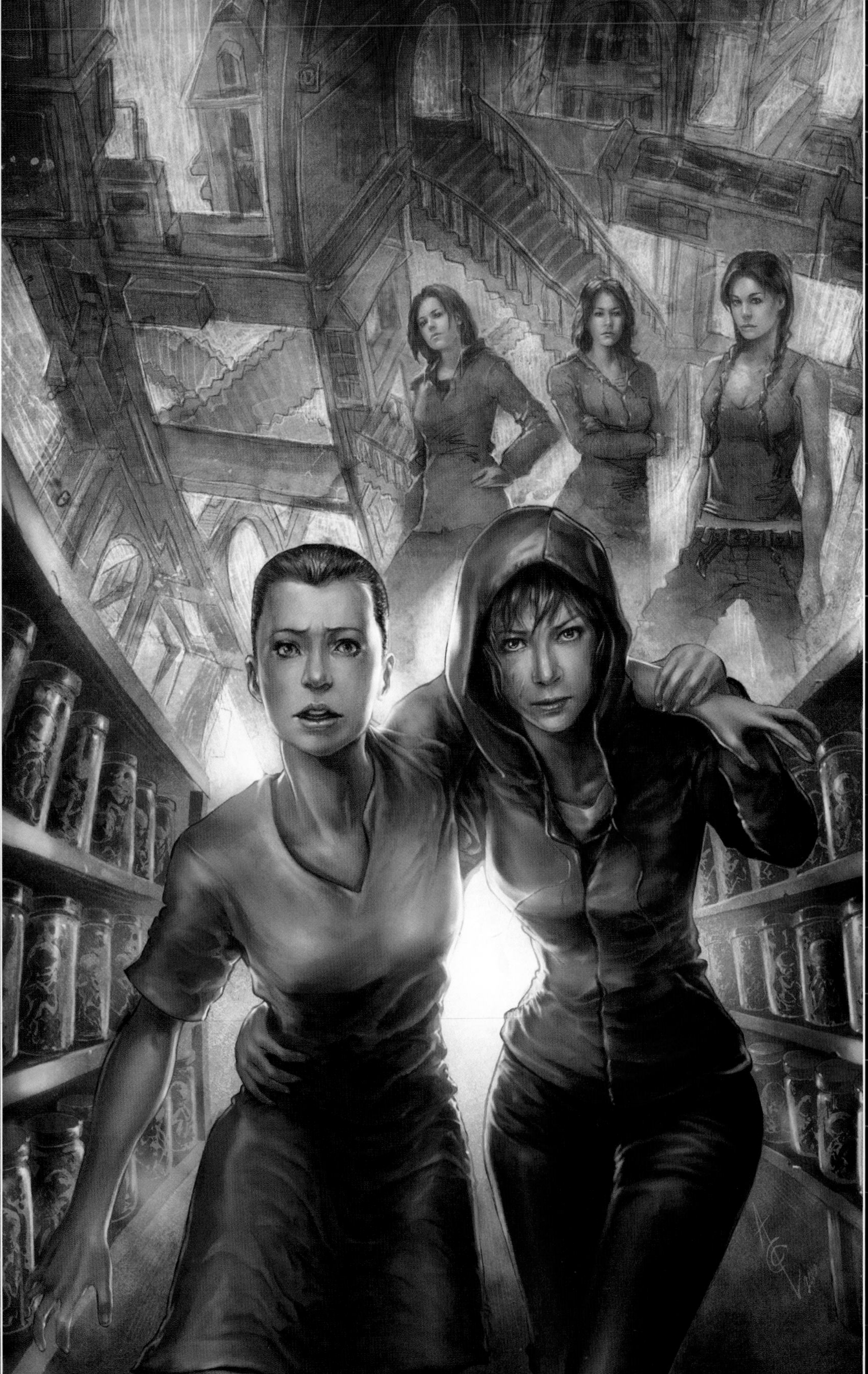

BY **ALAN QUAH**

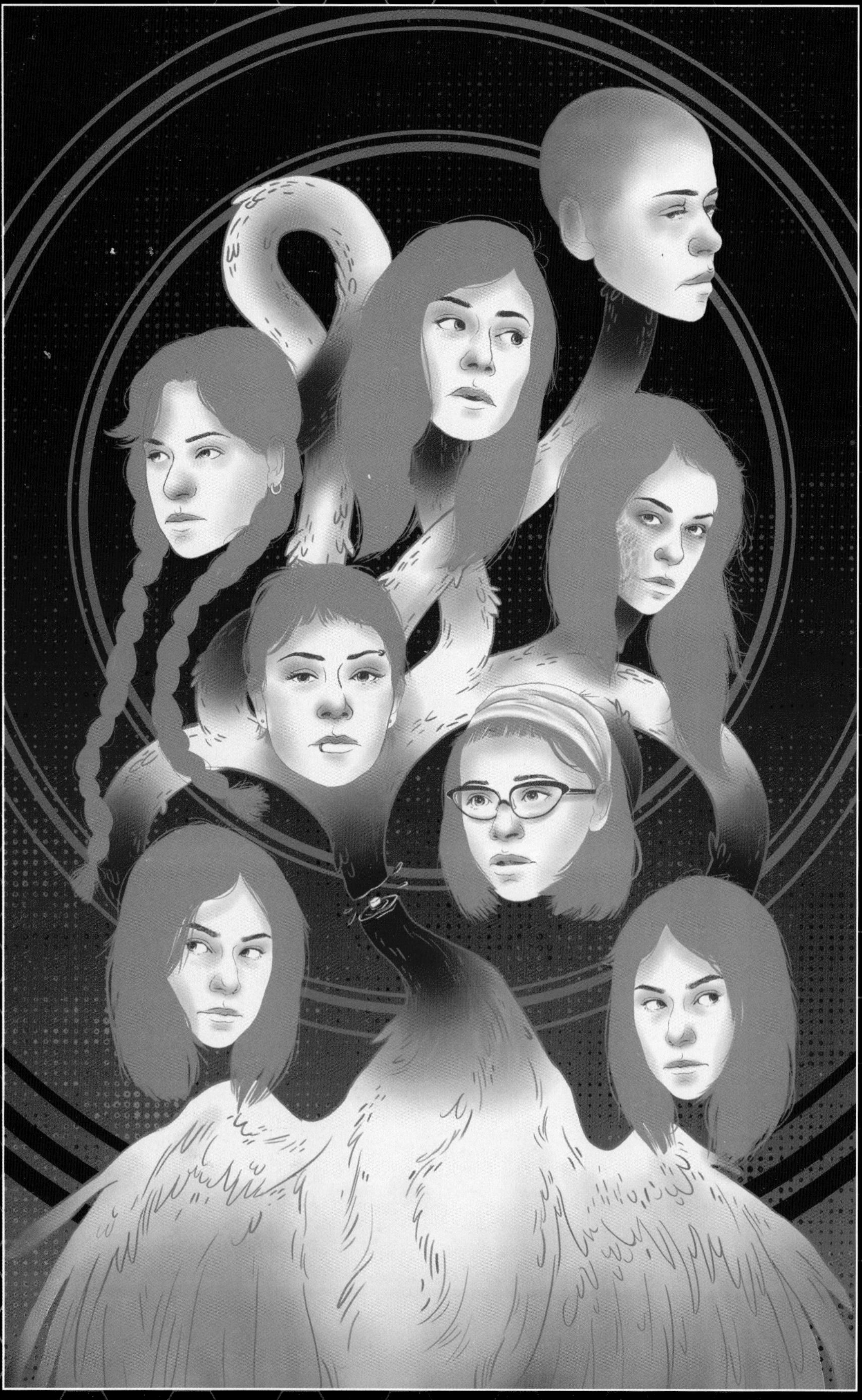

BY **AYNSLIE RISTO**